DEVELOPMENT IN CONTEXT
Acting and Thinking
in Specific Environments

The Jean Piaget Symposium Series
Available from LEA

OVERTON, W. F. (Ed.) • The Relationship Between Social and Cognitive Development

LIBEN, L. S. (Ed.). • Piaget and the Foundations of Knowledge

SCHOLNICK, E. K. (Ed.) • New Trends in Conceptual Representation: Challenges to Piaget's Theory?

NEIMARK, E. D., De LISI, R., & NEWMAN, J. L. (Eds.) • Moderators of Competence

BEARISON, D.J., & ZIMILES, H. (Eds.) • Thought and Emotion: Developmental Perspectives

LIBEN, L. S. (Ed.) • Development and Learning: Conflict or Congruence?

FORMAN, G., & PUFALL, P. B. (Eds.) • Constructivism in the Computer Age

OVERTON, W. F. (Ed.) • Reasoning, Necessity, and Logic: Developmental Perspectives

KEATING, D. P., & ROSEN, H. (Eds.) • Constructivist Perspectives on Developmental Psychopathology and Atypical Development

CAREY, S., & GELMAN, R. (Eds.) • The Epigensis of Mind: Essays on Biology and Cognition

BEILIN, H., & PUFALL, P. (Eds.) • Piaget's Theory: Prospects and Possibilities

WOZNIAK, R. H., & FISCHER, K. W. (Eds.) • Development in Context: Acting and Thinking in Specific Environments

DEVELOPMENT IN CONTEXT
Acting and Thinking
in Specific Environments

Edited by

Robert H. Wozniak
Bryn Mawr College

Kurt W. Fischer
Harvard University

LAWRENCE ERLBAUM ASSOCIATES, PUBLISHERS
1993   Hillsdale, New Jersey   Hove and London

Lawrence Erlbaum Associates, Inc., Publishers
365 Broadway
Hillsdale, New Jersey 07642

Library of Congress Cataloging-in-Publication Data

Development in context: acting and thinking in specific environments /
edited by Robert H. Wozniak, Kurt W. Fischer.
    p. cm.
    Chiefly papers presented at the Nineteenth Annual Symposium of the
Jean Piaget Society.
    Includes bibliographical references and index.
    ISBN 0-8058-0769-1 (hard)
    1. Cognition in children — Social aspects — Congresses.
2. Socialization — Congresses. 3. Environmental psychology —
Congresses. I. Wozniak, Robert H. II. Fischer, Kurt W.
BF723.C5S68   1993
155.9′2 — dc20   92-25908
                                                 CIP

Printed in the United States of America
10 9 8 7 6 5 4 3 2 1

Contents

SECTION IV   COMMENTARIES

Acknowledgments

This book originated with the 19th annual symposium of the Jean Piaget Society: Society for the Study of Knowledge and Development. The two of us were the official organizers of that meeting, but we were supported at every step by the board of directors and the officers of the society. We would especially like to thank William Gray, vice president (who coordinated the general program), Willis Overton, local arrangements director, and Rick Pollack, local arrangements assistant (both of whom arranged for the meeting site and dealt with the myriad specifics needed to make a meeting successful). After the symposium ended, other members of the society helped us to complete the book, especially Ellin Scholnick, editor of the JPS Series, and Jack Meacham, president of the society.

Most of the chapters in this volume were presented in earlier versions at the symposium, and the dialogue that resulted both at the meeting and subsequently has been exciting and productive. We feel that all the arguments have been substantially strengthened as a result.

In sponsoring meetings that focus on critical topics in the field, JPS plays an important role in promoting constructive dialogue that advances developmental theory and research. In a discipline that has often suffered from a narrowness of vision that blinds researchers to important phenomena in human behavior and to the diversity of useful theoretical perspectives, the Piaget Society has been unusual, especially for North America, both in organizing annual meetings around specific topics in development and in valuing theory as well as research.

Production of this book was supported not only by the society and the publishers but also by Bryn Mawr College and Harvard University, which support our research and writing.

Finally, we acknowledge the contributions of J. J. Gibson, Jean Piaget, and Lev Vygotsky to the work reported in this volume. And most of all we acknowledge the contributions of the authors, who responded patiently and constructively to our many comments and suggestions and produced a powerful set of chapters analyzing development in context.

Robert H. Wozniak
Kurt W. Fischer

Development in Context:
An Introduction

Robert H. Wozniak
Bryn Mawr College

Kurt W. Fischer
Harvard University

More than a decade ago, Urie Bronfenbrenner (1979) referred to developmental psychology as "the science of the strange behavior of children, in strange situations with strange adults for the briefest possible periods of time" (p. 19). In the intervening years, much has changed. In general, behavioral and developmental scholars have moved toward approaches that emphasize the particularities of persons in context. Instead of expecting explanations of behavior to take the form of a few simple universal principles similar to those in Newtonian physics, researchers and theorists have moved toward approaches that are rich in description. Analyses of the ecology and the dynamics of behavior have become popular, emphasizing the particulars of people acting in specific environments and the many complex factors of human body and mind that contribute to action and thought.

This volume brings together many of the current efforts to deal with development in this richly ecological, dynamic way. The research reported demonstrates that recent years have produced major shifts in approach. Activities are studied as they naturally occur in everyday contexts. Children's active construction of the world around them is treated as fundamentally social in nature, occurring in families, with peers, and in cultures. Behavior is studied not as something disembodied but within a rich matrix of body, emotion, belief, value, and physical world. Behavior is analyzed as changing dynamically, not only over seconds and minutes, but over hours, days, and years.

BASIC PROPOSITIONS

A few propositions have been fundamental to this shift toward ecological, dynamic psychology, and they are basic to most of the arguments presented in this volume:

1. Psychological events are transactions that take place between individuals and their specific environments. Psychological phenomena are explained with joint reference to active, constructive characteristics of both the individual and the interactional and physical contexts within which the individual acts.
2. The human mind is fundamentally social in nature. Human action and thought are built on social co-construction through joint activity, intersubjectivity, and acculturation.
3. The environment, both social and physical, is an exceedingly complex affair, and it participates directly in behavior. The contexts within which human beings develop are complex systems that exist at multiple levels from the microstructure of surfaces to the interinstitutional relationships of cultures.
4. Neither characteristics of individuals nor characteristics of the many contexts within which individuals live will, taken by themselves, be adequate to explain transactions. How we perceive the world, act on objects, interact with people, and generate symbols to represent events must be understood as the joint product of the physical and social situations that individuals find themselves in and the personal characteristics that individuals bring with them to these situations.

Along with these assumptions, several methodological orientations also permeate the new approach:

5. Development should be studied in its natural settings and in enriched laboratory situations that capture some of the complexity of naturalistic conditions.
6. To handle the complexities of person in context, researchers should study process with outcome, using appropriately complex methods such as the dynamic assessment of interaction as it unfolds over time, assessment in multiple contexts including variations in tasks and contextual supports, and participatory observation.

ORIGINS OF THE NEW ORIENTATION

This new orientation did not suddenly emerge *de novo*. It grew organically from work with its roots in a century of scholarship. Indeed, constructive interactionism (or transactionalism) is an old idea. James Mark Baldwin and his contemporary, John Dewey, were two of the most influential early exponents. In 1897, Baldwin argued that:

> the method of progress of society . . . analogous to [that] . . . in the child . . . is a circular movement of give-and-take between society and the individual. The form of collective organization cannot be social . . . without having first been individual . . . and the matter of social organization cannot be individual . . . without having first been social. (p. 543)

Some years later, Dewey (1916) articulated similar views, asserting that:

> development within the young . . . takes place through the intermediary of the environment . . . [,] the sum total of conditions which are concerned in the execution of the activity characteristic of a living being. The social environment consists of all the activities of fellow beings that are bound up in the carrying on of the activities of any one of its members. It is truly educative . . . in the degree in which an individual shares or participates in some conjoint activity. By doing his share in the associated activity, the individual appropriates the purpose which actuates it, becomes familiar with its methods and subject matters, acquires needed skill, and is saturated with its emotional spirit. (p. 26)

In the mid-1920s, in different parts of the world — Geneva, Moscow, and Berlin — three young psychologists continued to struggle with this problem. Jean Piaget first encountered Baldwin's work through Pierre Janet, who was lecturing at the Sorbonne during Piaget's stay in Paris from 1919 to 1921. He adopted Baldwin's concepts of assimilation, accommodation, and circular reaction and began to apply them to analysis of the sensorimotor intelligence of his first child. As Piaget (1936/1952) later wrote in *The Origins of Intelligence in Children:*

> Intelligence is an adaptation. In order to grasp its relation to life in general, it is therefore necessary to state precisely the relations that exist between the organism and the environment . . . Intelligence is assimilation to the extent that it incorporates all the given data of experience within its framework [but] . . . There can be no doubt either that mental life is an accommodation to the environment . . . Intellectual adaptation, like every other kind, consists of putting an assimilatory mechanism and a complementary accommodation into progressive equilibrium. (pp. 3, 6–7)

In Moscow at the Institute of Psychology, Lev Semenovich Vygotsky (1956), also familiar with the ideas of both Baldwin and Dewey, was working on a book, unpublished during his lifetime, on "The historical meaning of the crisis in psychology" (Wozniak, 1983). In this work,

Vygotsky argued against the dichotomy between consciousness and practical activity inherent in the then most prevalent approaches to psychology (introspectionism and behaviorism). A psychology of behavior that ignores the organizational function of consciousness, he suggested, is as incomplete as a psychology of consciousness divorced from practical activity in the real social/physical world.

Finally, in Berlin, Kurt Lewin (1926/1931) was completing his epochal *Vorsatz Wille und Bedürfniss,* in which he articulated the famous dictum that "the actual behavior of the child depends in every case both upon his individual characteristics and upon the momentary structure of the existing situation" (pp. 96–97).

Consideration of the problem of constructive interaction clearly has a long and distinguished history among developmental psychologists: What is the relationship of individual to society, biology to culture, universal to particular, maturation to learning, person to environment? Despite these broad theoretical currents, however, constructive interaction has long remained for most psychologists largely a promissory note. Myriad are the analyses of the psychological nature and function of the human individual, but until the recent past, attempts to offer even descriptive taxonomies, let alone theories, of the psychological environment have been rare indeed.

TOWARD POWERFUL ECOLOGICAL ANALYSES

Progress has come in recent years as new descriptions of the joint functioning of particular person and specific environment have begun to demonstrate their theoretical power. A landmark in this effort has been the ecological approach of J.J. Gibson introduced in *The Senses Considered as Perceptual Systems* (1966) and more fully elaborated in the *Ecological Approach to Visual Perception* (1979). Gibson's was the first attempt to provide a psychologically appropriate analysis of the physical environment, especially focusing on environmental affordances in visual perception. Gradually this approach has been assimilated into mainstream thinking in developmental psychology and expanded to new domains (Reed, chapter 2, this volume). The result has been powerful new ecological, dynamic analyses not only of developing perception and action but even of acculturation.

Vygotsky's legacy has also borne fruit with the emergence of "activity theory," originally developed as an extension and, to a certain extent, critique of Vygotsky by Leont'ev, Zaporozhets, and Zinchenko (Kozulin, 1986). A number of developmental researchers have focused on the role of conjoint adult–child activities in practical, everyday contexts reflecting the broader cultural and historical framework of the society within which a child develops (Rogoff, chapter 5, this volume). Children become like-minded members of their communities through joint participation in shared activities tied to the broader cultural institutions of those communities. The sociocultural environment is a complex, multiply embedded affair that extends from face-to-face interactions to the broadest reaches of culture and history.

For many years Urie Bronfenbrenner (chapter 1, this volume) has been an articulate, influential advocate for an ecological view. Influenced by Lewin, Bronfenbrenner has proposed a descriptive taxonomy of the environment, one especially sensitive to the social contexts within which children develop. In Bronfenbrenner's view, a complex ecology of development comprises home, neighborhood, school, parental work place, even the halls of government where public policy is made, together with all the many connections at all levels among these various contexts and the cultural and historical framework within which they exist.

Work strongly influenced by Piaget has likewise moved toward more powerful descriptions of person–environment interactions, often incorporating insights from Gibson, Vygotsky, Bronfenbrenner, and others. Some of these neo-constructive analyses have built upon Piaget's emphasis on the biological roots and endogenous development of action and logical operations by adding analysis of specific environmental constraints — how the characteristics of space shape the construction of symbols about the environment (Downs & Liben, chapter 6, this volume), how interaction in the family molds the child's cognitive development (Sigel, Stinson, & Kim, chapter 8, this volume), and how culture makes possible the development of prodigies (Feldman, chapter 9, this volume).

Others have characterized the dynamics of the co-construction of knowledge by people in pairs and triads. The developmental level of an individual child in a particular environment is determined jointly by the child's constructive efforts and the specific support contributed by another person interacting with the child — teacher, parent, peer, experimenter (Fischer, Bullock, Rotenberg, & Raya, chapter 4, this volume). The processes of co-construction of knowledge vary systematically in terms of both expertise and degree of collaboration to produce an array of qualitatively different types of co-construction (Granott, chapter 7, this volume). Development is thus an emergent characteristic of the person-in-context.

The complementarity of the traditions of Piaget, Vygotsky, and Gibson resonates throughout this book. Together, they may produce a grand theoretical framework broad enough to accommodate a concept of cognitive construction, a concern with acculturation through joint participation, and an ecological analysis of the environment (Wozniak, chapter 3, this volume).

Not surprisingly, in one or another fashion, most of the contributors to this volume look to an integration of Piaget with Vygotsky, or Piaget with Gibson, or Gibson with Vygotsky, to provide a theoretical heuristic for the development of a transactional, sociocultural, contextual, constructive approach to understanding the processes of development. The future will tell whether such an approach grows from rapprochement among these theories that in the past have often been treated as incompatible.

REFERENCE

Baldwin, J.M. (1897). *Social and ethical interpretations in mental development. A study in social psychology.* New York: Macmillan.

Bronfenbrenner, U. (1979). *The ecology of human development: Experiments by nature and design.* Cambridge: Harvard University Press.

Dewey, J. (1916). *Democracy and education. An introduction to the philosophy of education.* New York: Macmillan.

Gibson, J.J. (1966). *The senses considered as perceptual systems.* Boston: Houghton-Mifflin.

Gibson, J.J. (1979). *The ecological approach to visual perception.* Boston: Houghton-Mifflin.

Kozulin, A. (1986). Concept of activity in Soviet psychology: Vygotsky, his disciples, and critics. *American Psychologist, 41,* 264–274.

Lewin, K. (1926/1931). Environmental forces in child behavior and development. In C. Murchison (Ed.), *Handbook of child psychology.* Worcester, MA: Clark University Press.

Piaget, J. (1936/1952). *The origins of intelligence in children* (M. Cook, Trans.). New York: International Universities Press.

Vygotsky, L.S. (1956). *Isbrannye psikhologischeskie issledovaniaa* [Selected psychological investigations]. Moskva: RSFSR Akademia pedagogichesckii nauk.

Wozniak, R.H. (1983). Lev Semenovich Vygotsky (1896–1934). *History of Psychology Newsletter, 15,* 49–55.

ECOSYSTEMS, AFFORDANCES, TRANSACTIONS, AND SKILLS: THEORIES OF PERSON/SITUATION INTERACTION

1 The Ecology of Cognitive Development: Research Models and Fugitive Findings

Urie Bronfenbrenner
Cornell University

There is a text for this chapter. It is taken from the works of arguably the most cognitive of English 19th-century poets—Robert Browning. The familiar lines are from the imagined soliloquy of the painter, Andrea del Sarto:

> Ah, but a man's reach should exceed his grasp,
> Or what's a heaven for?

I am about to make that reach. My immodest aim is to move us toward a unifying theory of cognitive development. Whether the effort brings us closer to heaven or to hell remains to be seen. Perhaps the best I can hope for is to be left in limbo; by which I mean that the reader will reserve judgment, pending further developments. And, as becomes apparent here, further developments are indeed required. What I present here is less a theory than a theoretical perspective.

I must also admit my inadequacy to the task. The scope of that inadequacy becomes apparent once I lay out the dimensions of the endeavor. Under these circumstances, one may well ask why I presume to try. There is an answer. It is one that I give from time to time whenever I accept what I regard as our professional obligation to communicate to policymakers and to the public what we have learned from our research. I begin by acknowledging that there is much we do not know. I then go on to say: "We may not be very good, but, unfortunately we are the best there is." I then explain that, although we don't know many of the right answers, we do know how to ask the right questions. It is finding the right questions that is my aim here, not for social policy, but for science.

To turn to the task at hand. If the goal is to move toward a unifying theory, what is it that needs to be brought together? The first desired conceptual convergence is already implied in the first word of my title. Central to the ecological paradigm that I have proposed is a view of development as an evolving process of organism–environment interaction. I offer some notions about the nature of these interactive processes.

But the same ecological paradigm posits interaction not only between but also within each of its two constituent domains. Thus, the first comprehensive exposition of the theory, now a decade ago (Bronfenbrenner, 1979), was devoted primarily to what I then viewed as the necessary first task of constructing a differentiated conceptual framework for analyzing the developmental environment as a system of nested, interdependent, dynamic structures ranging from the proximal, consisting of immediate face-to-face settings, to the most distal, comprising broader social contexts such as classes and cultures. These constituent nested systems were also conceived as interdependent. In due course, I return to further consideration of these interactive contexts, and what I view as their critical role in cognitive development.

The task of constructing an analogous conceptual framework for analyzing the developmentally relevant characteristics of the person posed a different kind of challenge. Whereas in relation to the environment no such taxonomy existed, with respect to personal qualities the problem was one of overabundance. As I wrote in the 1979 monograph, in this domain, "the researcher has at his disposal a rich array of cognitive constructs, personality typologies, developmental stages, and dispositional tendencies, each equipped with ready-made measurement techniques" (pp. 16–17). How does one choose among them?

Nor is it simply a matter of too many disconnected concepts and variables. Beginning in the period after World War II, the discipline of psychology experienced rapid expansion accompanied by progressive, centrifugal fragmentation of the field, with the social-personality researchers ending up in one corner, cognitivists in another, and the biopsychologists in yet a third. Only in infancy could one still find an integrated organism, but the infant soon grew out of it, and conformed by breaking up into separate segments. For someone who had been trained in a generation taught that faculty psychology was extinct, it was an eerie feeling to see it coming back from the dead, but now garbed in modern dress, each faculty after its own fashion. (The cognitivists insisted on the most formal attire, but that was only after the learning theorists had lost their tails.)

And when that same someone was also attempting to develop an ecological paradigm for human development, the eerie feeling became an awesome obstacle. For within that paradigm, the human organism is conceived as a functional whole, an integrated system in its own right in which various psychological processes – cognitive, affective, emotional, motivational, and social – operate not in isolation, but in coordinated interaction with each other. From this perspective, research that deals only with one of these processes not only underspecifies the model, but risks overgeneralization of findings and, what is even more fatal for developmental science, can result in oversimplification and distortion of psychological realities.

The fact that intrapsychic processes are interdependent does not mean, however, that we cannot take one set of them, in this instance those in the cognitive domain, as a primary focus, and examine the systems in which they operate from that perspective.

Thus far, I have identified three systems – domains in which I attempt to effect some conceptual convergence. But there are still two other, often separated arenas that need to be linked – theory and reality.

It was Kurt Lewin who made the provocative assertion that "there is nothing so practical as a good theory." He then proceeded to demonstrate the validity of his claim by successfully applying his highly abstract, quasi-mathematical field theory to the design of effective programs of what he called "action research" for dealing with a variety of challenging problems confronting U.S. society, ranging from changing national food habits in order to cope with shortages during World War II (Lewin, 1943) to reducing racial tensions in New York City (Lewin, 1946).

I cite these examples in order to illustrate two essential requirements of a good theory: first, that it can be translated into concrete research designs; second, that it can be applied to the phenomena that it presumes to explain as they are manifested in the actual contexts in which they usually occur. Need I add that, in the case of human development, these are the contexts of everyday life.

I mention these two, perhaps seemingly obvious requirements, because not all developmental theories acknowledge their validity. Some remain so abstract as to defy unambiguous translation into research operations. Others confine such operations to settings so specialized as to preclude generalizing with any confidence to the environments in which human beings live and grow.

Accordingly, the fourth and final integration that this chapter attempts is that between theory and reality. Specifically, the abstract propositions or hypotheses I propose are followed, in due course, by the specification of research models appropriate for their operationalization in real-life settings.

Before beginning the integrative effort, I feel some obligation to try to forestall what I regard to be an altogether reasonable reaction to some of the material I present. Many psychologists are engaged in elegant research on specific domains of cognitive functioning, such as short-term memory, selective attention, encoding specificity, retrieval strategies, working memory capacity, and the like. These fundamental psychological processes may seem far removed from some of the topics I discuss here; for example, single-parent families, the relation between home and workplace peer groups, social class, ethnic differences in childrearing patterns, chaotic lifestyles, and, last but not least, the impact of historical events on life course development. One may well ask, with Hamlet, "What's Hecuba to me, or I to Hecuba?"

Or, in plainer English, "that's all well and good, but I am interested in basic cognitive processes that undergird behavior in all situations and are common to all human beings, no matter where they are. Moreover, these processes are best studied under uniform conditions, in which other factors are controlled, so that cognitive functions can become the principal focus of observation and interpretation."

To speak for myself, I regard scientific investigations of this kind as of the highest importance. But their very importance depends on the simultaneous conduct of scientific studies of the same processes in a rather different context; namely, in everyday life. Thus, it is equally essential for basic science that we understand how encoding operates in learning to read, how memory functions in courtroom testimony, or how selective attention operates in the family and the workplace, and how such processes develop.

But once the researcher admits to this broader kind of interest, the cognitive cat is out of the bag, no longer in a controlled environment, and other conditions and psychological processes come into play. In the case of species *Homo sapiens,* these conditions and processes become extraordinarily complex. This for two reasons. First, human beings are not only the partial products, but also the partial producers of their environments. Second, because of this species' unusual capacities for language and thought, the created environments are also symbolic in nature, and these symbols are not only cognitive in structure and content, they are also emotionally, socially, and motivationally loaded.

This means that once we as researchers become interested in cognition and cognitive development in everyday life, we need to develop more complex theoretical paradigms and research designs that are commensurate with the complexities of human beings functioning in human situations. This chapter represents one investigator's effort to contribute toward meeting this dual need. Need I add, there's a long way to go, and it will take many more of us, working from diverse perspectives, to make significant progress.

To turn, then, to the task at hand, I begin at the abstract level by presenting a formal definition of the general paradigm to which I have been referring. By now, the reader will find it somewhat familiar. The main reason for placing it before us is to provide the basis for expanding the terms in the definition.

Definition 1

The ecology of human development is the scientific study of the progressive, mutual accommodation, throughout the life course, between an active, growing, highly complex biopsychological organism — characterized by a distinctive complex of evolving interrelated, dynamic capacities for thought, feeling, and action — and the changing properties of the immediate settings in which the developing person lives, as this process is affected by the relations between these settings, and by the larger contexts in which the settings are embedded.

THE TRANSFORMED LEWINIAN EQUATION

When stated in this full, somewhat convoluted form, the definition hardly invites still further expansion and elaboration. But that is what has to be done if we are to translate the paradigm into operational form, as I promised to do. Paradoxically, we are going to accomplish that expansion first by contraction — that is, by collapsing each of the principal domains of the definition into a single term, and then expressing their relationship in the form of a seemingly simple equation. Those who are familiar with Lewinian theory, from which the ecological paradigm is in fact derived (Bronfenbrenner, 1977), will recognize this equation as a transformed and extended version of Kurt Lewin's (1935) classical formula:

$B = f(PE)$ [Behavior is a joint function of person and environment]

The transformation begins with a provocative substitution:

$D = f(PE)$ [Development is a joint function of person and environment]

The substitution is provocative because it focuses attention on the conceptual difference between "behavior" and "development." The key distinction lies in the fact that development involves a parameter not present in Lewin's original equation — the dimension of time.[1] The additional time factor can be represented in the formula itself by means of subscripts:

---

[1]The issue here raised is one that Lewin himself never directly addressed, or — perhaps putting it more precisely — it is an issue that he finessed by defining *psychology* as an ahistorical science. Lewin's failure to include this factor in his formula was not accidental, but deliberate. In his view, science was by its very nature ahistorical. In psychology as in physics, he argued, present events can be influenced only by forces existing in the present situation. In psychology, however, the latter consisted of what Lewin called the "psychological field"; that is, the situation defined not objectively but as perceived by the person. Hence, historical events could become "field forces" only to the extent that they existed in the person's present awareness. It was perhaps Lewin's predilection for the paradigms of physics, and their ahistorical orientation, that led him, and many other psychologists as well, to be far more interested in the study of behavior than of development. (For further discussion of these issues see Lewin, 1931, 1935.)

$$D_t = f_{(t-p)} \, (PE)_{(t-p)}$$

where t refers to the time at which a developmental outcome is observed and $t-p$ to the prior period, or periods, during which the joint forces, emanating both from the person and the environment, were operating over time to produce the outcome existing at the time of observation. To indicate that it is development in the cognitive sphere that is our primary focus of interest, we can add a second subscript c to the D on the left-hand side of the equation. It would not be appropriate, however, to add that same subscript to the term P on the right-hand side, for our ecological paradigm posits that other characteristics of the person, besides those that are strictly cognitive, play a critical role in shaping the course and content of intellectual development.

If we now relate this quasi-mathematical formula to the original definition for which it stands, it becomes apparent that the D term refers not to the phenomenon of development, but to its outcome at a particular point in time. Because as researchers we are concerned mainly not with effects, but with the processes that produce them, it is the right-hand side of the equation that identifies the focus of primary interest. Translating symbols into text, it defines development as the systematic study of the processes through which properties of the person and the environment interact to produce continuity and change in the characteristics of the person over the life course.

In the transformed equation, these processes are symbolized by the inconspicuous lower-case f, which stands for "function." As used by Lewin, this concept carries a signal implication that has also been incorporated in the ecological paradigm. Specifically, while indicating that the left-hand term of the equation is the joint result of some combination of forces arising from both the person and the environment, Lewin explicitly ruled out the assumption that the combination was only one of simple addition. The point is important because, despite occasional theoretical assertions to the contrary, many developmental investigations, including those in the cognitive sphere, employ analytic models that assume only *additive* effects; that is, the influences emanating from the person and the environment, as well as within each of these domains, are treated as operating independently of each other, with the net result estimated from an algebraic sum of the various factors included in the model.

Lewin used the terms *class-theoretical* and *field-theoretical* to distinguish between models in which the process was missing versus those in which it was explicitly defined. Class-theoretical models can provide useful information about how levels and modes of cognition vary in contrasting environments (e.g., cultures, social classes, types of family structure) and among groups with contrasting personal characteristics (such as gender and age). But they are limited by the fact that the processes producing the cognitive differences are left entirely open to speculation. For that reason, in the exposition that follows, I focus primarily on research that does not omit the f term in the revised Lewinian formula.

The last statement illustrates yet another feature of the transformed equation, one that provides a bridge from theory to practice. For, taken as a whole, that equation contains within it the full spectrum of operational models used and usable in developmental research. These models are defined by various combinations of the principal elements in the formula. Rather than present the full taxonomy in abstract terms, I identify each model as we encounter it in the context of specific studies. A systematic exposition and analysis of this taxonomy is presented elsewhere (Bronfenbrenner, 1988, 1989a).

PROPERTIES OF THE PERSON FROM AN ECOLOGICAL PERSPECTIVE

We are now in a position to expand each of the terms in the transformed Lewinian equation. Given our primary interest in the development of the cognitive characteristics of the *person,* it seems appropriate to begin the elaboration in that domain. However, because personal characteristics other than intellectual are presumed to play a critical role in affecting mental development, the appropriate question for guiding our inquiry becomes the following: What characteristics of the person are most likely to influence the course and outcome of subsequent cognitive development?

The results of a systematic effort to answer this question appear in a published chapter summarizing recent advances in theory and research on the ecology of human development (Bronfenbrenner, 1989a), and further work on this same theme is reported in Bronfenbrenner (1989b). For my purposes here, I focus on selected ideas and findings from both sources that seem especially relevant to research on cognitive functioning and growth.

As a first step in search of an answer to the question posed earlier, I undertook a survey of the relevant research literature to discover what personal characteristics had in fact been examined as possible antecedents of cognitive growth. Several instructive findings emerged from that inquiry. Perhaps most striking from a theoretical perspective was the discovery that the overwhelming majority of such characteristics are based on constructs that are *context free;* that is, the developmental attributes of the person are defined, both conceptually and operationally, without any explicit reference to the environment in which they occur, and are presumed to have the same psychological meaning irrespective of the culture, class, or setting in which they are observed, or in which the person lives. Examples of such noncontextual measures include conventional tests of intelligence and achievement, most analyses of Piagetian-type stages and processes, indices of cognitive style, or assessments based on theories of information processing and artificial intelligence.[2]

The tacit assumption of environmental generalizability, and I might add historical generalizability as well, underlay not only most cognitive studies but also, to no lesser degree, investigations of emotional, motivational, and social characteristics of the person—those traditionally included under the rubrics of temperament and personality. At the same time, the available empirical evidence does not support the underlying assumption (Bronfenbrenner, 1989a).

I describe some of this evidence later, but first I forestall a possible misinterpretation of the line of argument that I propose to take. In calling attention to the unwarranted assumptions typically underlying noncontextual assessments of cognitive and socioemotional functioning, I do not mean to imply that such indices are not appropriate in research based on an ecological paradigm. On the contrary, I contend here that the inclusion of such measures, and the constructs that underlie them, is invaluable in ecological research models when they also incorporate assessments of personal qualities based on context-oriented concepts.

An extended description and discussion of such concepts and associated measures appear in Bronfenbrenner (1989a). In this chapter, I focus on a particular type of context-oriented personal characteristic that, on theoretical grounds, emerges as most likely to exert influence on the course and content of subsequent psychological development in all spheres, including cognitive growth. I begin by tracing the theoretical roots of the concept.

Developmental Processes in the Immediate Setting

It is a first axiom of the ecological paradigm that development is an evolving function of person–environment interaction. It is a second axiom that, ultimately, this interaction must take place in the immediate, face-to-face setting in which the person exists, what I have referred to as the *microsystem*. What is the nature of the interactive developmental processes occurring at this, most proximal level of the environment?

Upon reviewing the research literature on this subject, I was somewhat surprised to discover that such processes are relatively few in number, at least in terms of existing knowledge. Essentially, they are of two general kinds. First, there are processes of social interaction between the developing person and one or more others, usually older, occasionally of the same age,

---

[2]For a fuller discussion of contextual versus noncontextual concepts of the person see Bronfenbrenner (1989a).

and rarely younger. (This unequal distribution reflects some tacit assumptions that can be called into question, but this is an issue beyond the scope of the present discussion.)

A second family of developmental processes has a rich theoretical base, but, as yet, is less grounded in systematic empirical work. I refer to the thesis, originally set forth by Lev Vygotsky (1978, 1979; Vygotsky & Luria, 1956) and subsequently further developed both by Soviet, and, more recently, U.S. scholars, that the principal engine of psychological, and especially cognitive, development is engagement in progressively more complex activities and tasks. Among Soviet psychologists, the key figure is Alexei Leont'ev (1932, 1959/1982, 1975/1978). On the U.S. side, the principal protagonists of activity theory have been Michael Cole, Barbara Rogoff, and James Wertsch (Cole, Gay, Glick, & Sharp, 1971; Laboratory of Comparative Human Cognition, 1983; Rogoff, 1990; Wertsch, 1985).

Given these two broad classes of proximal developmental processes, it appears plausible that, among the personal characteristics likely to be most potent in affecting the course of subsequent psychological growth, including cognitive development, are those that set in motion, sustain, and encourage processes of interaction between the person and two aspects of the proximal environment: first, the people present in the setting; and second, the physical and symbolic features of the setting that invite, permit, or inhibit engagement in sustained, progressively more complex interaction with and activity in the immediate environment.

In short, I propose that the attributes of the person most likely to shape the course of development, for better or for worse, are those that induce or inhibit dynamic dispositions toward the immediate environment. For great want of a better term I refer to such qualities as *developmentally instigative characteristics*.

Developmentally Instigative Characteristics

Four types of such characteristics are usefully distinguished. The first, and the one most often found in the research literature, consists of personal qualities that invite or discourage reactions from the environment of a kind that can disrupt or foster processes of psychological growth; for example, a fussy versus a happy baby; attractive versus unattractive physical appearance; or hyperactivity versus passivity. Half a century ago, Gordon Allport (1937), borrowing a term originally introduced by Mark A. May (1932), spoke of such characteristics as constituting *personality* defined in terms of its "social stimulus value." Accordingly, I refer to personal features of this kind as *personal stimulus characteristics*.

The developmental importance of such characteristics lies in the fact that they can set in motion reciprocal processes of interpersonal interaction, often escalating over time, that, in turn, can influence the course of development. Although a number of studies of the developmental effects of such characteristics have been conducted (e.g., Block, Buss, Block, & Gjerde, 1981; Caspi, Elder, & Bem, 1987, 1988; Gjerde, Block, & Block, 1986), almost all of them restrict themselves to looking for evidence for constancy over the years, while neglecting to investigate the complex of environmental forces and personal characteristics that produces departures from earlier patterns; this despite the fact that the data from such studies, when systematically examined, reveal that it is *discontinuity,* rather than continuity that is the rule.

The remaining three forms of developmentally instigative characteristics are probably even more powerful in their developmental impact, but have seldom been examined from this point of view. Attributes of this kind differ from social stimulus characteristics in the following respect: Rather than merely evoking a reaction from others, they share in common a differential responsiveness to, and an active, selective orientation toward, the environment—both social and physical. The three are distinguished from each other primarily on developmental grounds because they tend to emerge sequentially during childhood, and reflect progressively more complex levels of psychological functioning.

The first and earliest form of such an active orientation I call *selective responsivity.* It involves individual differences in reaction to, attraction by, and exploration of particular aspects of the physical and social environment.

The next type of developmentally instigative characteristic goes beyond individual differences in selective responsiveness to include the tendency to engage and persist in progressively more complex activities; for example, to elaborate, restructure, and even to create new features in one's environment—not only physical and social, but also symbolic. I refer to dispositions of this kind as *structuring proclivities.*

The transition from one to the other of these dynamic forms of psychological orientation during early childhood is illustrated in successive publications from a longitudinal study of infants being carried out by Leila Beckwith, Sarale Cohen, Claire Kopp, and Arthur Parmelee at UCLA (Beckwith & Cohen, 1984; Beckwith, Cohen, Kopp, Parmelee, & Marcy, 1976; Cohen & Beckwith, 1979; Cohen, Beckwith, & Parmelee, 1978; Cohen & Parmelee, 1983; Cohen, Parmelee, Beckwith, & Sigman, 1986). Their imaginative and careful work reveals a progressive sequence of such environmentally oriented orientations from birth through now 7 years of age. Thus, immediately after birth, infants are especially responsive to vestibular stimulation (being picked up and held in a vertical position close to the body), which has the effect of soothing the baby so that it begins to engage in mutual gazing; by 3 months, visual exploration extends beyond proximal objects, and it is the mother's voice that is most likely to elicit responses especially in the form of reciprocal vocalizations.

From about 6 months on, the infant begins actively to manipulate objects spontaneously in a purposeful way and to rearrange the physical environment. By now, both vocalization and gesture are being used to attract the parents' attention and to influence their behavior. In addition, there is a growing readiness, across modalities, to initiate and sustain reciprocal interaction with a widening circle of persons in the child's immediate environment. Here we see the emergence of what I have called "structuring proclivities."

A number of other investigations have yielded comparable findings, and have extended them to still other activity domains; for example, individual differences in children's creativity in play and fantasy behavior (Connolly & Doyle, 1984; MacDonald & Parke, 1984); Jean and Jack Block's longitudinal studies of "ego resiliency" and "ego control" (Block & Block, 1980; Block, Block, & Keyes, 1988); and, especially, the as-yet largely speculative ideas emerging from the field of behavioral genetics. Here, for example, Sandra Scarr (1988; Scarr & McCartney, 1983) and Robert Plomin (Plomin & Daniels, in press; Plomin & Nesselroade, in press) have proposed models emphasizing the emergence of genetically based dispositions to select, explore, conceptualize, elaborate, reorganize, and to construct physical, social, and symbolic environments both for the self and for the other. The possibility of developing reliable and valid measures of such dispositions does not seem to lie beyond the scope of our present knowledge and know-how.

The nature of the fourth and final class of developmentally instigative characteristics reflects the growing capacity and active propensity of children as they grow older to conceptualize their experience. It deals with what I have called *directive belief systems about the relation of the self to the environment,* or, for short, *directive beliefs.* The principal distinction between this construct and the familiar concepts of "locus of control" and "goal orientation" lies in the fact that they are conceived and analyzed not as developmental outcomes but as dynamic developmental forces interacting synergistically with particular features of the environment to produce successive levels of developmental advance or, as can and does happen in today's ecology, developmental stagnation and disarray.

These, then, are the four types of developmentally instigative characteristics that I propose for priority entry as "person" terms in ecological models for the study of human development. A number of them clearly involve cognitive components—especially in the case of structuring activities. But they also appear in the other spheres of selective responsiveness, belief systems, and even stimulus characteristics (e.g., the appearance of being intelligent or "not very bright").

In the analysis and interpretation of research findings in all four of these domains, it should be kept in mind that developmentally instigative characteristics do not *determine* the course of development; rather, they may be thought of as "putting a spin" on a body in motion. The effect of that spin depends on the other forces, and resources, in the total ecological system.

I am now in a position to provide a concrete illustration of my earlier assertion regarding the scientific importance of incorporating into ecological research designs more traditional, noncontextual measures of mental ability, cognitive process, as well as assessments of temperament or personality. All such assessments can be thought of as indexing *existing psychological resources and socioemotional states.* By combining such more static concepts with the dynamic element inherent in what I have called developmentally instigative characteristics, and then employing a design that can assess their joint, synergistic effect, the investigator can obtain a more powerful indication of the contribution of the person to his or her own development. To assess the one without the other treats the developing person either as devoid of psychological substance or of psychological force.

I refer to designs that meet the dual requirement as *force-resource* matches, or mismatches. An example might be the joint combination of levels of IQ with a measure of activity level. Where, as in this instance, one element of the dual combination involves a cognitive component, we can be more specific and speak of *force-resource cognitive matches.*

I recognize that what I am now expected to do is to provide some examples of the use of such force–resource combinations in developmental studies. But, alas, to date, I have not been able to find any. To be sure, there a number of investigations that have incorporated both static and dynamic personal characteristics in their research designs.[3] Upon closer examination, however, it becomes apparent that the design employed allowed only for assessment of additive effects thus providing no opportunity to detect any synergistic influence (positive or negative) of developmentally instigative

---

[3]Some outstanding examples are the California studies I have already mentioned, Helen Bee et al.'s (1982) investigation of cognitive and language development from early infancy through the preschool years, Lea Pulkkinen's (1982, 1983a, 1983b) follow-up studies in Finland of psychological development from preadolescence through early adulthood; and the work of Glen Elder and his colleagues (Elder, 1974; Elder & Caspi, 1988; Elder, Van Nguyen, & Caspi, 1985) in tracing the developmental consequences of the Great Depression of the 1930s now across three successive generations. All of these studies merit the attention of developmental researchers. Because some of the original sources are widely scattered, I have provided summaries in several of my own publications of the principal findings, and the research models employed (Bronfenbrenner, 1979, 1986, 1988, 1989a; Bronfenbrenner & Crouter, 1983).

characteristics on the realization of the person's psychological potential.[4]

Here then is a rich opportunity for future research in cognitive development. I suggest that the scientific yield of developmental investigations could be enhanced by incorporating prior assessments of such force-resource matches into the research design.

I hasten to add, however, that the sole inclusion of this one additional element is not likely to advance our knowledge by very much. Recall that, thus far, our concern has been focused on, and limited to, expansion only of the person term in the transformed Lewinian equation. Although context-oriented in their definition, developmentally instigative characteristics are properties of the person rather than of the external world. Unless appropriate complementary characteristics appear on the environmental side, we can hardly expect developmental processes to be substantially affected, one way or the other. It is time, then, to shift our attention to the environmental domain.

PROPERTIES OF CONTEXT FROM A DEVELOPMENTAL PERSPECTIVE

Paradoxically, the effort to identify and to conceptualize developmentally relevant characteristics of the person led to a reformulation of my earlier conceptualizations of the environment. Specifically, and not surprisingly, it suggested the notion of conceptualizing analogous developmentally instigative elements at each environmental systems level from the proximal to the distal.

The Microsystem in Action

For example, the definition of the *microsystem,* the immediate setting in which development ultimately occurs, has been expanded. The definition now reads as follows (I identify the added portion by italics):

Definition 2

A *microsystem* is a pattern of activities, roles, and interpersonal relations experienced by the developing person in a given face-to-face setting with particular physical, *social, and symbolic features that invite, permit, or inhibit, engagement in sustained, progressively more complex interaction with, and activity in, the immediate environment.*

---

[4]Should any colleagues know of any studies in which this scientific potential is realized, I would be most grateful for the information.

What does the addendum mean in concrete terms? The answer to this question is best conveyed by a concrete example. The research I have selected is well-suited for this purpose but unusual in its primary focus on the influence of the physical environment on cognitive development, although social factors are also brought into the picture in its later phases.

A decade ago, Theodore Wachs (1979) published a seminal paper in which he showed a consistent pattern of relationships between certain features in the physical environment of infants during the first 2 years of life and their cognitive development over this same period. Assessments in the latter sphere were based on the child's level of performance on the Uzgiris-Hunt Infant Development Scale, which was developed in an attempt to operationalize and standardize the concepts and techniques used by Piaget. The instrument is comprised of eight separate subscales corresponding to particular Piagetian processes, such as object permanence, perspective-taking, foresight, and the understanding of causality. Physical features of the home environment were assessed by means of an inventory covering a wide range of specific items such as the following: noise level, space for movement, sheltered areas, audio-visual responsive toys, ratio of rooms to people, and decorations in the child's room. To permit examining effects over time, data were grouped into successive 3-month blocks. The results are reported in the form of correlations between characteristics of the environment at an earlier time and developmental status at a later time.

The results of the study were quite complex. For purposes here, I focus on those physical features in the environment that were most frequently and strongly associated with various types of cognitive functioning. These included a physically responsive environment, presence of sheltered areas, "the degree to which the physical set-up of the home permits exploration", low level of noise and confusion, and "the degree of temporal regularity" (p. 30).

These, then, are some of the developmentally instigative characteristics now not of the person, but of the physical environment. In summary, it would appear that two general aspects of the physical environment can affect the course of cognitive development—one for better, the other for worse. On the constructive side are objects and areas that invite manipulation and exploration, whereas the instability, lack of clear structure, and unpredictability of events undermines the developmental process. As I have documented elsewhere (Bronfenbrenner 1986, 1989a), these same two vectors continue to exert their opposing effects at older ages as well.

In the light of an ecological paradigm, the existence of these countervailing forces in the physical environment highlights the unexploited opportunity to carry out an even more revealing analysis of the influence of the physical environment on cognitive functioning. The two principal analytic techniques employed by Wachs—correlations and canonical analyses—are both based on an additive model. Implicit in such a model, both methodologically and substantively, is the assumption that, in this particular instance, the positive environmental factors inviting manipulation and exploration have the same effect in a chaotic, unpredictable environment as in one that is stable; conversely, stable spatial and temporal structures exert the same positive influence whether or not the environment contains developmentally instigative features.

Such assumptions are of course incompatible with the ecological paradigm. To the contrary, the paradigm leads to the synergistic hypothesis that not only would developmentally instigative features of the surroundings have greater impact in more stable settings, but that they would also function as a buffer against the disruptive influences of disorganizing environments. Moreover, this hypothesis could be tested with data already available in Wach's pioneering research.

The availability of such data highlights another distinctive feature of Wach's investigation; namely, his use as a measure of developmental outcome of not a single composite index, like a Developmental Quotient (DQ), but a differentiated assessment of a pattern of cognitive processes.[5] Such assessments are of special importance for the simple reason that cognitive processes are in fact complex. Hence, as scientists, our primary interest should be not in the outcomes of cognition but the processes that produce it. Or, to put it another way, our main focus should be the forces that undergird the observed products, not the products themselves.

To return to — do I dare say — the "Wachsworks," thus far the findings discussed have dealt only with variations in cognitive outcomes as a function of characteristics of the environment. What about the characteristics of the person? Are all infants affected by the physical features of the setting in the same way? In his research design, Wachs included only one dimension in this person sphere, but its influence on the results, almost alone, justifies an affirmative answer to the question posed. All of his analyses were carried out separately for males and females.

In general, significant effects of the physical environment on cognitive development appeared much more frequently, and across a wider range of mental processes, for boys than for girls. Moreover, the features of the environment that were most influential differed in the two sexes. To quote Wachs' own summary:

Female development is positively and significantly related to long-term stimulus variety; males do not show this relationship. Male development is

---

[5]The progress that has been made over the past decade in the conceptualization and assessment of complex cognitive processes provides a far richer array of possible choices, both theoretically and operationally, than was available to Wachs at the time he carried out his pioneering study.

positively and significantly related to a lack of overcrowding; female development appears insensitive to overcrowding effects. Male development shows a significant and negative relationship between presence of noise-confusion in the home and the child's level of cognitive-intellectual development. For females the data indicate either non-significant or positive and significant relationships. (p. 28)

Beyond the specifics, we see here the beginnings of a general trend that continues to be observed through the life course, except perhaps during adolescence, when females begin to approach males in psychological vulnerability.[6]

In examining developmental outcomes as a joint function of characteristics of person and environment, Wachs' study provides an example of what I have called a *person–context* model. Because the processes underlying the observed variations in outcome remain unspecified, the design is still, in Lewin's terminology, only class-theoretical. Nevertheless, such models can often be useful, particularly in the early, exploratory phases of investigation. For example, at a purely descriptive level, the person–context model can be employed to identify what I have referred to as *ecological niches*. These are specified regions in the environment that are especially favorable or unfavorable to the development of individuals with particular personal characteristics. In the present instance, however, in which the design employed included only a single attribute of the person, gender — the niche is more properly called "sociological" than "ecological."

Yet, data already available within Wachs' study would in fact permit employing a highly informative person–context design that would define an entire complex of ecological niches, each associated with a possibly distinctive pattern of cognitive outcomes. The design becomes possible because the Uzgiris–Hunt assessment was administered every 3 months throughout the second year of life. Hence, the latest outcomes for the various Piagetian processes can be analyzed as a joint function of the corresponding earlier cognitive characteristics of the infant and of particular features of the environment. In the latter sphere, a 2×2 cross-classification by developmentally instigative versus disruptive elements of the setting would, in all likelihood, be particularly revealing.

But, at the moment, we can learn much more from Wachs' subsequent work. In his more recent investigations, he has focused on a question that is aptly defined by the title of an article currently in press: "Must the Physical Environment be Mediated by the Social Environment in Order to Influence Development: A Further Test" (Wachs, in press-a). Wachs addressed this problem in the following way. In addition to obtaining

---

[6]For evidence bearing on this point see Bronfenbrenner (1979, 1986, 1989a).

measures of the physical environment of the type previously described, he also administered an inventory of parental behaviors, such as responsiveness to the infant's vocalizations, involvement in child activities, and the use of parental coercion. Using the latter set as measures of the social environment, he then entered them first in a multiple regression equation, followed by assessments of the physical environment. The objective was to determine whether the latter still had a significant effect in predicting, in the first instance, language competence (Wachs & Chan, 1986), and then infant mastery as assessed in a play situation (Wachs, 1987a, 1987b).

In both cases, the effects of the physical environment — in particular, such factors as background noise, crowding, the presence of stimulus shelter, and the number of responsive toys — were still strong and significant after control for mother–child interaction. In the study of infant mastery, Wachs also reversed the order of entry, with the result that, after control for physical factors, socialization processes no longer exerted a significant effect, leading the author to conclude: "Contrary to what is commonly assumed, the physical environment acts to mediate the impact of the social environment and not the converse" (Wachs, 1987a, p. 10).

Is this interpretation correct? Yes and no. It is certainly the only conclusion that can be drawn, given the conceptual model implicit in the research design. An ecological paradigm, however, envisions a third possibility; namely, a synergistic interaction between the physical and social factors. Again, such a possibility could in fact be tested with the available data by comparing the effectiveness of socialization processes separately in developmentally "favorable" and "unfavorable" physical environments.[7]

The type of design I have just described represents a example of what I have called a *process–context model*. The defining property of such a model is that it allows for the possibility that the same process, in this instance, maternal socialization, may operate differently in different environments, here distinguished by the physical characteristics of the immediate setting. In this instance, the context in question is at the level of the *microsystem*. As I illustrate shortly, the same kind of design can also be applied in relation to broader environmental contexts.

At the moment, however, I want to take the opportunity provided by Wachs' pioneering research to introduce into his present model the missing domain of person characteristics. This is most easily done by asking whether the differing effects of context on the socialization process themselves vary as a function of the human beings involved. A simple way

---

[7]Wachs in fact envisaged such a possibility. In a footnote to his most recent published report he pointed out that "there is also [another] model, namely one in which physical and social factors co-vary in such a way that it is impossible to disentangle physical from social influences" (Wachs, in press-b).

to introduce this missing domain is to ask whether the effects of physical characteristics on socialization processes are the same for the two sexes. This is readily accomplished by analyzing the data separately for boys and girls, as Wachs had done in his first study.

Had he done so in the present investigation as well, we would have before us an example of a research design that incorporates all of the elements stipulated in the transformed Lewinian formula, and thereby implements an ecological paradigm of human development. I have referred to this type of design as a *process–person–context model*. Its distinctive feature is that it envisions the possibility of variation in developmental processes as a joint, synergistic function of the characteristics of the person and the environment.[8]

In surveying the research literature (Bronfenbrenner, 1989a), I found several studies that met at least the minimal requirements of this triadic model. None of them, however, focused explicitly on cognitive development, so that the best we will be able to do in this, our domain of primary interest is to infer the cognitive whole from its segmented parts. I proceed with that objective in view.

Note that in the examples examined thus far, the environment is limited to the immediate setting; that is, to a microsystem. We now move on to more distal ecological domains.

THE MESOSYSTEM: COGNITION FROM TWO SETTINGS

The next higher nested structure of the environment is briefly, accurately, but not very informatively defined as a system of two or more microsystems. Implied in this definition are a number of criteria. To begin with the most obvious, a mesosystem involves two or more settings frequented by the same person; for example, home and day care; day care and school, family and peer group, or, to mention a linkage of growing importance for both socioemotional and cognitive development in modern times from adolescence onward — school and workplace. Of course, higher order

---

[8]It is a further indication of Wachs' scientific prescience that he foresaw the possibility of applying just such a model in the next phase of his own research, and is currently engaged in that task. Witness the following concluding statement from an as-yet-unpublished symposium paper (Wachs, 1987b) in which he proposed:

> what I have called the "hypothesis of age specificity" — different aspects of the environment are relevant for development at different ages. I hope in the near future to begin to test this hypothesis, through longitudinal follow up of the comparative salience of physical and social environments upon the infant's development across the first few years of life.

combinations are also possible, but have rarely been investigated, despite the fact that, from a purely methodological perspective, this is not much more difficult to accomplish because, by definition, the same persons are to be found in every setting of a mesosystem. The difficulty derives from the fact that the mere availability of data from or about more than one setting is a necessary but not sufficient criterion for defining a mesosystem.

Perhaps the best way to convey the nature of the additional requirements is again by means of a concrete example. For this purpose I have selected a recent study by Laurence Steinberg and Bradford Brown (1989) that had as an explicit aim defining and demonstrating the distinctive properties of a mesosystem model. Substantively, the investigation focused on the impact on school performance of parental and peer support of academic activities and goals among high school students. The measure of parental influence was based on students' responses to items dealing with such topics as parental monitoring of homework and school performance, the parents' involvement in school programs and activities, and the encouragement of scholastic effort by their children. Corresponding items on the peer side concerned the importance to their close friends of doing well in school, of completing high school, and of going on to college.

Note that we are dealing here with the corresponding *belief systems* that each group holds with respect to the desirability and importance of academic achievement. Here we see another instance in which a characteristic originally defined as an attribute of the developing person becomes a feature of that person's environment when it occurs as a quality present in others who play an important role in that person's life.

The outcome measures in this study included a self-reported grade point average, a scale of how much the student enjoyed and valued going to school, and assessments of educational aspirations and expectations.

The authors' description of the conceptual model guiding their analysis of the data merits our attention. It reads as follows:

> There has been little effort among educational researchers devoted toward understanding how parental and peer influences may operate simultaneously, perhaps because the working model has been for so long that peer and parental influences are inherently antagonistic, with peers constantly trying to undermine the best intentions of parents. To draw on the ecological model proposed by Bronfenbrenner, most studies have focused on the microsystem of the family or the microsystem of the peer group, and not at all on the mesosystem that connects them . . . The failure of researchers to look jointly at parent and peer influences has left open important questions about (1) how these influences may themselves be related (e.g., are they antagonistic, independent, or synergistic) and (2) how the manner in which these influences are related may affect the school performance and behavior of the individual adolescent? (p. 2)

In sum, in terms of our ecological taxonomy, what the authors have described is a process–context model at the level of the mesosystem — a model that allows for detecting both additive and interactive effects of influences emanating from different settings, in this instance, home and school.

Application of the model yielded an informative set of findings, particularly with respect to synergistic effects. Contrary to the conventional cross-pressure conception of parent–peer influences, the data revealed no evidence of opposing forces. Without exception, both influences operated in the same direction, but the relative power of parents versus peers varied depending on the outcome being assessed. Thus, parents exerted a more powerful effect on educational aspirations, but peers were more influential with regard to day-to-day attitudes and behaviors. Finally, with respect to academic achievement, parental support was particularly effective when peers were nonsupportive, but this pattern was not reciprocated; that is, peers did not exhibit a special compensatory power when parental support was not forthcoming.

In their conclusion, the authors argued for a reorientation in the way in which researchers have usually conceived of multiple environmental influences on development: "Our position is that we may oversimplify the picture by continuing to study one [source of] influence without taking account of the concurrent influence of the other." In their view, the failure to assess synergistic processes contributes to the typically low proportion of explained variance in developmental research.

In the light of these considerations, we are now in a position to formulate a more expanded definition of the mesosystem as follows:

Definition 3

A *mesosystem* comprises the linkages and processes taking place between two or more settings containing the developing person. *Special attention is focused on the synergistic effects created by the interaction of developmentally instigative or inhibitory features and processes present in each setting.*

In the light of this definition it should be noted that, strictly speaking, Steinberg and Brown's design does not meet full the requirements for a mesosystem model, since no direct evidence is provided regarding the nature of the synergistic process taking place. For example, is it a function of the degree of face-to-face interaction between parents and peers, the knowledge and perceptions that each group has about the other, or the extent to which parents, peers, or children themselves play a role in the choice of their children's companions?

The preceding series of questions illustrates one of the fringe benefits of ecological models; namely, their capacity to call attention to missing elements and ambiguities of interpretation characterizing a particular set of findings or plan of investigation.

But, to return to our principal concern, what are the implications of a mesosystem model for research on cognitive development. Although it would be an interesting possibility, the implications do not lie primarily in the fact that one could substitute for, or perhaps more informatively add to, the single outcome measure in the above design, assessments of theoretically more significant and complex cognitive outcomes. Rather, in my view, the richest scientific opportunity involves introducing measures of actual processes of cognitive development as the operators in the mesosystem equation. There are a number of theoretically enticing possibilities. My own first choice derives from Vygotsky's theory of *activities* as the principal agents of cognitive development. Thus, I would propose introducing as the process element in the research design indices of the extent to which parents and peers have engaged the young person in reciprocal activities that become progressively more complex versus those that do not involve this presumed developmentally instigative characteristic.

It would also be important to introduce another factor not included in Steinberg and Brown's design; namely, the gender of all parties involved. Particularly in adolescence, there is reason to expect that the same processes of cognitive socialization may operate differently for males and females and for same-sex versus cross-sex dyads. Note that, once sex of subject is included in the design, we again have met the minimal criteria for a process–person–context model. The model would of course becomes far more informative if the entries in the person domain went beyond gender to include psychological characteristics, in particular those that I have referred to as developmentally instigative. If the beliefs of others regarding the importance of intellectual activities influence cognitive growth, then surely researchers should not overlook the person's own beliefs in that domain.

Although the research of Steinberg and his colleagues provides an excellent illustration of a mesosystem model at work, the use of grade point average as an outcome measure hardly qualifies it as truly a study of cognitive development. That criterion is clearly met, however, in a recent report by Morrison (1988) on the "five to seven shift." In order to investigate the factors involved in this phenomenon, Morrison employed a mesosystem design with the following features. The sample of Canadian 5- to 7-year-olds was divided into those whose birthdays fell just short of the cutoff for school, and those who were just beyond it. The two groups, equated on IQ and a variety of other cognitive measures assessed at age 5, differed in mean age by about 1 month, but the older group started schooling 1 year sooner. Both samples were then followed up at 1-year intervals over a 3-year period in order to evaluate progress in a variety of cognitive acquisitions, between ages 5 and 7, in such areas as concept formation, clustering, and short-term memory. Morrison then applied a regression model to evaluate the relative contributions of age, baseline competence scores, and schooling to the outcome measures. The results revealed that, at each follow-up, it was mainly the specific processes associated with formal schooling, and not age or prior cognitive status, that accounted for the observed gains in specific mental processes.

We see here the effects of transition to a new setting on changes in cognitive growth that cannot be attributed solely to maturation. At the same time, however, the analytic model is restricted only to the detection of additive effects. By treating both age and prior mental status as moderator variables, it would have been possible to determine the extent to which the cognitive advance instigated by transition to a new cognitive environment was in fact a joint, synergistic function of the interaction between the developmentally instigative properties of the new setting and the developmentally instigative characteristics of the person.

DEVELOPMENT AND THE BROADER ENVIRONMENT: EXOSYSTEMS AND MACROSYSTEMS

Thus far, we have been concerned only with developmental influences occurring in environments in which the developing person is actually present, and can therefore directly interact with persons and objects in the immediate situation. We turn next to environmental contexts in which such direct interaction is not possible because the environments are, so to speak, "out of reach."

Such environments are of two kinds. Because the next research example illustrates both, I present and discuss their definitions one after the other.

Definition 4

The *exosystem* comprises the linkages and processes taking place between two or more settings, at least one of which does not contain the developing person, but in which events occur that indirectly influence processes within the immediate setting in which the developing person lives.

An example for the developing child is the link between the home and the parent's workplace. Examples for developing adults are the link between the home and their children's peer group, or, increasingly nowadays, between the home or workplace and government offices, whatever they may be.

The definition of the *macrosystem* is more complex, both in relation to other, lower order systems, and to the original conceptualization of this overarching sphere. As in the case of the microsystem, this expansion was a by-product of the effort to develop a more differentiated conceptualization of the characteristics of the developing person, and it was again a Vygotskian construct that paved the way.

In his theory of the "sociohistorical evolution of the mind," Vygotsky (1978; Vygotsky & Luria, 1956) had set forth the thesis that the potential options for individual development are defined and delimited by the possibilities available in a given culture at a given point in its history. This means, for example, that, in a particular microsystem setting—such as the home, day-care setting, the classroom, or the workplace—the structure and content of the setting, and the forms of developmental process that can, or cannot, take place within it, are to a large extent provided by the culture, subculture, or other macrosystem structure in which the microsystem is embedded. It follows that the definition of the macrosystem should include provision for recognizing the developmentally instigative properties that it incorporates. Accordingly, the original definition of the macrosystem has been expanded as follows:

Definition 5

The *macrosystem* consists of the overarching pattern of micro- meso- and exosystems characteristic of a given culture, subculture, or other extended social structure, *with particular reference to the developmentally instigative belief systems, resources, hazards, lifestyles, opportunity structures, life course options and patterns of social interchange that are embedded in such overarching systems.*

This expanded definition has powerful implications at two levels, first in the realm of developmental theory, second with respect to research design. On the former count, the reformulation implies that developmental processes are likely to differ significantly—not just statistically, but substantively—from one macrosystem to the next. With respect to study design, it argues for the representation of characteristics of the culture, or of any other macrosystem, as a critical feature of research models for investigating developmental processes and outcomes—particularly, I would add, in the cognitive sphere.

Evidence in support of both of these propositions appears in the remaining research examples that I now present. It is my hope that that evidence is both provocative and persuasive.

The "Children of the Great Depression" Grow Up

The first example is the most recent report (Elder & Caspi, 1990) from Glen Elder's classic, now three-generational study of children from families that were either smitten or spared by the Great Depression of the 1930s (Elder, 1974). The present report describes and analyzes the contrasting life trajectories of the two original cohorts born, respectively, in the early and late 1920s. Its key feature derives from the fact that the two groups encountered profound social changes at *different ages and stages* of their lives. The second and more traditional design element was the inclusion of two control groups, corresponding in age, but differing in the fact that the family breadwinner (in those days, of course, the father) did not lose his job during the Great Depression.

The developmental consequences by young adulthood of this historical accident can be summarized as follows. The impact of economic hardship differed substantially as a joint function of both the subjects' gender, and the age at which their families suffered a heavy financial blow, with the most severe effects on psychological development occurring for boys who were of preschool age when the Depression hit. The principal shortcoming of this investigation from the perspective of our particular interest is the absence of more specific information about cognitive functioning at adolescence. From the perspective of an ecological model, one would expect that differences in cognitive processes and outcomes would have paralleled those documented in other psychological domains.

What is available, however, is information about the sequential chain of events and processes that produced the paradoxical pattern of developmental outcomes during adolescence and youth. Any summary does injustice both to the richness of the findings and the theoretical and methodological sophistication of the authors. In the hope that justice will be blind in this instance, I proceed to commit the crime of condensation, relying heavily on the authors' own words.

The "changes in family relationship initiated by men's loss of earning and job" . . . increased the relative power of mothers, reduced the level and effectiveness of paternal control, and diminished the attractiveness of fathers as role models" (p. 223). These changes in turn resulted in greater family "tensions, conflicts, and violence" with particular disruption of psychological functioning of men as manifested in "heavy drinking, emotional depression and health disabilities," and — what proved to be especially critical for the development of their young sons — "inconsistent discipline of their children" (p. 224).

Why were older sons not affected? Again in the authors' words: "As the economy worsened, their family hardship meant adult-like responsibilities . . . These, in turn, "enhanced their social and family independence and reduced their exposure to conflict and turmoil in the home." As a net result, "boys were more apt to aspire to grown-up status and to enter adult roles" (pp. 224–225).

And what about the girls? Theirs is a different story. To the extent that they were affected at all, the pattern by age appears to have been reversed, with the older ones at greater risk than the younger. The authors remain strangely silent about this phenomenon and its possible origins — at least in this report.[9]

The story for boys, however, not only continues but has a surprise happy ending. Contrary to the expectation that "young boys in the Great Depression would become a blighted generation, . . . these dire predictions did not materialize . . . By mid-life, a surprising number of men from deprived backgrounds were successful by any standard of work achievement." Employing a series of what we have called process–person–context models, the investigators trace the developmental turnabout to what they refer to as three "institutionalized transitions that involve new responsibilities and privileges"; the three are military service (mainly in the Korean War), further education, and marriage.

What were the distinguishing characteristics of the three settings in this sequential mesosystem that set in motion and propelled a rising developmental trajectory? Necessarily skipping over details of both substance and method, I can point to a complex of interactive factors and processes common to each of the three sequential experiences of those males who, seemingly fated for failure by early deprivation, emerged successful as adults. These critical elements were: an opportunity for a fresh start, the presence of both challenge and support in a new, complex but stable environment; and recognition of accomplishment in the new setting. Engagement in challenging activities within such settings ultimately led to greater competence on the job, more rapid advancement, and higher levels of occupational attainment. Especially significant is the fact that, in each setting, the presence of these elements had a greater positive effect on those men who had experienced deprivation in childhood.

Where do the characteristics of the person appear in this equation? In this domain the results are not as explicit, but some evidence nevertheless exists for the influence of individuals on their own development. The evidence is most clearly detectable in the contrasting characteristics of the young men from deprived and nondeprived backgrounds who entered the armed

---

[9]In an earlier study, Elder, Downey, and Cross (1986) traced the psychological life course of the women in the younger cohort — those who were young children when their families experienced the brunt of the Great Depression. On the basis of their findings, the authors suggest the following explanation for the absence of disruptive developmental effects of economic hardship in this group: "Mothers' and daughters' reactions to financial stress and its consequences facilitate an affectionate relationship that may protect daughters from the harshness of their fathers" (p. 162).

No comparable analysis appears to have been carried out for the older female cohort nor has there been any systematic assessment of differences in developmental processes and trajectories occurring for women in the two cohorts.

services. To begin with, those from disadvantaged backgrounds were not only more likely to enlist, but also to do so at an earlier age—that is, in late adolescence. Moreover, compared with age-mates from nondeprived backgrounds, they had ranked "at the bottom on adolescent competence," having emerged as less "assertive, self-confident, and ambitious" on previously administered project measures. The authors interpret such findings as indicating a "link between an incompetent self (e.g., feelings of self-inadequacy, passivity, lack of self-direction) and the appeal of military options" (p. 35). The investigators go on to state:

> Moreover, the early joiners, most of whom came from deprived circumstances, represent the clearest case of personal choice in the self-selection process. Indeed, their early history of social and psychological disadvantage suggests a self-enhancing choice; the selection of a setting may act as a resocialization mechanism . . . In particular, we have some evidence that military service, and especially early entry into the service, was a "planned" decision among adolescents from deprived circumstances . . . Indeed, cognate research on the psychological risk associated with early adversity (e.g., Rutter & Quinton, 1984) suggests that the tendency to exercise foresight or planning in dealing with environmental challenges is a critical variable in the reduction of continued risk. (pp. 35–38)

The foregoing pattern constitutes an example of what I referred to earlier as a "force–resource" combination of personal characteristics, in which cognitive capacities are coupled with developmentally instigative dynamic dispositions. Moreover, here we observe the formation of this fusion as a developmental change instigated by exposure to stress. One recalls the words of the Banished Duke in the Forest of Arden:

> Even till I shrink with cold, I smile and say
> 'This is not flattery; these are counsellors
> That feelingly persuade me what I am.'
> Sweet are the uses of adversity;
> Which, like the toad, ugly and venomous,
> Wears yet a precious jewel in his head.
>
> *As You Like It* (Act ii, Scene i)

Note where the hard-won gains of adversity are stored, and where they shine.

Still, is there any evidence that the subsequent experience in young adulthood brought about advancement not only in the outer world, but also in the inner workings of the mind? The results of identical psychological tests administered in adolescence and at mid-life revealed that early enlistees from deprived backgrounds, when compared both to late entrants and nonveterans, had, over the intervening period, felt less inadequate, less submissive, and more socially competent.

The developmental effects of further education were even more pronounced. Deprived men who had gone on to college surpassed nondeprived graduates on a wide range of psychological characteristics, including "achievement via independence," "flexibility," "spontaneity," "intellectual efficiency," and "ability to influence others." Although no comparable measures for the same set of variables were available from a prior period, the sharp contrast with the psychological picture presented by the same group at adolescence constitutes powerful evidence for the occurrence of substantial developmental changes as a function of having experienced and surmounted difficulties earlier in life.

Not, however, without some cost. In their final analysis, the authors obtained self-reports from their subjects on health and psychosomatic problems experienced at mid-life, including, for example, chronic fatigue, energy decline, and heavy drinking. Not only were such difficulties more prevalent among men from deprived families, but problems were reported most often by those from disadvantaged circumstances who had gone on to college, thus opening the way to higher job status. The authors report these findings under a poignant heading: "The Hidden Stresses of Surmounting Early Deprivation."

In the work of Elder and Caspi, we have followed development through space and time, and observed the forces and processes that resulted both in constancy and change in the characteristics of the person over the life course. But in one of the three principal domains of the ecological paradigm, the only *cited evidence* has been indirect rather than direct, more inferred than observed. I refer to the presumably ever-present influence of the person on his or her own development. The inference was mainly based on the general knowledge that the majority of early entrants into the military during the period in question were volunteers, and hence, by enlisting, had taken an action of their own free will.

In the preceding paragraph, I have italicized the words *cited evidence* for a reason. In point of fact, additional data were available in earlier assessments that could have been analyzed to provide direct evidence on the issue. These data were of two kinds. First, there were the personality scales administered at adolescence. Among the qualities assessed were the following: *goal orientation* (e.g., "high aspirations"), *self-inadequacy* (e.g., "feels victimized,"), and *social competence* (e.g., "arouses liking and acceptance"). You will recognize in these several of what I distinguished earlier as developmentally instigative characteristics. In addition, in the analyses conducted at mid-life, one of the control factors used as a covariate in assessing the effects of military schooling and adult education was "childhood IQ."

Taken together, these two types of personal characteristics meet the requirements of what I have called a "force-resource" model—one that provides not only an index of capacity but also of motivational disposition. Thus, the availability of these two types of data for the childhood period makes it possible to examine the extent to which the "recovery" from psychological disarray during adolescence was a function not only of environmental opportunities but also of the earlier cognitive assets and dynamic orientations of the individual.

The preceding "Gedanken Experiment" provides a cogent illustration of the importance and use of conventional measures of intelligence in developmental research; namely, they provide an assessment of the intellectual resources that the person has at his or her disposal for future development. The fact that such resources themselves reflect the prior interactive influence of both genetic and environmental factors underscores their theoretical significance and, hence, the desirability of including them in the research design not merely as controls, but as critical elements in the person domain of the ecological paradigm.

But even without the additional evidence that such an analysis would have provided, the scientific life story of the "Children of the Great Depression" is well worth the researcher's reading. For the particular purposes of this chapter, it provides a rich and powerful example of the uses and yield of a process–person–context model, here applied not only through the life course, but across generations. At a more concrete level, it illustrates three basic premises of an ecological paradigm of human development. The first is the principle that development occurs through organism–environment interaction through the life course, here manifested in the successive interplay between environmental stresses, personal initiatives, and environmental opportunities. Second, the study demonstrates the systems character of the human organism functioning as a whole, as reflected in the intricate interdependence of psychological resources and dispositions within the person—cognitive, emotional, motivational, and social. Finally, the research reveals the dynamic interactive relationships operating between different environmental contexts, beginning with the dramatic impact of an exosystem event—the unemployment of the father—on developmental processes taking placing in the child's family, and then radiating outward into the mesosystems of school, military service, college, and workplace, with processes and outcomes in each setting influencing their sequelae in the next.

This entire succession of environments, however, is itself embedded within the overarching context of U.S. society and its distinctive institutions, customs, belief systems, and aspirations at particular critical points in its history—economic depression, war, and economic recovery. In the words of my Cornell colleague, Rick Canfield, what Glen Elder and his coworkers have done is to deliver on Vygotsky's promissory note without ever having owed the debt. Thus, their work gives elegant support to the central Vygotskian thesis that psychological development, in all its aspects, is a function of the flow of history. In accord with that thesis, the generalization applies in the cognitive realm no less, and perhaps even more, than in any other. Across the centuries, there have been special ecologies for special qualities of mind — ancient Athens, Alexandria in its prime, Florence in the 15th century, Paris in the 19th, Vienna before World War II, and Berlin just afterward — not to mention New Orleans, and the College of the City of New York!

But once again, Hecuba, what is she to us and we to her? What do such flowery, and far-flung generalizations have to do with what we do? I feel reasonably confident that few are about to undertake a three-generational study across historical time. Nevertheless, the work of Elder and of other students on the impact of human history on human development does have relevance for what we do. That relevance lies in the fact that whatever psychological phenomena we study, they are taking place in a particular culture at a particular point in its history. And, as we have seen in Elder's work, the prevailing Zeitgeist of the period leaves a heavy imprint not only on what people think, but how they learn to think — or don't. As I have argued elsewhere (Bronfenbrenner, 1989c), the present crises we are experiencing in American education and, thereby, in the competence of the American work force, have to do not only with the way in which we teach reading, math, and science in our schools. The roots of our difficulties lie in the major changes now taking place in American society that are disruptive to basic processes of psychological development and cognitive growth.

The preceding considerations raise a question regarding the extent to which the processes, contexts, and personal characteristics analyzed by Elder and his colleagues — all of these distinctively American in provenience — are applicable to other groups with differing cultural and historical roots and experiences. The concluding section of this exposition addresses this challenging query.

Cognition in Context: Microprocesses in a Macroworld

Some provocative findings bearing on this issue appear in a series of reports from two collaborative programs of research, one directed by Sanford Dornbusch at Stanford University (Dornbusch, 1987; Dornbusch, Ritter, Leiderman, Roberts, & Fraleigh, 1987), and the other by Laurence Steinberg, now at Temple University (Mounts, Lamborn, & Steinberg, 1989; Steinberg, 1989). Taking as their point of departure the classic and frequently replicated work of Diana Baumrind (1966, 1971, 1973; Baumrind & Black, 1967) on the superiority of authoritative parental styles over either permissiveness or authoritarianism, both groups of investigators have demonstrated that these parental patterns have reliably and dramatically different, and even contradictory, cognitive effects when separately examined in the four principal ethnic groups in the United States—Whites, Blacks, Hispanics, and Asians.

Specifically, in the first study, Dornbusch and his colleagues (1987), using a sample of over 7,000 adolescents enrolled in six high schools in the San Francisco Bay area, found that, in general, effects on school performance of parental style, and of other family characteristics as well, were substantially greater for Whites than for any other ethnic group. The Whites benefited most from an authoritative style, suffered most from authoritarianism, and were the only group to show a significant negative impact of permissiveness. Next in line were the Asians, but, for them, only authoritarianism produced its expected negative impact, albeit in reduced measure; permissiveness had virtually no influence; and the effect of the presumably optimal authoritative style was not only nonsignificant, but negative in sign. By contrast, for Hispanics, authoritativeness showed some positive effects, but authoritarianism exerted an influence only on females. Finally, for Black students, none of the three parenting styles produced any significant effects whatsoever.

I should mention that the foregoing pattern of results was still in evidence after control for the following possibly confounding factors: the subject's gender and age (14 to 18), parental education (used as a measure of social class), and family structure (one-parent, two-parent, and stepparent). The control was accomplished by calculating separate regression equations within each ethnic group, with all of these factors entered as covariates. (By now, I expect at least a raised eyebrow—if not a rising gorge—when you hear that familiar formula.)

Steinberg and his colleagues obtained essentially the same pattern of varying, if not contradictory, findings. Perhaps the most striking paradox is one highlighted by Dornbusch. Taking note of "the success of Asian children in our public schools," he commented as follows:

> Compared to whites, Asian high school students of both sexes reported that their families were higher on the index of authoritarian parenting and lower on the index of authoritative parenting. Yet, counter to the general association of such parenting patterns to grades, the Asians as a group were receiving higher grades in school. In addition, while authoritarian parenting was significantly associated with lower grades among Asians, there was no significant relation between grades and the other two parenting styles. This article concludes with more questions than answers in examining Asian parenting practices and school performance (Dornbusch et al., 1987, p. 1256)

How is one to make sense of such a melange? Why should the "same" socialization processes lead to such contrasting outcomes in different ethnic groups? An ecological paradigm reminds us that the outcome of a socialization process depends not only on the behavior of the socializing agent but also on the characteristics of the person being socialized. This was indeed the line of inquiry pursued by both groups of investigators. The personal quality selected for study was what Steinberg called "work orientation" measured by the adolescent's response on a 10-item scale composed of statements like the following: "Hard work is never fun," "I finish any work I'm supposed to do." Note that this concept meets the criteria for what I have referred to as a developmentally instigative characteristic of the person.

The measure of work orientation turned out to be a stronger and more consistent predictor of academic performance than was parental style. But, as with parental behavior, the effect of this orientation was more powerful among White and, especially, Asian students, and weakest among Blacks.

Equally instructive was an analysis reported by Dornbusch (1987) in which both types of variables were combined, thus permitting an assessment of their possible synergistic effects in what I have referred to as a force–resource cognitive match. The pattern of results provides a clue to the mystery, but, I hasten to add, hardly a solution. Specifically, work orientation predicts grades more strongly among families in which the level of authoritarianism is low, with the difference being most pronounced among Blacks—especially Black males—and least evident among Whites—especially females. In fact, for sons of Black authoritarian parents, the correlation is not merely low and unreliable, but negative in sign. Black families also obtained the highest scores on authoritarianism, and Whites the lowest.

What these findings suggest is that processes of cognitive socialization, and perhaps cognitive outcomes as well, may have different meanings, and hence different effects, in different contexts. In the absence of further clues from the data, we do well, in the continuing effort to detect some order in the seeming confusion, to return once again to the formal definition of the macrosystem and its specification of the critical elements embedded in this overarching environmental context. These specified elements are: developmentally instigative belief systems, resources, hazards, lifestyles, opportunity structures, life course options, and patterns of social interchange.

One has only to see the words "resources" and "hazards"—let alone "opportunity structures" and "life course options"—to recognize that these are hardly equally distributed among the four ethnic groups as they exist in the American context.

But is not that problem met by the control variables included in the analysis—in particular, social class (as indexed by parental education) and the three forms of family structure—two-parent, one-parent, and stepparent? After all, the analytic procedure employed, that of treating such potentially confounding factors as covariates in a regression analysis, is one of the most generally accepted and widely used in contemporary social research.

By now it should be clear that the answer to the question just posed is a resounding "No!". Moreover, the rejection is based even more on theoretical than on methodological grounds. The grounds are that such an analytic procedure assumes that the processes or relationships under investigation operate in the same way and to the same degree with respect to each of the person and context characteristics being treated as control variables. It is precisely this assumption, of course, that is challenged by an ecological paradigm. It is not that the paradigm rejects the assumption as invalid a priori, but rather that the question always be left open both as a theoretical and empirical possibility.[10]

In the present instance, it is highly unlikely that the assumption is justified, primarily for the reason that both of the contexts in question possess the stipulated characteristics of macrosystems. To be more precise, the intersection of the two domains with each other defines a set of four macrosystems, each of which meets the formal definition. As I have written elsewhere:

> In the last analysis, what defines the macrosystem is sharing in common the kinds of characteristics specified in the above formal definition (i.e., similar belief systems, social and economic resources, hazards, life styles, etc.). *From this perspective, social classes, ethnic or religious groups, or persons living in particular regions, communities, neighborhoods, or other types of broader social structures constitute a subculture whenever the above conditions are met.* This also means that, over the course of history, newly evolving social structures have the potential of turning into subcultures by developing a characteristic set of values, life style, and other defining features of a subculture. A case in point is what can now justifiably be called the "institution of single parenthood" in the United States. Another example is the two-wage-earner family. From an ecological perspective, the test of whether the label of subculture is legitimately applied to both of these phenomena is the demonstration that such structures do in fact exhibit the defining characteristics specified in the above definition of a macrosystem. There is a

---

[10]The assumption also has its methodological analogue in statistical theory; in that context it is known as "the assumption of homogeneity of regression." When the assumption is not justified, the use of statistical controls can produce distorted results that have no correspondence in reality. What, then, can be done? Both on theoretical and statistical grounds there is the same simple answer: Each process must be examined separately in the context or population in which it occurs.

growing body of research evidence indicating that the criteria are indeed well met. (Bronfenbrenner, 1989a, p. 229)

From this perspective, the designs employed in both the Dornbusch and the Steinberg studies represent a confounding of macrosystems defined by ethnicity, with others distinguished both by social class and family structure. This confounding could be clarified, however, by applying a more differentiated design to data that are already available. Given the large sample size in both of these studies, it would probably be possible to stratify most ethnic groups by both of the latter factors and then examine the socialization processes in each. Especially revealing would be a comparison of ethnic differences in the effect of family styles separately for the two most contrasting groups: middle-class two-parent families and poor single-parent households.

In general, one would expect that, within each ethnic group, the effects of parental style on school performance would be higher in two-parent middle-class families than in single-parent disadvantaged households. But, at the same time, this difference should be less pronounced the greater the degree of discrimination and denigration to which each ethnic minority is subjected in American society. Specifically, the very term *denigration* points to Blacks as the group for whom parental styles may make little difference even in those families with both parents present who have achieved middle-class status. In any event, the results of such an analysis should provide a clearer—and one would hope more theoretically coherent—picture of ethnic differences in cognitive socialization as they vary, or persist, across both class and family structure.

Even before such a model is applied, however, its very conceptualization already permits a more coherent interpretation of the paradoxical findings reported by Dornbusch, Steinberg, and their colleagues. Thus, an analysis of the developmental research literature in an ecological perspective (Bronfenbrenner, 1989c) indicates that the impact of family processes and conditions decreases with age, with the decline being most rapid and most pronounced for families living under the most disadvantaged circumstances. The finding that family styles were most predictive for Whites and Asians, less so for Hispanics, and least for Blacks is consistent with trend just discussed.

Nor were parental styles the only family characteristic to exhibit the same pattern of decreasing predictiveness across ethnic groups ranked by socioeconomic status. In reporting results of the separate analyses conducted for each ethnic group, Dornbusch and his colleagues cited regression coefficients for all control variables, including both social class and family structure. These, too, showed a similar decline in parental power across the four ethnic groups (Dornbusch et al., 1987, p. 1254, Table 3).

At a broader level, the preceding findings are consistent with the general ecological hypothesis (Bronfenbrenner, 1989a, 1989b) that, by adolescence, the power of constructive family processes is effectively undermined in macrosystems characterized by high levels of stress and disorganization.

This hypothesis calls attention to another major finding in the research of Dornbusch and his colleagues. The finding emerged from the initial analysis of the entire sample, including all four ethnic groups, and is described by the authors as follows:

> But the mean grades of students in pure authoritarian or pure permissive families were not the lowest. The lowest grades were found among students whose family parenting style is inconsistent, especially with combinations that include authoritarian parenting . . . We speculate that inconsistency in the home environment creates anxiety among children, and that the anxiety reduces the relation between students' effort in school and the grade received. (Dornbusch et al., p. 1255)

Regrettably, the investigators did not include the measure of parental inconsistency in their separate analyses for each ethnic group. The results of other studies (see Bronfenbrenner, 1986, 1989a) indicate that inconsistency in parental behavior is more likely to occur both in disadvantaged and in single-parent families. Hence, a design that permits assessment of its presumed disruptive synergistic effects should further contribute to disentangling and clarifying the distinctive contribution of ethnic macrosystems in contrasting socioeconomic and structural contexts.

Moreover, there is evidence in the reported results suggesting that such a distinctive contribution in fact exists. It is seen primarily in the already mentioned paradoxical findings for the Asian sample. Thus, it is difficult to see how socioeconomic conditions and family structure could account for the academic success of Asian students despite the fact that their families were both more authoritarian and less authoritative than were White parents.[11] Nor do these structural factors explain the fact that the Asians were the only group not showing a significant gender difference in academic performance favoring females over males. (The means for the two genders for Asian students were essentially identical.) Asians were also the group most handicapped by having either a single parent or a stepparent.

---

[11]Unfortunately, because of limitations in sample size, it was not possible to conduct independent analyses for each of the ethnic subgroups within the Asian sample. Dornbusch (1987) was able, however, to carry out, within both the Asian and Hispanic samples, a separate analysis by generation, with the following result. The earlier a family had emigrated to the United States, the more that pattern of socialization effects resembled that of U.S. Whites. Regrettably, the report cites only correlations and does not include average scores by generation either for parental variables or for academic achievement.

Perhaps a key to such structural variation lies in the extent to which parents employing different styles also engage in progressively more complex activities — that is, in processes more closely related to the development of cognitive competence. The inclusion of measures of such processes as elements in a force–resource model could help to clarify these issues. But all this would require getting additional information not now available.

With respect to analyses of existing data, I do not mean to imply that the mere employment of a design that also incorporates the factors of socioeconomic status and family structure will resolve such mysteries. We need but recall that these factors are solely class-theoretical concepts to recognize that the most they can contribute to our knowledge is to indicate which persons in what contexts are most affected by the processes being assessed. To realize the full potential of an ecological paradigm, the research design must go beyond the conventional labels used to distinguish various social groups in a society. It is necessary, in addition, to gather specific information about one or more of the substantive domains specified in the definition of the macrosystem.

Even with this further substantive differentiation, however, the design would remain a process–context model that leaves unexplored, for example, any intellectual resources or developmentally instigative cognitive characteristics of the person that might also affect the differential impact of parental styles among different ethnic groups living in otherwise comparable macrosystem worlds.

Cognition and Culture. In such a process–person–context model, it is important to recognize that the person domain is also culturally rooted. A growing body of research testifies to the validity of this proposition. It begins with the ethnographic studies of the English anthropologist, W. H. R. Rivers (1926), on whose ideas Vygotsky drew in developing his theory of the sociohistorical evolution of the mind. That theory, in turn, served as the basis for the extraordinary expedition to remote regions in Soviet Asia, conceived by Vygotsky and carried out by his students — Luria and Zaporozhets, with the aim of assessing the impact on thought processes brought about by the social and technological changes associated with the Russian Revolution (Luria, 1931, 1979).

In the present generation, the same thesis has received more sophisticated and systematic support from the work of contemporary ethnologists, and psychologists. As an example of a recent, concerted effort to assess cognition in context, I can do no better than to cite the work of my colleague, Stephen Ceci (1990), an experimental psychologist briefly turned anthropologist who then returned to his root discipline by putting the laboratory itself in context. In a series of experimental studies, Ceci and his colleagues demonstrated that the same cognitive processes, in both children and adults, varied appreciably both in complexity and efficiency as a function of the context in which they were embedded. For example, processes supporting prospective memory progressively increased in efficiency as the same experiment was conducted with samples of children in a physics laboratory, a laboratory in a home economics building, and in the children's own home (Ceci & Bronfenbrenner, 1985). In a second experiment (Ceci, 1990), the ability to educe complex visual patterns showed a quantum gain when the same stimulus patterns were depicted as small pictures of familiar objects embedded in a video game instead of by abstract geometrical figures embedded within a laboratory task. In a third study, appropriately titled "A Day at the Races" (Ceci & Liker, 1986), highly successful racetrack bettors were asked to handicap 60 actual and experimentally contrived races.

> The analysis revealed that expert handicapping was a cognitively sophisticated enterprise, with experts using a mental model that contained multiple interaction effects and nonlinearity . . . involving as many as seven variables [pertaining to the characteristics of the horse, the jockey, the other horses in the field, the weather, etc.]. (Ceci & Liker, 1986, p. 255)

Measures of expertise, however, were not correlated with the subjects' IQs, and four of the top handicappers had IQ scores in the lower to mid-80s.

On the basis of their findings, Ceci, Bronfenbrenner, and Baker (1988) concluded that "the context in which cognition takes place is not simply an adjunct to the cognition, but a constituent of it" (p. 243).

Some Preposterous Proposals

Ceci's scientific aphorism has important implications for research on cognitive development in general? The reader may recall a statement I made earlier, which, at the time, may have seemed perplexing if not preposterous. I asserted, without further elaboration, that the definition of a macrosystem argued for "the representation of characteristics of the culture, or of any other macrosystem, as a critical feature of research models for investigating developmental processes and outcomes-particularly in the cognitive sphere."

I now offer two recommendations that spell out what the term *representation* implies in terms of research design. These recommendations may make the original statement less perplexing, but probably even more preposterous.

Recommendation 1

Because the psychological meaning of particular characteristics of process, person, and context depends on the particular macrosystem in which these phenomena occur, it is important to include in every research design some assessment of the meaning to the research subjects of key elements of the model to which they are exposed. Such assessment can usually be most easily carried by interviewing a subsample of the subjects or requesting their responses to an open-ended questionnaire.

For example, in the studies of parental style, it would have been instructive to ask representatives of each ethnic group what their opinion is of a parent who is authoritarian, and what the significance of grade point average is in their lives. To illustrate what can be learned from posing such questions, I quote the response of a Chinese-American student in my class. When I asked what Asians thought about authoritarian parents, he replied, with a smile: "That's how we know our parents love us."

It should be clear that what I am recommending here is an ecological analogue to Piaget's classic clinical interview.

The second recommendation goes even farther:

Recommendation 2

To the extent that is practically possible, every program of research on human development should include, at an early stage, a contrast between at least two macrosystems most relevant to the developmental phenomenon under investigation, represented not just by a label, but by psychological substance.

Why should such an outlandish provision be desirable, let alone necessary? I offer what I hope are two compelling reasons. First, the recommended procedure provides one of the most effective checks against arriving at, and publishing, a false conclusion. Second, and even more important for scientific advance, the strategy constitutes one of the most powerful tools we have for illuminating our understanding of how developmental processes function in species *Homo sapiens*. In the words of a leading British neuropsychologist, "We are a species wired for culture." Short of trying to change human beings, an effort for which the chances of success are not particularly high, our next best hope as scientists is to try to understand how human nature does that very job. And macrosystems are where we humans do it on the grandest scale, the better or the worse for our own development — cognitive and otherwise.

*   *   *

At the beginning of this chapter I promised to present research models and fugitive findings. By now it should be clear what I meant by research models; some are real, but most are imagined, waiting for someone rash enough to try to transform methodological fantasy into methodological fact.

And what about fugitive findings? Even the meaning of this expression is ambiguous. In the Oxford English Dictionary, the adjective "fugitive" has several definitions. One is "fleeting, evanescent, subject to change"; in other words, the findings I have cited may not stand up. But there is another definition, even more disconcerting: "running away, or intending flight"; in short, escaping consequences by dodging the issues.

It is true that many of the findings I have presented relate to cognition only by analogy, and for some, a connection to cognitive development may seem more imagined than real. I am unhappily reminded of Hotspur's response to old Glendower (in *Henry the Fourth, Part I*). The latter had been expanding upon the scope of his own remarkable powers, and finished with a flourish: "I can call spirits from the vasty deep." To which Hotspur retorted: "But will they come when you do call for them?"

I must acknowledge that this chapter consists more of dreams than of data. Earlier on, I invoked Lewin's classic dictum: "There is nothing so practical as a good theory." It would seem to follow that there is nothing so useless as a bad one. I close with the ardent hope that some of the ideas presented here may turn out to be useful.

ACKNOWLEDGMENTS

I am indebted to my colleagues Richard Canfield and Stephen J. Ceci for their insightful criticisms and creative suggestions, and to Avshalom Caspi and Glen H. Elder, Jr. for copies of graphs from their research reports.

REFERENCES

Allport, G. W. (1937). *Personality: A psychosocial interpretation*. New York: Holt.

Baumrind, D. (1966). Effects of authoritative parental control on child behavior. *Child Development, 37*, 887–907.

Baumrind, D. (1971). Current patterns of parental authority. *Developmental Psychology Monograph 4*, 1–103.

Baumrind, D. (1973). The development of instrumental competence through socialization. In A. D. Pick (Ed.), *Minnesota symposium on child psychology* (Vol. 7, pp. 3–46). Minneapolis: University of Minnesota Press.

Baumrind, D., & Black, A. E. (1967). Socialization practices associated with dimensions of competence in preschool boys and girls. *Child Development, 38*, 291–327.

Beckwith, L., & Cohen, S. E. (1984). Home environment and cognitive competence in preterm children during the first 5 years. In A. W. Gottfried (Ed.), *Home environments and early mental development*. New York: Academic Press.

Beckwith, L., Cohen, S. E., Kopp, C. B., Parmelee, A. H., & Marcy, T. G. (1976). *Child Development, 47*, 579–587.

Bee, H. L., Barnard, K. E., Eyeres, S. J., Gray, C. A., Hammond, M. A., Spietz, A. L., Snyder, C., & Clark, B. C. (1982). Prediction of IQ and language skill from perinatal status, childhood performance, family characteristics, and mother-infant interaction. *Child Development, 53,* 1134-1156.

Block, J. H., & Block, J. (1980). The role of ego-control and ego-resiliency in the organization of behavior. In W. A. Collins, (Ed.), *Minnesota symposia on child psychology, Vol. 13: Development of cognition, affect, and social relations* (pp. 39-101). Hillsdale, NJ: Lawrence Erlbaum Associates.

Block, J., Block, J. H., & Keyes, S. (1988). Longitudinally foretelling drug usage in adolescence: Early childhood personality and environmental precursors. *Child Development, 59,* 336-355.

Block, J., Buss, D. M., Block, J. H., & Gjerde, P. F. (1981). The cognitive style of breadth of categorization: Longitudinal consistency of personality correlates. *Journal of Personality and Social Psychology, 40,* 770-779.

Bronfenbrenner, U. (1977). Lewinian space and ecological substance. *Journal of Social Issues, 33,* 199-212.

Bronfenbrenner, U. (1979). *The ecology of human development.* Cambridge, MA: Harvard University Press.

Bronfenbrenner, U. (1986). Ecology of the family as a context for human development. *Developmental Psychology, 22,* 723-742.

Bronfenbrenner, U. (1988). Interacting systems in human development: Research paradigms: present and future. In N. Bolger, A. Caspi, G. Downey, & M. Moorehouse (Eds.), *Persons in context: Developmental processes* (pp. 25-49). New York: Cambridge University Press.

Bronfenbrenner, U. (1989a). Ecological systems theory. In R. Vasta (Ed.), *Six theories of child development* (pp. 185-246). Greenwich, CT: JAI Press.

Bronfenbrenner, U. (1989b, April). *The developing ecology of human development: Paradigm lost or paradigm regained?* Paper presented at a symposium on "Theories of Child Development: Updates and Reformulations" at the biennial meeting of the Society for Research in child Development, Kansas City, MO.

Bronfenbrenner, U. (1989c). *On making human beings human.* Unpublished manuscript.

Bronfenbrenner, U., & Crouter, A. C. (1983). The evolution of environmental models in developmental research. In P. H. Mussen (Series Ed.) & W. Kessen (Vol. Ed.), *Handbook of child psychology: Vol. 4. History, theory, and methods* (pp. 357-414). New York: Wiley.

Caspi, A., Elder, G. H., Jr., & Bem, D. J. (1987). Moving against the world: Life-course patterns of explosive children. *Developmental Psychology, 22,* 303-308.

Caspi, A., Elder, G. H., Jr., & Bem, D. J. (1988). Moving against the world: Life-course patterns of shy children. *Developmental Psychology, 24,* 824-831.

Ceci, S. H. (1990). *On intelligence: A bioecological view of intellectual development* (Century Series in Psychology). Englewood Cliffs: NJ: Prentice-Hall.

Ceci, S. J., & Bronfenbrenner, U. (1985). "Don't forget to take the cupcakes out of the oven": Prospective memory, strategic time-monitoring, and context. *Child Development, 56,* 150-165.

Ceci, S. J., Bronfenbrenner, U., & Baker, J. G. (1988). Memory in context: The case of prospective memory. In F. Weinert & M. Perlmutter (Eds.), *Universals and changes in memory development* (pp. 243-256). Hillsdale, NJ: Lawrence Erlbaum Associates.

Ceci, S. J., & Liker, J. (1986). A day at the races: IQ, expertise, and cognitive complexity. *Journal of Experimental Psychology: General, 115,* 255-266.

Cohen, S. E., & Beckwith, L. (1979). Preterm infant interaction with the caregiver in the first year of live and competence at age two. *Child Development, 50,* 767-776.

Cohen, S. E., Beckwith, L., & Parmelee, A. H. (1978). Receptive language development in preterm children as related to caregiver-child interaction. *Pediatrics, 61,* 16-20.

Cohen, S. E., & Parmelee, A. H. (1983). Prediction of five-Stanford-Binet scores in preterm infants. *Child Development, 54,* 1242–1253.

Cohen, S. E., Parmelee, A. H., Beckwith, L., & Sigman, M. (1986). Cognitive development in preterm infants: Birth to 8 years. *Developmental and Behavioral Pediatrics, 7,* 102–110.

Cole, M. J., Gay, J., Glick, J., & Sharp, D. W. (1971). *The cultural context of learning and thinking.* New York: Basic Books.

Cole, M., & Scribner, S. (1974). *Culture and thought.* New York: Wiley.

Connolly, J. A., & Doyle, A. (1984). Relation of social fantasy play to social competence in preschoolers. *Developmental Psychology, 20,* 797–806.

Dornbusch, S. M. (1987, April). *Adolescent behavior and school problems: The importance of context.* Paper presented at the meetings of the Society for Research in Child Development, Baltimore, MD.

Dornbusch, S. M., Ritter, P. L., Leiderman, P. H., Roberts, D. F., & Fraleigh, M. J. (1987). The relation of parenting style to adolescent school performance. *Child Development, 58,* 1244–1257.

Elder, G. H., Jr. (1974). *Children of the Great Depression.* Chicago: University of Chicago Press.

Elder, G. H., Jr., & Caspi, A. (1988). Human development and social change: An emerging perspective on the life course. In N. Bolger, A. Caspi, G. Downey, & M. Moorehouse (Eds.), *Persons in context: Developmental processes* (pp. 77–113). New York: Cambridge University Press.

Elder, G. H., Jr., & Caspi, A. (1990). Studying lives in a changing society: Sociological and personological explanations. In A. I. Rabin, R. A. Zucker, & S. Frank (Eds.), *Studying persons and lives* (pp. 201–247). New York: Springer.

Elder, G. H., Jr., Downey, G., & Cross, C. E. (1986). Family ties and life chances: Hard times and hard choices in women's lives since the 1930s. In N. Datan, A. L. Greene, & H. W. Reese (Eds.), *Life-span developmental psychology: Intergenerational relations* (pp. 151–183). Hillsdale, NJ: Lawrence Erlbaum Associates.

Elder, G. H., Jr., Van Nguyen, T. V., & Caspi, A. (1985). Linking family hardship to children's lives. *Child Development, 56,* 361–375.

Gjerde, P. F., Block, J., & Block, J. H. (1986). Egocentrism and ego resiliency: Personality characteristics associated with perspective-taking from early childhood to adolescence. *Journal of Personality and Social Psychology, 51,* 423–434.

Laboratory of Comparative Human Cognition. (1983). Culture and cognitive development. In P. H. Mussen (Series Ed.) & W. Kessen (Vol. Ed.), *Handbook of child psychology: Vol. 1. History, theory, and methods* (4th ed., pp. 295–356). New York: Wiley.

Leont'ev, A. N. (1932). The development of voluntary attention in the child. *Journal of Genetic Psychology, 40,* 52–83.

Leont'ev, A. N. (1982). *Problems in the development of mind.* Moscow: Progress Publishers. (Original Work published 1959)

Leont'ev, A. N. (1978). *Activity, consciousness, personality.* Englewood Cliffs, NJ: Prentice-Hall. (Original Work published 1975)

Lewin, K. (1931). The conflict between Aristotelian and Galilean modes of thought in contemporary psychology. *Journal of Genetic Psychology, 5,* 141–177.

Lewin, K. (1935). *A dynamic theory of personality.* New York: McGraw-Hill.

Lewin, K. (1943). Forces behind food habits and methods of change. *National Research Council Bulletin, 108,* 35–65.

Lewin, K. (1946). Action Research and minority problems. *Journal of Social Issues, 2,* 34–46.

Luria, A. R. (1931). Psychological expedition to Central Asia. *Science, 74,* 383–384.

Luria, A. R. (1979). *The making of mind.* Cambridge, MA: Harvard University Press.

MacDonald, K., & Parke, R. D. (1984). Bridging the gap: Parent-child play interaction and peer interactive competence. *Child development, 55,* 1265–1277.

May, M. A. (1932). The foundations of personality. In P. S. Achilles (Ed.), *Psychology at work* (pp. 81–101). New York: McGraw-Hill.

Morrison, F. J. (1988). *The "Five-to-Seven Shift Revisited: A natural experiment."* Paper presented at the meeting of the Psychonomic Association, Chicago, IL.

Mounts, N. S., Lamborn, S. D., & Steinberg, L. (1989, April). *Relations between family processes and school achievement in different ethnic contexts.* Paper presented at the biennial meeting of the Society for Research in Child Development, Kansas City, MO.

Plomin, R., & Daniels, S. (1987). Why are children in the same family so different from one another? *Brain and Behavioral Sciences, 10,* 1–16.

Plomin, R., & Nesselroade, J. R. (1990). Behavior genetics and personality change. *Journal of Personality, 58,* 191–220.

Pulkkinen, L. (1982). Self control and continuity from childhood to late adolescence. In P. Baltes & O. Brim (Eds.), *Life span development and behavior* (Vol. 4, pp. 64–102). New York: Academic Press.

Pulkkinen, L. (1983a). Finland: The search for alternatives to aggression. In A. P. Goldstein & M. Segall (Eds.) *Aggression in global perspective* (pp. 104–144). New York: Pergamon Press.

Pulkkinen, L. (1983b). Youthful smoking and drinking in longitudinal perspective. *Journal of Youth and Adolescence, 12,* 253–283.

Rivers, W. H. R. (1926). *Psychology and ethnology.* New York: Harcourt, Brace.

Rogoff, B. (1990). *Apprenticeship in thinking.* New York: Oxford University Press.

Rutter, M., & Quinton, D. (1984). Long-term follow-up of women institutionalized in childhood: Factors promoting good functioning in adulthood. *British Journal of Developmental Psychology, 2,* 191–204.

Scarr, S. (1988). How genotypes and environments combine: Development and individual differences. In N. Bolger, A. Caspi, G. Downey, & M. Moorehouse (Eds.), *Persons in context: Developmental processes* (pp. 217–244). New York: Cambridge University Press.

Scarr, S., & McCartney, K. (1983). How people make their own environments: A theory of genotype-environment effects. *Child Development, 54,* 424–435.

Steinberg, L. (1989, March). *Parenting academic achievers: When families make a difference (and when they don't).* Paper presented at the annual meetings of the American Educational Research Association, San Francisco, CA.

Steinberg, L., & Brown, B. B. (1989, March). *Beyond the classroom: Parental and peer influences on high school achievement.* Invited paper presented to the Families as Educators Special Interest Group at the annual meetings of the American Educational Research Association, San Francisco, CA.

Super, C. M. (1980). Cognitive development: Looking across at growing up. In C. Super & M. Harkness (Eds.), *New directions for child development: Anthropological perspectives on child development* (Vol. 8, pp. 59–69). San Francisco: Jossey-Bass.

Vygotsky, L. S. (1929). II. The problem of the cultural development of the child. *Journal of Genetic Psychology, 36,* 415–434.

Vygotsky, L. S. (1978). *Mind in society.* Cambridge, MA: Harvard University Press.

Vygotsky, L. S. (1979). Consciousness as a problem in the psychology of behavior. *Soviet Psychology, 17,* 3–35.

Vygotsky, L. S., & Luria, A. R. (1956). *Psikhoilogicheskie vozzreniia Vygotskogo* [Vygotsky's views on psychology]. In L. Vygotsky (Ed.), *Izbrannye psikhologicheskie issledovaniiia.* Moscow: Academy of Pedagogical Sciences.

Wachs, T. D. (1979). Proximal experience and early cognitive intellectual development: The physical environment. *Merrill-Palmer Quarterly, 25,* 3–41.

Wachs, T. D. (1987a). Specificity of environmental action as manifest in environmental correlates of infants's mastery motivation. *Developmental Psychology, 23,* 782–790.

Wachs, T. D. (1987b, April). *Comparative salience of physical and social environmental differences.* Paper presented at the biennial meeting of the Society for Research in Child Development. Baltimore, MD.

Wachs, T. D. (1989). The nature of the physical micro-environment: An expanded classification system. *Merrill-Palmer Quarterly, 35,* 399–419.

Wachs, T. D. (1990). Must the physical environment be mediated by the social environment in order to influence development?: A further test. *Journal of Applied Developmental Psychology, 11,* 163–178.

Wachs, T. D., & Chan, A. (1986). Specificity of environmental action as seen in environmental correlates of infants' communication performance. *Child Development, 57,* 1464–1474.

Wertsch, J. V. (1985). *Vygotsky and the social formation of mind.* Cambridge, MA: Harvard University Press.

2

The Intention to Use a Specific Affordance: A Conceptual Framework for Psychology

Edward S. Reed
Franklin and Marshall College

The theme of this volume, the role of specific environments in cognitive development, has been central to my theorizing. Influenced by both Charles Darwin and James and Eleanor Gibson, my approach to action has always begun with an analysis of what Darwin preferred to call the "habits of life" of a species, and the evolutionary constraints on those habits. To use Gibsonian language, I have been interested in the evolution and development of the ability to use those affordances of the environment that are basic to the fundamental human econiche. The use of these affordances reflects what Piaget would have considered a very sophisticated kind of biological regulatory process, in which both skill and knowledge become progressively adapted to a wide variety of behavioral contexts. This ontogenetic process of adaptation is intrinsically social—and here I follow Marx and Vygotsky, the fourth of my influences.

Any account of the "psychological environment" that hopes to deal with human development in an acceptable way, must necessarily include an adequate descriptive theory of the animal in its environment that provides concepts for making sense of variation at all these different levels. I believe that, finally, psychology is near this important goal, thanks to James Gibson's theory of the environment to be perceived, acted upon, and known. Gibson's fundamental concept is that of an affordance of the environment for behavior; but, from the outset, Gibson was keenly aware that any higher animal's perception of and action on the affordances surrounding it was a matter of intentional direction of both knowledge and skill (J. Gibson, 1966; see Reed, 1988a, chapter 16). In the following overview of this "ecological approach" to the concept of environments for

cognition I try to make clear the twin roles played by these two concepts —
affordance and intentionality.

The ecological approach to cognitive development that I present rests on
two ideas: First, an account of the relationship between an individual's
intentions and the affordances he or she uses. Second, an account of how
two or more individuals establish joint intentions, and the fundamental role
played by joint intentions in the processes of learning and cognitive
development. I argue that in any situation, an individual's intentions serve
to *select* a small number of the potential affordances available in that
situation. This selection is reflected in the organization of the individual's
attention and activity, and therefore plays a major role in shaping the
knowledge acquisition process. I also argue that, for social creatures like
human beings, the formation of intentions is frequently an interpsychic and
dialectical process, in which more than one individual is involved, and in
which social constraints and cultural norms play a major role.

Existing theories of cognition are "claustrophobic," as Lave (1988) nicely
put it. They assume that cognition is a private, internal, mental affair, and
they also tend to assume that what is cognized are the sorts of abstract
entities and rules found nowadays in schools. The Gibsonian theory of
cognition adumbrated here treats cognition as ecological, as both public
and mental (cf. Rogoff, 1982). It construes the environment as a rich and
meaningful place within which purposeful agents can learn, cooperate, and
conflict, an environment within which realistic cognitive skills could evolve
and develop.

Gibson, Perception, and Cognition

The great potential of James Gibson's ecological psychology for improving
our understanding of cognition has been obscured by the rather vitriolic
debate surrounding his ecological theory of perception (Cutting, 1986;
Fodor & Pylyshyn, 1981; Hagen, 1985; Reed, 1988a; Turvey, Shaw, Reed,
& Mace, 1981; Ullman, 1980). The greater proportion of this debate has
been fueled by a misapprehension: Proponents and opponents of Gibson's
views alike have assumed that perception, at least in Gibson's sense of the
term, should be *contrasted* with cognition. But this is a false contrast.
According to Gibson, perception is one kind — the most basic kind — of
cognition (J. Gibson, 1966, p. 91; cf. Reed, 1987, 1988a, p. 298f.; Shaw &
Bransford, 1977).

Throughout this chapter, *cognition* is used to refer to any and all
psychological processes that function to give an organism knowledge about
its environment, and its situation within the environment. By knowledge I
mean any functional awareness of aspects of the environment as they exist
(perception), or as they have existed (memory), or as they should come to

exist (insight and anticipation), or even as they ought to exist (planning). By functional awareness I mean any capacity to guide action and thought, whether conscious or not. The distinctions among these different types of cognition are not sharp—indeed, it is notoriously difficult to demarcate certain kinds of perception, memory, and anticipation (Bartlett, 1932; J. Gibson, 1966, chapter 13). But all of these knowledge-yielding processes can and should be distinguished from *non*cognitive processes, those psychological processes that do not yield knowledge of the actual environment. Among these noncognitive psychological processes are dreaming, imagining (in the strict sense), guessing, or wishing. It can be difficult to determine whether a given performance is cognitive or noncognitive, and this is no trivial matter. Nevertheless, for purposes of conceptual analysis, the distinction is clear.

According to the present perspective, perception is cognitive because it yields knowledge, not because it is based on information-processing mechanisms, as much of contemporary cognitive psychology holds. Perception is a basic cognitive function because it yields knowledge of the psychologically most basic aspects of our environment—what Gibson called the *affordances of the environment*. Other modes of cognition, such as those involving the use of gestures, symbols (linguistic or numerical), or depictions can bring us knowledge of other aspects of the environment, such as abstract properties (color, metrical shape, cultural significances). J. Gibson (1966, p. 282; cf. Reed, 1988a, p. 306f) rightly argued that these other modes of cognition have the very important effect of reorganizing and securing the knowledge gained via perception, and he explicitly held that most adult human apprehension involved combinations of several modes of cognition.

Once the false antagonism between perception and cognition is removed, it becomes possible to extend Gibson's description of the environment to be perceived so as to develop a general description of the environment to be cognized, acted upon, and shared. Such a project is a major undertaking (to put it mildly!), but a necessary one. Ever since its inception, psychology has run afoul of the problem of not having an adequate account of the rich environmental structures and events in which all psychological development occurs. Behaviorists ludicrously try to reduce this environment to "stimuli" (see J. Gibson, 1960/1982a). That obviously does not work. More recently, information-processing psychologists have tried to solve the problem by pretending it does not exist, and allowing all manner of items—from electric shocks to stories—to be called *stimuli,* focusing instead on attempts to model the knowledge structure supposedly built up from experience.

This tendency in contemporary psychology—to be concerned with the knowledge structure an individual builds up on the basis of experience with one sort of stimuli or another—is perhaps an improvement over behaviorist concerns. Nevertheless, if one is ever to evaluate the cognitive status of this learning, one still needs to have an independent account of *what* a subject has learned. Such an account can and should combine biological and cultural realism, but it must not presuppose aspects of individuals' experiences in describing what it is that people learn, at risk of circularity or vacuousness. The environment is so rich that diametrically opposed conceptions of knowledge structure—such as analog versus propositional representations—have been posited of single cognitive systems (Anderson, 1978). Worse, it is now becoming apparent that any given cognitive system can also be modeled by a number of neural networks, making comparative testing of cognitive models even less precise. Cognitive psychology must concern itself with the ecology of human behavior and knowledge, or risk being buried beneath the weight of theories that are top-heavy with untestable assumptions.

THE ECOLOGY OF PERCEIVING, ACTING, AND KNOWING

In the first part of his last book, *The Ecological Approach to Visual Perception,* J. Gibson (1979) provided a rich description of what the environment surrounding all cognizing organisms is composed of. He showed how substantial surfaces aggregate into objects and layouts, within which events can occur, and he provided a taxonomy of kinds of events as well. The basic "furniture of the world" for sentient animals according to this theory is objects, places, events, and other animals. What we perceive of these things, Gibson argued, is first and foremost what they afford us for action. An object might be graspable, a place a good hiding spot, an event cause for flight or approach, and an other might be friend or foe. Far from considering these use values as abstractions to be inferred by observers on the basis of sensory data or mental representations of various properties of these objects, Gibson claimed that affordances are the primary perceptibles, from which the perception of features, surfaces, representations, and the like are derived. More importantly, J. Gibson (1979, p. 135) also emphasized that among the most important results of perceptual development is the ability to perceive what things afford for others as well as for oneself. Later in this chapter, I show how important this concept of a shared environment is for theorizing about cognitive development.

Perception and Action

What is typically called the *inanimate environment,* on its own, affords only action to an animal. The ground affords locomotion, a small rock affords grasping, whereas a large boulder might afford sitting or climbing. Places, such as caves, can afford concealment or shelter, whereas other places, such as a field, might afford a variety of activities to be done in the open. Events, such as the coming of night or of rainfall, may afford sufficient danger to cause one to take shelter. If Gibson is correct, all higher animals can understand and act upon these meaningful properties of the environment without the intermediation of symbols at all, whether external or mental.

Studies with human infants have demonstrated that even the youngest of human beings—who are capable of only a limited set of actions—can perceive many of the meaningful properties of their environment. Ongoing research is revealing how prelocomoting infants perceive the graspability (in hand and mouth) of objects of various sizes, shapes, and substances (Rochat, 1989), and how locomoting infants perceive the traversability of surfaces with different properties of resistance and resilience (E. Gibson et al., 1987; E. Gibson & Schmuckler, 1989). An excellent example of this sort of research is Gustafson's (1984) work on the effects of using a walker on prelocomoting infants. Gustafson showed that such infants quickly adapt to the new possibilities afforded by the walker, revealing sophisticated patterns of perception that are "preadapted" for the needs of locomotion. Upon use of the walker, Gustafson's infants quickly began to look at far away objects to which they had not previously attended, and they also began to interact more with adults. This illustrates a central theme of my theory: As the environment to be acted upon changes, the developing person him or herself changes, reorganizing his or her action systems. We make ourselves as persons, albeit not under conditions of our own choosing, as Marx said.

Interaction

The conditions in which we find ourselves include not just the biosphere, but also a particular human culture, with its historically specific institutions of family, lifestyle, language, education, and the like. The environment in which we live is thus a "populated" one, as J. Gibson (1982b, p. 411) said. Animals live surrounded by life, and especially by other animals. Social vertebrates, such as human beings, are constantly perceiving and acting in the presence of others. Other animals are not mere objects, even objects considered to have special affordances, for they are objects that perceive and act in their own right. When we perceive another animal, we also perceive it perceiving us, and perceive its capacities for action. We share the affordances of the environment with others of our own species, and even with other kinds of animals. We also compete for these affordances. In many instances, we may also be sharing awarenesses of affordances, as well as sharing the affordances themselves. The predatory wolf and the human being share the affordances of the terrestrial ground for locomotion, but only the human can climb that tree—and both the wolf and human share this knowledge, which has a strong effect on their actions.

Eisenberg (1981), in his review of the major mammalian radiations, goes so far as to suggest that there is a generalized mammalian "interaction system." Certainly, when two mammals meet, each is active and capable of perceiving much of what the other is doing and about to do. If there is a generalized mammalian (and bird?) interaction system, it would have evolved because of the importance of the shared environment:

> The richest and most elaborate affordances of the environment are provided by other animals and, for us, other people. . . . They move from place to place, changing the postures of their bodies, ingesting and emitting certain substances, and doing all this spontaneously, which is to say their movements are animate. . . . They are so different from plants and ordinary objects that infants learn almost immediately to distinguish them from plants and non-living things. When touched they touch back, when struck they strike back; in short they *interact* with the observer and with one another. Behavior affords behavior, and the whole subject matter of psychology and of the social sciences can be seen as an elaboration of this basic fact. (Gibson, 1979, p. 135)

The ecological ubiquity of interaction has meant that there has occurred considerable selection on those specific components of behavior that are most relevant to interaction. Darwin (1872) long ago noted a number of special kinds of selection that applied only to animal signals and gestures, and much of his thinking on this subject is still accepted, in slightly modified form (Smith, 1977). Darwin argued that those behavioral patterns that are perceptible and associated with communication or emotional states will undergo selection not only in terms of the fitness they confer on an animal in an intrinsic way, but also in terms of the fitness they confer on that animal in its social context. Hence, for example, there will be considerable selection for gestures to be based on what later ethologists speak of as "intention movements"—brief and simple movement patterns that reliably reveal an animal's next course of action. This means that an individual can perceive not only what another conspecific affords him or her, but also can perceive affordances *indicated* by another's signals or gestures, and, at least in some cases, to perceive what the other is aware of.

Signal systems allow conspecifics to live in a shared environment, and this is a basic fact of all social structure. Evidence abounds that higher mammals and birds have repeatedly evolved signal systems by which they share both the affordances of their surroundings, and knowledge of those affordances (Cheyney & Seyfarth, 1991). Evidence is also accumulating that human infants spontaneously develop signals and gestures that enable them to share not only their needs with caretakers, but also to communicate about things and events with them. For example, Acredolo and Goodwyn (1988) found over 100 creatively invented gestures being used to indicate objects in their study of children in the second year of life. These gestures are idiosyncratic and, unlike verbalizations, understood by at most a handful of people. Such gestures represent the child's own effort to share his or her environment and experience with others. The need to share in this way, and the limitations of such individualistic systems, plays a major role in facilitating the entry of children into language systems, and probably also plays a role in contributing variation to those systems.

The emergence of symbolic gesture (including true language) in the second year of life, alongside of the emergence of tool use, has suggested to Vygotsky and many others that there is a relationship between symbols and tools. There is also considerable ethological evidence for this apparent parallelism between tools and symbols (Ingold, 1987, chapter 3; Woolfson, 1982). Symbolic gestures appear to function as tools only in populated environments, in which the symbolizer can cooperate sufficiently with others so as to share either idiosyncratic acts of reference, or more systematic symbol systems. But the individual self who is symbolizing is also a part of this environment, and these various "tools" of communication and symbolizing are brought to bear self-referentially, as well as in communication. In Vygotsky's terminology, one "internalizes" symbols and language, and thus alters one's cognitive and action capacities.

Words serve as invariant information structures that bring new things into awareness, or new action capacities under control (J. Gibson, 1966, p. 281f; Vygotsky, 1934/1986). Even proto-words can serve this function. A toddler who can manage to reliably utter some two syllable proto-word with the right prosody can invariable get a caretaker to play "bouncy" or some equally fun game. The utterance soon comes to symbolize this desired interaction, to the caretaker as well as to the child, thus reorganizing both of their action patterns within an interactive context. Vygotsky emphasized that words are "given" from a culture to a child, but that the child then uses these items to reorganize his or her understanding of the world. The discovery of a label for a game, or of a request word (e.g., "more") helps the child to attend to and act upon things he or she did not before. This process of internalization of symbols (as Vygotsky considered it) and reorganization can only occur in a socially organized environment, hence Vygotsky's emphasis on what he termed the transition from inter- to intrapsychic functioning.

Proper Action

Human interaction involves even more than knowledge of affordances and shared knowledge of affordances. J. Gibson (1979) commented that "only when each child perceives the values of things for others as well as for herself does she begin to be socialized" (p. 141). But this is a rudimentary form of socialization, at best. The wolf and I may both perceive the value of the tree for affording me safety, but little socialization is involved in this shared knowledge. What Gibson left out here is that social animals live in populations that have *specializations* (age, gender, and social status-related) in behavior. These specializations produce constraints on *what* affordances can be utilized, *by whom,* and *when.* These are social norms that are *constraints on action,* not on affordances. For example, when a child is toilet trained he or she learns a number of taboos about the acts of defecation and urination as well as the affordances of the various tools we use as toilets.

To describe these phenomena, I have adapted J. Gibson's (1950) earlier distinction between the *expedient* use of affordances—with concern only for the utility of the outcome—and acting *with propriety*—acting with concern for the socially established norms (see Reed, 1988a, chapter 6). It is important to note that social norms are not private, subjective states, they are public and *exist in the environment.* To be part of the cultural environment is not to be nonexistent; nor does it imply that norms are somehow "mental" or "subjective" as opposed to "physical" and "objective" affordances (Ingold, 1987, chapters 1 & 2; Reed, 1988b). The activities of caretakers in toilet training—a classic instance of socialization—are both mental and physical, and are public to the child, as well as affecting him or her privately. In any case, these toilet-training activities are certainly as real and publicly verifiable as the toilet technology itself.

The learning of affordances and the learning of norms typically are very different processes. When one learns about the affordances of things—even about the interactive affordances of others—one is learning about properties of objects, events, and places with respect to one's own actions. When one learns about norms, one is learning about properties of one's own actions (and their objects) with respect to the awarenesses and activities of others. To learn that the cookie jar is a place for concealing cookies requires understanding permanence and placement. To learn that obtaining cookies from the jar is to be done only with parental permission involves, in addition to the above cognitive skills, a considerable array of social knowledge about interactions concerning food, and the social classification of certain items as "treats."

The Nature of Social Affordances

One of the standard criticisms of Gibson's concept of affordances for behavior is that these are necessarily restricted to the "physical environment" and cannot be of use in understanding the social world (Noble, 1981;

B. Schmitt, 1987). If this were true, the ecological approach to describing the environment would be of little use to anyone who wanted to have anything to say about real human endeavors. However, the argument is spurious precisely because it overlooks Gibson's important attempt to transcend the usual dichotomy between the social and the physical environment (J. Gibson, 1966, p. 26; Reed, 1988a, p. 309f; cf. Ingold, 1987). J. Gibson (1979) was willing to say of even such a culturally specific object as a mailbox that it affords mailing:

> For Koffka it was the *phenomenal* mailbox that invited letter-writing, not the *physical* postbox. But this duality is pernicious. I prefer to say that the real postbox (the only one) affords letter-mailing to a letter-writing human in a community with a postal system. This fact is perceived when the postbox is identified as such, and it is apprehended whether the postbox is in sight or out of sight. To feel a special attraction to it when one has a letter to mail is not surprising, but the main fact is that it is perceived as part of the environment — as an item of the neighborhood in which we live. Everyone above the age of six knows what it is for and where the nearest one is . . . (p. 139)

B. Schmitt (1987, p. 274) asked "how could these generalized expectations, these social norms, be specified in a physical stimulus?" He seems to think that it is only a colored, odd-shaped box that is perceived and known. But Gibson's point is that what "everyone above the age of 6" knows about is a complex social arrangement, involving a variety of events, from letter-writing, to the posting and receiving of mail. The box is seen as it is because it is seen as an object within that system, an "item" in our "neighborhood." Just as one typically learns that a bat affords hitting a ball by seeing it as a component of a complex event in which balls are thrown and swung at, so the postbox is seen as affording sending mail by being seen in a context. In the case of the bat the context can be said to be "physical" only because of the convention of overlooking the cultural forces that shape bats, balls, and the rules of the game. In the case of the mailbox, the context can be said to be social only because of the convention of overlooking the physical embodiments of things like postal systems. However, the events involved in posting are no less observable than those involved in hitting, and Gibson's claim is equally appropriate in both cases. Socially produced entities, such as postboxes (or bats!), are just as real as and exist in the environment alongside of naturally produced objects, such as trees.

The Field of Promoted Action

It is the *perception* or *use* of affordances that can be culturally biased, not the existence of the affordances. Individual human beings develop within a family context, which itself exists as a subsector of a particular culture. Indeed, what we now think of as the family unit itself only originated within the past 1,000 years (Herlihy, 1988), and has undergone considerable change over time (Aries, 1962; Casey, 1989; Engels, 1885). Within this cultural subhabitat, individuals are exposed to their environment (both physical and cultural) in a specific manner, according to the peculiar customs of that subcultural group (Gramsci, 1988). An individual who came from a culture in which mailing letters was unknown might well have a most difficult time learning what a postbox was. And a person from a cricket-playing culture will certainly have some difficulty grasping at least the finer points of batting in baseball (and vice versa). These facts of cultural variation should not be interpreted ontologically, however. The affordances for an entire population do not change, even though people's knowledge, perception, and skill differ within that population, or between members of different populations. Cow's milk is still a nutritious drink for humans, even though many people cannot digest it without some additional processing, via cooking or fermenting.

Ingold (1987) remarked: "put a spear into my untutored hand, and I would be no more capable of hunting than without it" (p. 28). Now, obviously, a spear is a weapon that affords important activities involved in hunting. But, given to an individual who has never been encouraged to attend to or to learn about those hunting-relevant properties of the spear, and who has little or no experience of the exigencies of hunting — torn away from the kind of culturally based, interpersonal learning that characterizes all human skill — a spear cannot, of itself, create a hunter.

An object affords what it does because it is what it is, because it has certain specific properties. But these properties are not intrinsic to the object; on the contrary, they are properties taken with reference to agents who will perceive or use the object. The nutritive value of milk must be taken with reference to a human drinker. A spear — or any human tool — has the affordances it has because of its relation to human manipulative abilities, to human body and arm size, and so on. To realize these affordance properties requires that an agent regulate his or her activity according to fairly precise information concerning both the tool and the agent's own postures and movements. Many of the affordances we use unthinkingly and habitually in daily life requires extensive experience and learning to be perceived or to be used. Such skill requires practice and learning, and this typically requires encouragement and even instruction from other individuals, and the same goes for learning to eat or drink certain foods. Instruction in the sense of helping others to learn the affordances of objects and tools within the context of a given skill (as opposed to more formal methods of teaching) has only just begun to be studied, and promises to be an exciting area of research (Rogoff, chapter 5, this volume).

Affordances are thus entities with relatively variable persistences. (The same holds for any biological resource, such as a food item.) The affordance of the ground for terrestrial locomotion is of long-term phylogenetic significance, and has exerted important selection pressure on countless generations of creatures. At the other extreme, the affordance of a particular apple for eating persists only through a single act of a single animal. In our human econiche there are species-specific affordances (e.g., the graspability of branches and other sticks of approximately hand width), many of which become modified and shaped by cultural practices into more specialized affordances (e.g., a spear). The history of technological and cultural diffusion strongly suggests that cultural modifications of affordances are specializations, not complete transformations (Basalla, 1988). The current intellectual fashion of cultural relativism simply overlooks the fact that we humans all live in a shared environment. Many Asians find cheese unpalatable, just as many Europeans find Hundred Year Old Egg noisome, but in both instances individuals can see how these items do afford eating to someone. And, although I may be incapable of using a spear, I can understand how it is a useful tool (Reed, 1988b).

The environment is not so much altered by cultures as it is articulated and modified. Cultures only exist as populations of individuals who select a typical and culture-specific set of affordances to live among. I call those aspects of the environment to which an individual attends because of consistent encouragement from others the field of promoted action (FPA). (The idea is borrowed with modification from Valsiner, 1987.) This field is necessarily part of the shared environment, and it typically changes over time for a given individual. Our human specializations for selecting information, gesturing, indicating, depicting, and symbolizing has allowed us to create large and well articulated FPAs. Research in cross-cultural psychology suggests that cultural differences among FPAs are one of the most important factors leading to cognitive differences among peoples of different cultural background (Cole & Scribner, 1981; Laboratory of Comparative Human Cognition, 1982; Lave, 1988). The processes underlying the establishment and maintenance of FPAs are discussed later.

INFORMATION IN THE ENVIRONMENT

The ecological approach to psychology begins, as I have here, with an analysis of what exists in the environment of perceiving, acting, and knowing creatures. The ecological approach attempts to analyze the information on the basis of which animals and people can and do come to learn about their environment. As mentioned earlier, Gibson's claims about the nature of the information that exists for the perception of the affordances of the environment have aroused considerable controversy. Much of that controversy, however, is due to confusion concerning the meaning of the term *information*. Other aspects of the controversy are due to a failure to realize the limitations Gibson placed on his claims about the kind of information that gives rise to perception, and his emphasis on the different kinds of information that are involved in various cognitive skills. This description of the psychological environment can thus provide us with a helpful framework for understanding how, according to Gibson, *ecological* information provides a basis for perceptual knowledge, whereas other forms of information, primarily informative structures created by people for communicative purposes, provide the bases for different modes of cognition.

Information and Cognition

In this chapter, *cognition* is taken to be the set of capacities by which observers gain knowledge of their environment. We have seen that the animate, populated environment is quite complex, including everything from simple objects, to intricate patterns of interaction, ritual, and social norms. It should not be expected that knowledge of such diverse things is based exclusively on a single kind of information. We should also be quite careful to distinguish cognitive from noncognitive mental functions. Imagining, guessing, and dreaming are all psychological processes of great importance, and all of them use information in some way, but none of them are cognitive, in the sense meant here of reflecting processes that further an individual's knowledge of the environment. These noncognitive processes can play an indirect role in cognition, by facilitating cognitive processes in one way or another. A daydream might help one remember something, but it is the remembering that is cognitive, not the dreaming on its own (Freud, 1900/1933).

Ecological Information and Direct Perception of the Environment

Gibson's greatest contribution to psychology was his concept of *ecological* information. This is the kind of information that is available in ambient energy sources to an active, exploring observer, and that specifies its source in the environment. Specificity means that the detection of such information is tantamount to the perception of the source of that information, including the activities of the observer. Thus, if the horizon is specified in the optic array by the largest inclusive visual solid angle (and it is), then the detection of that angle, or of information equivalent to that, by any observer will mean that the observer perceives him or herself in the midst of a place reaching off to the horizon (see Sedgwick, 1980). As I have shown at length elsewhere (Reed, 1986, 1988a), in his own research Gibson showed how one could use this concept of information to test concrete hypotheses concerning the perception of many important aspects of the environment, from spatial layout to the line of sight of other people (J. Gibson, 1950; J. Gibson & Danielson, 1963), from the motion of objects, to the controlling of self-locomotion (Gibson, 1958, 1968), from the shapes and textures of objects, to the perception of complex events within environments cluttered with objects (J. Gibson, 1950, 1979), from the perception of pictures to the perception of places (Gibson, 1971; Gibson, Purdy, & Lawrence, 1955).

Throughout this program of research, Gibson's goal was to show that the meaningful aspects of the environment could be perceived directly, by which he meant that the process underlying cognition of these things was a process of information detection, not one of symbolic interpretation, or the formation of mental representations (J. Gibson, 1960/1982a; Reed, 1987, 1988a). According to Gibson, almost everything within the environment is sufficiently embodied so that some aspect of it is perceptible. Even social rituals must be embodied in ecological events, and at least some aspects of those events will be perceptible, especially to those who have experience of the ritual and therefore understand the subtleties of what information to attend to. It is because visual perception is so informative about the environment, including the social events surrounding one, that cultures are able to use movements and postures of the hands, arms, body, and face, to communicate about emotions, intentions, and other social relations.

Gibson argued that in all instances in which affordances are perceived, no matter how complex the property to be cognized, our awareness of it is necessarily rooted in perception. For example, in referring to Kohler's studies on how chimpanzees learned to use a stick as a rake to gather food, J. Gibson (1966) wrote: "The perceiving of rake-character may have developed slowly, after much . . . manipulation . . . The point is that these meanings do not consist of the memories of past manipulations, or of the acquired motor tendencies to manipulate. The acts of picking up and reaching with *reveal* certain facts about objects, they do not *create* them" (p. 274).

Selections of Information

Although it is true that ecological information is a potential source of knowledge about almost every aspect of the environment, on its own, information is not an adequate basis for cognition of all aspects of our habitat. It has already been mentioned that many species of higher mammals and birds have developed complex signal systems for communicating about dangers or opportunities. There has thus been considerable selection pressure in a diversity of econiches for the capacity to select particular aspects of information. It is through these various ways of selecting information that one observer becomes capable of making another observer aware of something. I refer to this active process of making others aware of something as *indication* (Reed, 1981).

Information that has the capacity to indicate is rather different from information that can specify. Like most environmental events, a gesture specifies itself; that is, whatever postures and movements out of which it is composed. But what a gesture indicates is something beyond itself, some affordance of a different environmental object, place, event, or creature of which the observer should take note. In effect, a bodily gesture is information that causes the observer of the gesture to take notice of some *further* information in the environment. When a child comes to understand pointing, what he or she has learned is to attend not to the pointing person, but to the information that specifies that which the pointer is pointing at. In the absence of other information, the awareness of the display or gesture is direct, but the awareness of what is indicated is indirect, because it is mediated by the display. Typically, when indirect perception functions in the control of action, it does so by leading to further direct perception: to the pickup of information specifying that which is indicated. But indirect perception can also be used to mislead, as well as to lead.

In social creatures, indications and socially mediated attention are ubiquitous. Much of human psychological development involves this doubly dialectical process between direct and indirect cognition and individual and socially mediated experience. It is important to avoid collapsing these two distinctions. With the advent of "internalization," it is quite possible for individuals to guide their own actions (or misguide them) via indirect cognition, controlling their own actions via gestures and symbols acquired through interaction, as Vygotsky emphasized. But it is also certainly possible for a group of people to share in the direct perception of an event, without significant social mediation.

Varieties of Indication

There are several varieties of indication. Indication always involves some sort of selection of information, but there are a diversity of ways in which information can be selected. Information can be embodied in gesture, bodily or verbal. This is the simplest form of indication, for it involves nothing more than the discovery by one observer of an efficacious way of causing another observer to attend to already available ecological information. Information can be selected and depicted on a surface, as in picturing, which involves a much more active process of noticing information structures in the environment, and modifying a surface so that it presents similar structures. *Systems* of gesturing and signaling would only evolve later, after repeated uses of particular indications in particular contexts gave rise to selection pressures for systematicity in symbolizing. For example, it is possible for nonsegmented vocalizations to indicate a large variety of things in the environment. But without segmentation of vocalization into re-assortable units like phonemes, so that an indefinite number of larger units can be created, there will be limits to the communicative efficacy of vocalization (Studdert-Kennedy, 1986, 1987).

Indication, in whatever form, still relies heavily on perception, for each form of indication succeeds only because observers of the selected information can use it as a guide to help them to perceive what the selector intended. Information can also be selected and encoded in a variety of symbolic forms, such as language, number, and a plethora of measuring systems. It is useful to distinguish this encoding of information by the term *predication* (see Searle, 1969, for more on the distinction between mere reference or indication and predication). Whereas the process of selection allows one to manipulate existing information and thereby refer to things, the process of encoding actually allows one to manipulate information itself and to make statements, questions, or commands. Human societies specialize in instruments for embodying combinations of predications and indications, such as maps, game charts and boards, currency, memory strings (quipus), and so on. Depiction, symbolic coding, and devices for representation seem to be highly specialized in human cultures and found rarely, if at all, elsewhere.

Symbols and Language

It is important to note that the present definition of displays or representations is at variance with current practice in semiotic theory and cognitive science. Roger Brown (1987) said that the standard definition of a symbol is "a token that is associated with and represents a referent on the basis of arbitrary convention" (p. 443). According to my account, *representations— even words or numbers—are not entities that stand for other entities in any way* (either "conventionally" or "naturally.") On the contrary, they are entities that partially embody ecological information in some way, or allow experienced observers to detect specific kinds of information. Thus, if an observer has knowledge of the representation system being used, he or she will be able to apprehend what is represented by a display, even if, prior to this, that represented object was unknown to the observer.

Words cannot stand for things. They cannot even stand for information.

They do not have the kinds of patterns of invariance across extensive transformation that characterizes either ecological objects or information. It is, after all, this relative lack of variability that makes them so useful. What words do is facilitate awareness by facilitating the listeners' use of information, as Vygotsky seems to have realized with his strong emphasis on the social-semiotic nature of mature human behavior. The important thing about words and symbols is that the ability to use them entails the ability to better perceive and act upon what the words and symbols represent, even when one has not directly experienced what they represent. This capacity of symbols is tied up with the definition of indirect perception as given earlier: that certain kinds of selected information can be utilized to make others aware of things.

According to the present view, even the learning of speech is not the learning of one set of things (words) that stand for other things (ideas, objects, meaning, whatever). On the contrary, the learning of speech is the learning of an amodal system (for words can be vocal, manual, or written) that enables one to refine and organize one's own and others' ability to use ecological information to regulate both acting and knowing. Above all else, language is selective, and what it selects is the ability to detect information and thereby regulate action. Speech can help children regulate their action and interactions prior to and independently of its ability to help them label the world. In fact, it is because speech functions in this regulatory fashion, that it can be helpful in labeling as well. When language is understood in this way—as a means for sharing awareness of the world to be acted upon through encoded information, not just the abstract encoding process itself—it becomes clear that the existence of language itself requires such phenomena as commands, questions, and statements. Language itself is not a code, but a culturally based tool for acting and thinking: "A language is more than a code because it permits predications as well as labellings. It has a grammar as well as a vocabulary. The child's discovery of facts about the world can be predicated in sentences, not simply stereotyped in words" (J. Gibson, 1966, pp. 281–282).

The structure of language in the environment is necessarily multimodal, because language, when produced, is an expression of the speaker's entire person, and even some of the context, not merely the production of a vocal tract. It has become clear that even relatively young infants appreciate the multimodal structure of language, and exhibit sensitivities to both the auditory and visual events comprising speech (Kuhl & Meltzoff, 1987). As J. Gibson (1966) said, echoing Vygotsky's half-century old analysis: ". . . words are not simply auditory stimuli or vocal responses. They embody stimulus information, especially invariant information about the regularities of the environment. They consolidate the growing ability of the child to detect and abstract" the information (p. 281). Utterances thus become "extracortical" connections that serve a crucial role in relating and integrating divergent aspects of the developing child's experience. A simple word like "uh-oh" helps to consolidate the 20-month-old's growing awareness of the causal structure of events. Similarly, words used to label categories (correctly or not) serve to regulate and reorganize the child's thinking and acting (Gopnik & Meltzoff, 1986, 1987).

A child with the ability to detect information and to recognize gestures and other displays but with no language skills at all could learn a great deal about the affordances of the environment for action and interaction, but would learn little about the proprieties of the particular human environment in which he or she finds him or herself. The FPA of every culture is intimately tied up with language, and there appear to be characteristic modes of address even to infants, who obviously do not understand the content of the talk, but who are thereby slowly brought into that culture's shared environment. In early conversation, according to Cazden (1979, cited in Rogoff & Gardner, 1984):

> The mothers work to maintain a conversation despite the inadequacies of their conversational partners. At first they accept burps, yawns, and coughs as well as laughs and coos — but not arm-waving or head movements — as the baby's turn. They fill in for the babies by asking and answering their own questions, and by phrasing questions so that a minimal response can be treated as a reply. Then by 7 months the babies become considerably more active partners, and the mothers no longer accept all of the baby's vocalizations, only vocalic or consonantal babbles. As the mother raises the ante, the child's development proceeds. (p. 105)

INTENTIONS AND THE SELECTION OF AFFORDANCES

What are Intentions?

Intention is typically used to refer to a mental state. In particular, the idea has been that intentions are mental states that cause actions. This theory leads to profound philosophical problems (What causes intentions? How can mental states cause embodied actions?). But, more importantly for present purposes, this mental state theory of intention has a number of problematic methodological results. If intentions are mental states that cause acts, then the only evidence we can have for them, outside of introspection, is evidence of spontaneous, even capricious acts (i.e., actions not under "stimulus control"). Such spontaneous acts are precisely what neurologists look for when they try to identify intentions. Yet surely the development of intention and volition is far more than the growth of spontaneity.

In the present view, intentional action is a prime example of just how "spread out" cognition is. To have an intention requires objects as well as subjects (Fischer et al., chapter 4, this volume). And both objects and subjects must be situated in a setting (Bronfenbrenner, chapter 1, this volume; cf. Heft, 1988, 1989). Intentions are thus not discrete, static, internal, mental events. They are continuous, dynamic, contextualized, public events.[1] To identify an intention—the entire complex organization of action and knowledge—with its earliest mental components is as grave a fallacy as identifying a hurricane with its first gales.

From an ecological point of view, intentions are not causes of action, but patterns of organization of action; they are not mental as opposed to physical, but are instead embodied in the kinds of performances most likely found in cognitively capable creatures. Intention is characterized by *directedness, persistence, and resilience:* directedness toward objects, places, or events relevant to the intender's situation; persistence until the intention is met, and recognized as having been met by the agent; resilience in the face of perturbation, whether environmental or personal. The development of intention is thus the development of the ability to nest bouts of exploratory and performatory behavior so as to achieve desired outcomes. The purely cognitive ability to think of things or to plan activities is a component of intention, but only one small component of a much larger, more complex process.

Intention is a phenomenon that only emerges when a complex organism finds itself in a complex environment. Roughly speaking, intention can emerge (but may not) whenever there is a real possibility of choice among affordances. For example, an apple affords both eating and throwing as a missile to higher primates. What will a given animal do with the apple? Why will one affordance be realized and not the other? Or why will this object be passed by entirely, and another activity take place? Young children show

---

[1]I find that even the most "contextualist" of cognitivists demur at my claim that the intentions in actions are "public." But what is a nonpublic intention? It is either a public lie or a private lie. In the former case at least some aspect of the intentional act is public, and in the latter there is no intentional act of the sort supposed. The paradigmatic case of "private intention" is an internal monolog. For example, an agent may take umbrage at what someone does, without expressing this in public. Thus, the agent lies in public, acting politely while all the time thinking and plotting revenge. Here the intentional act is *to deceive,* and it is public (whether successful or not). A second case of private intention is a lie to oneself, where one formulates an intention in thought ("I will begin that diet tomorrow . . .") but with a more or less inchoate caveat against carrying it out. In this sort of case it is unclear whether there is any intentional action at all. In any event, these subtle internalized forms of intending have barely begun to develop in young school-aged children, and are far from the fundamental cases of intentional action with which this chapter is concerned.

evidence of components of intentionality: They can understand situations, plan, and act up to a point. But the resilience and persistence required for successful voluntary action in a broad range of contexts is missing in young children, and develops only slowly.

The Context of Behavior

The present description of the psychological environment, the information for knowing the environment, and the concept of intention as a complex process of using information to guide performance would seem to have introduced such a bewildering array of concepts and issues that no theory could be constructed to unite and integrate them. It would therefore seem that such extensive and intensive diversity would force anyone who wished to attempt to develop a cognitive psychology of everyday life to work largely at a descriptive level, focusing on contextual determination of phenomena.

For those who seek scientific explanations of psychological phenomena, as I do, the appeal to context, although increasingly heard throughout psychology these days, is of little use. If we don't understand, for example, how a person comes to know about a certain kind of object (e.g., a container), saying that the knowledge gathered and the underlying processes are different in different contexts offers no further contribution at all. Instead, one is beset by a new set of questions: What counts as a context? Are contexts physical or mental (or must we repeat these same old dichotomies)? And how are contexts known?

The best way to resolve the problems raised by a cognitive psychology of real, everyday activities is to follow the path blazed by Lave (1988) and others, and to push out from the "claustrophobic concept of cognition" currently used. We need to study cognition in the settings in which it is actually found, to establish how it is organized and reorganized to meet the needs of different situations and intentions (Reed, 1991). But this alone is not enough. Altering the notion of context from a mental space to the real world is helpful, but only insofar as one seeks a valid *description* of cognitive phenomena. To *explain* the complex, contextually varying phenomena of cognition will require a theory that is rich enough to explain how *patterns of coherence can and do emerge from ranges of variation.*

In my own work on the description of intentional action in the traumatically brain damaged, we confront this problem of coherence within apparent chaos at every step. Patients suffering from traumatic closed head injuries — typically from traffic accidents — manifest severe but relatively diffuse brain damage. A significant percentage of these individuals appear to have lost the ability to understand and act on their environments to accomplish basic goals of everyday life. Their behavior is typically slow and halting, and they appear confused: They will try to put one shoe over another, to mix peculiar food items (tomato juice as "syrup" for waffles), to "lose their place" (to forget to bathe, or to repeat the process indefinitely). In one detailed case study, for example (see Mayer et al., 1990; Schwartz, Reed, Montgomery, Palmer, & Mayer, 1991), we analyzed 28 days of breakfast eating over a period of 2 months in one patient. We found several hundred significant errors, and nearly 100 errors in the act of making and drinking coffee alone. Often incorrect items were put into the coffee (e.g., oatmeal), or the different items required to make coffee were never brought together properly (e.g., sugar put in the hot water, but nothing else). Despite such apparent chaos, not once did this individual pour a liquid onto his plate, or attempt to transport a liquid via a knife or fork. Even such disordered action revealed marked limits to its variability—limits almost certainly related to the preservation of the understanding of certain basic affordances, despite a failure to organize coherent skilled behavior.

Heretofore ecological psychologists of all schools have been content to point to contextual variability and take note of its extent and importance. But how can one explain such variability in performance and knowledge? How is a person in a setting so constrained that even the behavior of seriously brain damaged individuals reveals coherence at the level of affordance usage, despite lack of selection of appropriate affordances?

The Need for a Selective Retention Theory

The best examples of theories that can explain how variation is constrained within coherent ranges come from population biology (Ghiselin, 1969; Lewontin, 1970; Reed, 1978, 1989). These theories begin with populations of varying entities (cells or organisms) that compete for resources, and that are capable of replication, again with variation. Patterns of environmental support and pressure emerge from this combination of population growth dynamics and competition and shape the range of variation. These *selective retention theories* do not segregate context from the events under study; on the contrary, they attempt to describe and explain the entire complex pattern of interrelationship between organism and environment.

In a provocative recent review, Siegler (1989) argued that evidence in several areas of developmental research implicates competition/selection mechanisms as playing an important role in cognitive change and growth. In a variety of cases, he argued, "competition seems to serve the same function. The multiple competing entities provide the variability needed to adapt to changing environments, contextual demands, and organismic capabilities" (p. 376). This is in agreement with the ideas offered here. The ecological approach to cognitive development offered here differs from Siegler's primarily in the assessment of what should count as the "units" of the selection and competition processes. Existing competition models in cognitive psychology tend to assign these units in an ad hoc fashion, and even go so far as to *assume* the existence of stable units (cf. Siegler's, 1989, discussion of MacWhinney at p. 362). However, as Darwin long ago emphasized, the units of selective retention systems are not stable, they are dynamic. Moreover, competition frequently occurs across several levels at which different units cohere. For example, in neuroembryogenesis, there is cell–cell competition, but also competition among groups of cells (Edelman, 1987, 1988; Reed, 1989). Thus, one needs to identify the *bounds* of competition; especially the lowest levels of a system at which meaningful competition occurs, and the level at which change in units is especially significant. This is why Darwin emphasized competition among individual organisms leading to changes at the species level. The following is an attempt to use the ecological psychology of the environment to help us seek both the levels at which meaningful competition occurs in cognitive systems, and the kinds of specific units of knowing and acting that emerge from that competition.

The theory proposed here is that, within any real-world task context, the emergence of intentions is the growth of the ability to select specific affordances for the observer to become aware of and to use. This selection process operates on all kinds of affordances and situations, from the simplest to the most complex. It also operates in cases of joint intention, that is, where a caretaker is scaffolding a situation for a child, or other learner. Intentions thus set limits on the range of variation in activity that will count as contributing to the task at hand. Intentions are thus the "species" that emerge out of competition among perceptual and action processes for utilizing affordances. I call the smallest units of this competition perception action cycles (PACs), and, as described here, these PACs can and do aggregate into diverse, more complex units. Even our very confused brain damaged patients understood at least that liquids are to be poured only into certain kinds of vessels (cups and bowls) and not other places; and they also understood that other food items might best be put on plates. Thus, these individuals oriented their action systems to various tasks subsidiary to eating (e.g., pouring liquids into containers) and oriented their perceptual systems accordingly (e.g., monitoring their pouring so that little or no spillage occurred). Some patients are typically quite successful in these subsidiary tasks while being unsuccessful in organizing these various PACs into the coherent accomplishment of the overall task of eating and drinking. Cognitive development (and, I would add, the development of volition as well) involves the child's increasing awareness of intention-generated limits, the ability to work within these limits, and to accomplish goals under these constraints. The theory is summarized in Table 2.1 and the rest of this section is devoted to explicating these ideas.

TABLE 2.1
Elements of a Selectionist Theory of Cognitive Development

Component Processes:	Perception action cycle (PACs)
Principle of Variation:	Equifinality of PACs for a given goal
Principle of Selection:	Task constraints
	Bringing attention under the control of intention
Intentions:	Emerge from variation + selection
Joint Intention:	Selection + interaction + proper action
	Acculturation of attention
Fields and Zones of Action:	Field of free action
	Field of promoted action
	Zone of proximal development

The Process of Affordance Selection

Component Processes. The component processes underlying all affordance use can be broken down into two kinds of activity, *exploratory* and *performatory* (E. Gibson, 1988; Reed, 1982). Perception in particular, and cognition in general, cannot occur except as the result of exploratory activity, in which the goal is *the detection and use of available information about affordances.* Even the most passive of thinkers, lost in a reverie, is thinking about things at least some of which were originally discovered through exploratory activities. (The recent emphasis of cognitivists on the centrality of analogies of experience in thinking is very much in the spirit of the present theory. See especially Johnson, 1987.) Performatory activity means any kind of action in which some affordance of the environment (and this includes the social environment) is altered. (Note that, in the limiting case at least, performatory and exploratory activity are necessarily distinct.) These two modes of activity are complimentary, and when they work together as they normally do, I speak of a PAC. To become aware of affordances requires exploration of information, to use an affordance, requires performance, and this includes the regulation of performance via both information related to the nature of the task to be achieved, and previously acquired experience and knowledge.

The basic units of action on which psychological developmental selection can operate are, therefore, typically comprised of one or more PACs. As we see here, skilled cognition operates on several levels simultaneously, and it is very doubtful that there could be a single kind of behavioral or cognitive unit on which selection will occur.

Principle of Variation. Because the environment is extremely complex, it is inevitable that a large set of varying PACs is capable of accomplishing the same exploratory and performatory goals. I can stir milk in and slowly sip from the spoon to make sure that my coffee is not too hot to drink, or

I can blow on it in the mug. Either way, I am changing my environment as I want it to be, and monitoring the change accordingly. That the same goals can be accomplished by diverse means is a fundamental fact of cognition and action, at any level of analysis.

Just as a given goal cannot imply a single action pattern, so a given situation is not a single, univocal context. On the contrary, one and the same situation or object may afford a considerable diversity of actions. The stick that affords poking holes in the ground for planting may also afford raking-in fruit from a high tree branch, or it may afford hitting another person, and so on. There is so much information available in any given situation that not all of it can be detected and used. And, similarly, there are so many possibilities for action in a single situation that not all of them can be detected and used. Our brain damaged patients often use an affordance of a given object, but not the affordance that would help them accomplish their goal. Cups are good for helping one rinse out the sink — but this action is irrelevant if the task at hand is brushing one's hair.

Principle of Selection. With such a rich and complex environment, what is to keep anyone from attempting to use every affordance she detects? Or, conversely, what is to keep anyone from detecting a seemingly endless series of affordances, without ever settling down to doing anything? At this point, there will be those who are tempted to invoke innate constraints, at least for the case of some animals. Although it might explain certain special cases, this cannot work as a general answer. The idea that there exist innate constraints on the nervous system causing it to selectively attend to and utilize certain kinds of information and affordances is tempting. But this notion overlooks the incredible variability of information and affordances in the real environment. Although it is true that there may be a relatively small set of highly important affordances needed by a given animal, those affordances will be found in a complex environment, under such a variety of circumstances, that no amount of genetic preprogramming could account for adequate detection of these environmental values. At best, what can be innate are certain tendencies and motivations to utilize specific kinds of affordances as opposed to others.

The hypothesis that I have been evaluating and testing is that every intention selects information and affordances relevant to it out of the complex environmental circumstances in which any animal finds itself. The affordances that an observer attends to and utilizes are thus determined not only by what affordances and information are available in the environment, but by the observer's intention. Note, by the way, that the affordances are not created by the intention, just attended to because of it. This selection process brings attention increasingly under the control of the subject's intentions, as E. Gibson and N. Rader (1979) argued.

A child who has little experience with a given task, or who finds him or herself interested in several tasks within a given setting, will show apparently less stable action and knowledge of the affordances of the child than a more "single-minded" child. But what allows the development of this single-mindedness? When does the child in an object concept situation learn to ignore the interesting event of covering and focus attention on the covered object and only that? Why do some of our brain damaged clients start out to brush their teeth but end up playing with water in the sink? Clients (and children) who do this are typically labeled *distractable* but this is a misnomer. To be distractable is to have an attentional deficit. Yet most of these individuals demonstrate considerable deliberation and attention to the "nonpreferred" tasks they end up doing. The problem here is one of intention, not attention — in particular, a problem of bringing one's attention under the control of one's intentions.

Research on private speech and the verbal regulation of action takes on new significance within the present conceptual framework. Vygotsky and Luria argued that internalizable symbols (like words) were a necessary precursor to the development of voluntary, knowledge-based, activity. The surprisingly sophisticated cognitive and action skills of preverbal infants would seem to cast doubt on this idea. Nevertheless, Vygotsky would almost certainly have concurred with the present argument that symbol skills consolidate and reorganize the developing child's action systems. Variable and unstable courses of action can be stabilized and canalized by words and, once the beginnings of this channeling are available, repetition and competition will lead to further reorganizations, especially to sequential and nested organizations of activity under the selection pressure of an intention.

The present argument would seem to be in line with Gopnik and Meltzoff's (1986, 1987) specificity hypothesis. These writers argued that it is not general cognitive skills that are associated with the verbal "take-off" around 18 months. Instead, they argue, the take-off emerges from a small set of specific cognitive skills that enable the child to comprehend the meanings of key words and phrases (and vice versa). For example, nouns and category terms are associated specifically with object knowledge; and certain verbs and other words of agency are associated with the child's increasingly rich understanding of events and causality. In this regard, it is significant that the kinds of utterances produced in private speech also appear to reflect some cognitive-functional specialization. Terms of self-regulation, self-description, and expressive content are more likely to appear in a 2-year-old's self-directed speech than in his other-directed utterances (Furrow, 1984).

Intentions.   On the present view, intentions are spread out across mind, body, information, ecological context, and social setting. Development of the ability to act intentionally requires not only knowledge of how the self should perform in a situation to achieve a goal, but also the ability to regulate cognition and action so that only the intended affordances are attended to and utilized. This regulation involves organizing one's activity so that most or all of the unit PACs are "on task" and that the groupings of PACs that emerge in the activity progressively help the subject to gain knowledge of the relevant affordances, or to use them in the intended manner.

Joint Intention.   Most human learning occurs in an interactive, acculturating context. The cognition we use most in daily life thus only emerges in a system in which there exists, at the very least, a scaffolder as well as a learner. The relative "helplessness" of human infants in their first few seasons guarantees that much early human experience is interpersonal (Kaye, 1982; Trevarthen, 1988). However, because intentions are manifested in diverse situations, it is not always possible for scaffolders to be sure that learners share their intentions. When one says "look at the dog" the child may, after all, look at the tree next to the dog. According to some thinkers, this ambiguity of reference is inevitable (Quine, 1969) and therefore we can only come to share meanings and intentions if a number of assumptions are built into our cognitive systems. This is simply a mistake, one that ignores the cultural, selective context in which joint intention is established.

Joint intention cannot be imposed. Even if a scaffolder wanted to, he or she would have no means available of insuring that the learner attended to precisely the same information and affordances as the scaffolder intended. For one thing, the affordances of the environment are typically very different for adults and children, just by virtue of their differences in size. Furthermore, no human language has, or could have, a sufficiently rich vocabulary to capture all the distinctions and dimensions available in perception. Despite this, the scaffolder can and does attend to what the learner does, and, similarly, many learners attend carefully to the scaffolder. Through his or her action the scaffolder establishes *boundary conditions,* which is to say, a set of criteria for what will count as satisfactory performance. A child being taught to walk on his or her own will be encouraged to walk without aid, but a gentle holding by one hand might well count as satisfactory early on in the learning of the skill. The boundary may well move, and the criteria shift as the child gains skill and confidence, as suggested in Cazden's account of the growth of speech skills.

The scaffolder in these situations thus acts as part of the selection process affecting the learner, and the attentive scaffolder finds his or her own intentions subject to selection pressures from the learner. (Darwin actually spoke of "unconscious selection" in the shaping of behavior in domesticated animals.) What matters is not that the learner and scaffolder necessarily share identical intentions, but that the two are sufficiently close, and that the direction of change is appropriate. The field of promoted action thus feeds into cognitive development in several ways: by constraining, in increasingly specific ways, what affordances are to be attended to and used; by encouraging one set of intentionally guided PACs, and discouraging others; by creating subsidiary environments in which certain kinds of repetitions (i.e., repetitions of PACs within certain tolerances of variation) are emphasized.

Fields of Action.   As a human child develops, there is an inherently social process of encouraging the formation and carrying out of certain intentions, and discouraging the formation and execution of others. This social structuring involves alterations of the child's environment, and the information available to the child within that environment, as well as alterations of the child's behavior. The field of promoted action (FPA), as described earlier, encompasses those affordances (natural or social) to which a child's attention and activities are directed by others. There is also a field of free action (FFA) (again, these are modifications of concepts of Valsiner's, 1987, chapter 4). The FFA encompasses those affordances and activities that the individual is both capable of accomplishing on his or her own, and is allowed by social circumstances to do so.

In cognitive development, there is an overall increase in the FFA, along with a progressive refinement and sophistication within the FPA. Cognitive development does not simply mean that the individual can do more things (although that is certainly an important part of cognitive growth); it also means that the individual can understand progressively subtler and more complicated instructions and ideas. In Valsiner's (1987) case studies of the development of mealtime skills, for instance, it is shown that the FFA is typically highly restricted at mealtime for middle-class children in the United States. (There is even a technology for accomplishing this restriction, the "high chair" and the newer "sassy seat.") But this restriction on the FFA would seem to be designed to facilitate a focusing of instruction, so that discrete and episodic intervention by caretakers concerning what to eat and how to do so will have a significant effect on the child. For the same child at "free play" there might be a considerably expanded FFA, but also a less articulated FPA. For example, banging is an exploratory activity favored by 6- to 12-month-old infants specifically for hard objects (Palmer, 1989). The same child might be free to bang a spoon at playtime, or even encouraged to do so, but not allowed to do so (i.e., the spoon may be taken away) at mealtime.

This subtle relationship between the FPA and the FFA determine what Vygotsky dubbed the zone of proximal development (ZPD). It would seem, however, that Vygotsky viewed the ZPD as a general phenomenon, reflecting the general difference between a child's individual cognitive function and that same child's ability to function with instruction. From an ecological point of view, such a notion of the ZPD as a general range is not viable. The ZPD does not even emerge except in highly channeled and specialized environments. The causes of its emergence will differ for different skills, and will be strongly affected by ecological, cultural, and individual factors. Thus, I argue that there is no general ZPD, only specific ZPDs for specific skills, reflecting particular relationships that emerge between FPAs and FFAs. The only sense in which a general ZPD can be said to exist is in terms of a set of specific, culturally determined developmental tasks which tend to be assigned in each child's FPA, and reflected in the growth of their FFAs.

To summarize, the modified concept of the ZPD, as used here, emerges from the new concepts of FFA and FPA. These are defined as follows:

Field of promoted action (FPA): Those objects, places, events, and their affordances, which an individual is encouraged to realize. This field changes from object to object, place to place, event to event, but persistent and invariant patterns of encouragement are hypothesized to exist for given individuals, families, and other cultural groupings.

Field of free action (FFA): Those objects, places, events, and their affordances that an individual can realize on his or her own, and that the individual is allowed to use. This field expands and contracts reciprocally to the field of promoted action.

Zone of proximal (potential) development (ZPD): For any given skill, the difference between the FPA and the FFA. This represents the range of affordances and the variety of contexts within which social scaffolding facilitates affordance usage.

CONCLUSION

Cognition, like all forms of animate activity, begins with use values, with the affordances of the environment for action. At the outset, then, cognition is a specific relation between organism and environment (Holt, 1915). This relation is made possible by the existence of ecological information specifying the situation of an active observer within his or her surroundings (J. Gibson, 1966, 1979), and by each organism's capacity to detect that information, and to develop improved processes of detection (E. Gibson, 1969, 1984). The complexity of the environment is such that the specific relations of affordance use inevitably come into conflict, and successful organisms must develop processes of selection whereby the pattern and sequence of their affordance use is made to be appropriate for their current situation.

In social animals, all these processes, from the simplest act of affordance detection, to the most sophisticated patterning of choice, are mediated in part through interactions as well as actions. Further, social animals' actions and interactions are themselves mediated in part by information that has been selected and coded by other social animals. Not only do attention and performance become increasingly selective and attuned to the environment and information around us, they become increasingly acculturated as well. We make ourselves, Marx long ago emphasized, but not under conditions of our own choosing (R. Schmitt, 1987). Our cognitive skills do not determine our social reality, nor does our social reality determine our cognition. Rather, our social mode of existence is a kind of life within which cognitive skills emerge, develop, and are refined. And, at bottom, all human modes of life, however cognitively or socially refined, require that nature provide us with the means of life: "whatever social form it may take, wealth always consists in use-values" (Marx, 1859, p. 27).

The task of ecological developmental psychology is to help us understand the intricate structure of affordance use in acculturated settings that characterizes all human behavior. The theory proposed here is primarily descriptive. My hope is that the concepts described here — affordances, information, the fields of promoted and free action, the concept of selective retention among general affordances to yield task specificity — are both rich enough and concrete enough to enable empirical tests of real, everyday behavior.

ACKNOWLEDGMENTS

I want to thank the Piaget Society, and especially the organizers of the 1989 symposium, Rob Wozniak and Kurt Fischer, for inviting me to speak for making the symposium such an intellectually stimulating event, and for their detailed and helpful comments on an earlier version of this chapter. I benefited greatly from both the formal and informal remarks of all the other participants in this symposium. I also thank the following individuals for reading an earlier version of this chapter and giving me a great deal of good advice on the issues, most of which I have tried to follow: Paul Callagy, Tom Ferguson, Carol Fowler, Eleanor Gibson, Gene Goldfield, Andrew Meltzoff, Carolyn Palmer, Anne Pick, and Pete Pufall. Although herein I do not discuss the issues of rehabilitation of patients with traumatic brain injury, almost all of the ideas presented in this chapter emerged out of my work on studying everyday activities in the context of rehabilitation at The Drucker Brain Injury Center of Moss Rehabilitation Hospital, ably supported by Nathaniel Mayer, MD and Myrna Schwartz. This research was supported by a Mary Switzer Fellowship from the National Institute on Disability and Rehabilitation Research (1987–1988) and a grant from the Moss Hospital Research Committee (1989–1990).

REFERENCES

Acredolo, L., & Goodwyn, S. (1988). Symbolic gesturing in normal infants. *Child Development, 59,* 450–466.

Anderson, J. (1978). Arguments concerning representations for mental imagery. *Psychological Review, 85,* 249–278.

Aries, P. (1962). *Centuries of childhood.* New York: Random House.

Bartlett, F. W. (1932). *Remembering.* Cambridge: Cambridge University Press.

Basalla, G. (1988). *The evolution of technology.* New York: Cambridge University Press.

Brown, R. (1987). *Social psychology* (2nd ed.). New York: Basic Books.

Casey, J. (1989). *The history of the family.* New York: Cambridge University Press.

Cheney, D. L., & Seyfarth, R. M. (1991). *How monkeys see the world.* Chicago: University of Chicago Press.

Cole, M., & Scribner, S. (1981). *The psychology of literacy.* Cambridge, MA: Harvard University Press.

Cutting, J. (1982). Two ecological perspectives. *American Journal of Psychology, 95,* 199–222.

Darwin, C. (1872). *The expression of the emotions in men and animals.* London: John Murray.

Edelman, G. (1987). *Neural Darwinism.* New York: Basic Books.

Edelman, G. (1988). *Topobiology.* New York: Basic Books.

Eisenberg, J. (1981). *The mammalian radiations.* Chicago: University of Chicago Press.

Engels, F. (1885). *The origin of the family, private property, and the state.* Peking: Foreign Language Publishers.

Fodor, J., & Pylyshyn, Z. (1981). How direct is perception? *Cognition, 9,* 139–196.

Freud, S. (1931). *The interpretation of dreams* (A. A. Brill, Trans.). New York: Random House. (Original work published 1900)

Furrow, D. (1984). Social and private aspects of speech at two years. *Child Development, 55,* 355–362.

Ghiselin, M. T. (1969). *The triumph of the Darwinian method.* Los Angeles: University of California.

Gibson, E. J. (1969). *Principles of perceptual learning and development.* Englewood Cliffs, NJ: Prentice-Hall.

Gibson, E. J. (1984). Perceptual development from the ecological approach. *Advances in Developmental Psychology, 3,* 243–286.

Gibson, E. J. (1988). Exploratory behavior in the development of perceiving, acting, and the acquiring of knowledge. *Annual Review of Psychology, 39,* 1–41.

Gibson, E. J., & Rader, N. (1979). The perceiver as performer. In G. Hale & M. Lewis (Eds.), *Attention and cognitive development* (pp. 1–21). New York: Academic Press.

Gibson, E. J., Riccio, G., Schmuckler, M., Stoffregen, T., Rosenberg, D., & Taormino, J. (1987). Detection of traversability of surfaces by crawling and walking infants, *Journal of Experimental Psychology: Human Perception and Performance, 13,* 533–544.

Gibson, E. J., & Schmuckler, M. (1989). Going somewhere: An ecological and experimental approach to development of mobility. *Ecological Psychology, 1,* 3–27.

Gibson, J. J. (1950). *The perception of the visual world.* Boston: Houghton-Mifflin.

Gibson, J. J. (1958). Visually controlled locomotion and visual orientation in animals. *British Journal of Psychology, 49,* 182–194.

Gibson, J. J. (1968). What gives rise to the perception of motion? *Psychological Review, 75,* 335–346.

Gibson, J. J. (1966). *The senses considered as perceptual systems.* Boston: Houghton-Mifflin.

Gibson, J. J. (1971). The information available in pictures. *Leonardo, 4,* 27–35.

Gibson, J. J. (1979). *The ecological approach to visual perception.* Boston: Houghton-Mifflin.

Gibson, J. J. (1982a). The concept of stimulus in psychology. In E. Reed & R. Jones (Eds.), *Reasons for realism: Selected essays of James J Gibson* Hillsdale, NJ: Lawrence Erlbaum Associates. (Original work published 1960)

Gibson, J. J. (1982b). Perceiving in a populated environment. In E. Reid & R. Jones (Eds.), *Reasons for realism: Selected essays of James J. Gibson.* Hillsdale, NJ: Lawrence Erlbaum Associates.

Gibson, J. J., & Danielson, A. (1963). The perception of another person's looking behavior. *American Journal of Psychology, 76,* 386–394.

Gibson, J. J., Purdy, J., & Lawrence, L. (1955). A method of controlling stimulation for the study of space perception: The optical tunnel. *Journal of Experimental Psychology, 50,* 1–14.

Gopnik, A., & Meltzoff, A. (1986). Relations between semantic and cognitive development in the one word stage: the specificity hypothesis. *Child Development, 57,* 1040–1053.

Gopnik, A., & Meltzoff, A. (1987). The development of categorization in the second year and its relationship to other cognitive and linguistic developments. *Child Development, 58,* 1523–1531.

Gramsci, A. (1988). Philosophy, common sense, language, and folklore. In D. Forgacs (Ed.), *An Antonio Gramsci reader.* New York: Schocken.

Gustafson, G. (1984). The effect of the ability to locomote on infants' social and exploratory skills. *Developmental Psychology, 20,* 397–405.

Hagen, M. A. (1985). The ecological approach to visual perception. In S. Koch & D. Leary (Eds.), *A century of scientific psychology* (pp. 231–250). New York: McGraw Hill.

Heft, H. (1988). The affordances of children's environments. *Children's Environments Quarterly, 5,* 29–37.

Heft, H. (1989). Affordances and the body: An intentional analysis. *Journal for the Theory of Social Behaviour, 19,* 1–30.

Herlihy, D. (1988). *Medieval households.* Cambridge, MA: Harvard University Press.

Holt, E. B. (1915). *The Freudian wish and its place in ethics.* New York: Holt.

Ingold, T. (1987). *The appropriation of nature.* Manchester: Manchester University Press.

Johnson, M. (1987). *The body in the mind.* Chicago, IL: University of Chicago Press.

Kaye, K. (1982). Organism, apprentice, and person. In E. Z. Tronick (Ed.), *Social interchange in infancy* (pp. 89–105). Baltimore: University Park Press.

Kuhl, P., & Meltzoff, A. (1987). Speech as an intermodal object of perception. In A. Yonas (Ed.), *Perceptual development in infancy. Minnesota Symposium in Child Psychology* (Vol. 20, pp. 235–266). Hillsdale, NJ: Lawrence Erlbaum Associates.

Laboratory of Comparative Human Cognition. (1983). In P. H. Mussen (Series Ed.) & Culture and cognition. W. Kessen (Vol. Ed.), *Handbook of child psychology: Vol. 1. History, theory, and methods* (4th ed. pp. 295–356). New York: Wiley.

Lave, J. (1988). Cognition in practice. Cambridge: Cambridge University Press

Lewontin, R. (1970). The units of selection. *Annual Review of Systematics and Ecology, 11,* 1–18.

Marx, K. (1859). *A contribution to the critique of political economy.* Moscow: Progress Publishers.

Mayer, N., Reed, E., Schwartz, M., Montgomery, M., & Palmer, C. (in 1990). Buttering a hot cup of coffee: An approach to the study of errors of action in brain damaged patients. In D. Tupper & K. Cicerone (Eds.), *The neuropsychology of everyday life, Vol. 2: Assessment and basic competencies.* Boston: Kluwer.

Noble, W. (1981). Gibsonian theory and the ecological perspective. *Journal for the Theory of Social Behavior, 11,* 65–85.

Palmer, C. A. (1989). The discriminating nature of the infants' exploratory actions. *Developmental Psychology, 25* 885–893.

Quine, W. V. O. (1969). *The roots of reference.* La Salle, IL: Open Court.

Reed, E. S. (1978). Darwin's philosophy of nature: The laws of chage. *Acta Biotheoretica, 27,* 201-235.

Reed, E. S. (1981). *Indirect action.* Unpublished manuscript.

Reed, E. S. (1982). An outline of a theory of action systems: *Journal of Motor Behavior, 14,* 98-134.

Reed, E. S. (1986). James J. Gibson's ecological revolution in perceptual psychology: A case study in the transformation of scientific ideas. *Studies in the History and Philosophy of Science, 17,* 65-99.

Reed, E. S. (1987). James Gibson's ecological approach to cognition. In A. Costall & A. Still (Eds.), *Alternatives to cognitivism.* Brighton: Harvester.

Reed, E. S. (1988a). *James J. Gibson and the psychology of perception.* New Haven, CT: Yale University Press

Reed, E. S. (1988b). The affordances of the animate environment: Social science from an ecological point of view. In T. Ingold (Ed.), *What is an animal?* London: Unwin & Hyman.

Reed, E. S. (1989). The neural regulation of adaptive behavior. *Ecological Psychology, 1,* 97-117

Reed, E. S. (1991). Cognition as the cooperative appropriation of affordances. *Ecological Psychology, 3,* 135-158.

Rochat, P. (1989). Object manipulation and exploration in 2- to 5-month old infants. *Developmental Psychology, 25,* 871-884.

Rogoff, B. (1982). Integrating context and cognition. *Advances in Developmental Psychology, 2,* 128-170.

Rogoff, B., & Gardner, W. (1984). Guidance in cognitive development: An examination of mother-child interaction. In B. Rogoff & J. Lave (Eds.), *Everyday cognition: Its development and social context.* Cambridge, MA: Harvard University Press.

Rogoff, B., & Lave, J. (Eds.). (1984). *Everyday cognition: Its development in a social context.* Cambridge, MA: Harvard University Press.

Schmitt, B. (1987). The ecological approach to social perception: A conceptual critique. *Journal for the Theory of Social Behavior, 17,* 261-278.

Schmitt, R. (1987). *An introduction to Marx and Engels.* Boulder: Westview

Schwartz, M., Reed E., Montgomery, M., Palmer, C., Mayer, N. (1991). The quantitative description of action disorganisation after brain damage: A case study. *Cognitive Neuropsychology, 8,* 381-414.

Searle, J. (1969). *Speech acts.* Cambridge: Cambridge University Press.

Sedgwick, H. (1980). The geometry of spatial layout in pictures. In M. A. Hagen (Ed.), *The perception of pictures* (Vol. 1). New York: Academic Press.

Shaw, R., & Bransford, J. (1977). Introduction. In R. Shaw & J. Bransford (Eds.), *Perceiving, acting, and knowing: Towards an ecological psychology.* Hillsdale, NJ: Lawrence Erlbaum Associates.

Siegler, R. (1989). Mechanisms of cognitive development. *Annual Review of Psychology, 40,* 353-380.

Smith, W. J. (1977). *Animal communication.* Cambridge, MA: Harvard University Press

Studdert-Kennedy, M. (1986). Sources of variability in early speech development. In J. Perkell & D. Klatt (Eds.), *Invariance and variability in speech processes.* Hillsdale, NJ: Lawrence Erlbaum Associates.

Studdert-Kennedy, M. (1987). The phoneme as a perceptuomotor structure. In D. Allport, D. MacKay, E. Scheerer, & W. Prinz (Eds.), *Language perception and production.* New York: Academic Press.

Trevarthen, C. (1988). Universal cooperative motives: How infants begin to know the language and culture of their parents. In G. Jahoda & M. Lewis (Eds.), *Acquiring culture: Cross-cultural studies in child development* (pp. 37-90). London: Croom Helm.

Turvey, M., Shaw, R., Reed, E., & Mace, W. (1981). Ecological laws of perceiving and acting. *Cognition, 9,* 237–304.

Ullman, S. (1980). Against direct perception. *The Behavioral and Brain Sciences, 3,* 373–415.

Valsiner, J. (1987). *Culture and the development of cognition.* New York: Academic Press.

Vygotsky, L. S. (1986). Thought and language (A. Kozulin, Trans.). Cambridge: MIT Press. (Original work published 1934)

Vygotsky, L. S. (1988). *Collected works, Vol. 1 Problems of general psychology* (R. Rieber & A. Carton, Eds.). New York: Plenum.

3
Co-Constructive Metatheory for Psychology: Implications for an Analysis of Families as Specific Social Contexts for Development

Robert H. Wozniak
Bryn Mawr College

In this chapter, I present a brief overview of an approach to the explanation of psychological phenomena with which I have long been concerned (Wozniak, 1975, 1981, 1983, 1985, 1987, 1992). This approach was inspired originally by my attempt to make sense of formal characteristics shared by the constructivism of Piaget (Piaget & Inhelder, 1969), the sociohistorical theory of Vygotsky (1956), and the ecological psychology of Gibson (1966, 1979). The perspective that has emerged from this effort is transactional, intersubjective, and constructivist in orientation.

In offering this overview, I emphasize metatheoretical and theoretical principles that are relevant to a discussion of social ecology—to our understanding of the nature of social experience (or perception), the defining characteristics of human sociality, distinctive features of the physical and social environments, and the psychological nature of the family as the primary social structure within which children develop. Then, in the light of these principles, I raise a few questions concerning the study of families as specific social contexts for development and acculturation.

CO-CONSTRUCTIVE EXPLANATION IN DEVELOPMENTAL PSYCHOLOGY

The theoretical views presented here have been developed within a meta-theoretical framework that takes a particular position with respect to the nature of psychological explanation (see Wozniak, 1985, for a longer discussion of this view). From this perspective, the explanation of psychological phenomena requires theories of mind, theories of the environment, and theories of mind–environment interaction. Psychological phenomena, in other words, are presumed to be constructed as transactions between minds and the social and physical ecologies that they inhabit.[1]

At the individual level of analysis, these transactional phenomena can be exhaustively classified into three mutually exclusive but closely related categories: experience, semiotic activity, and action (more about each of these later). Human experiences, symbolic productions, and actions, in other words, are constructed as joint functions of structures and processes of a knowing, valuing, meaning-creating mind, on the one hand, and structures and processes of a psychologically relevant (ecological) physical and social world on the other. At the social level of analysis, categories of transactional psychological phenomena from dyadic interaction to the totality of culture must be explained, in turn, with joint reference to the intersubjective experiences, semiotic activities, and actions of the various individuals who together construct the relevant social system. The implications of this approach for explanation become evident in the discussion that follows.

EXPERIENCE AND THE PERCEPTION OF SOCIAL EVENTS

The term *experience,* as it is used here, is roughly equivalent to *consciousness* as it was used in an earlier era by psychologists such as James (1890). Experience consists of phenomena such as seeing a landscape, hearing a dog bark, tasting a persimmon, and feeling a rush of anger or the dull pain of an aching muscle. Experience arises in the interaction of mind and environment.

Gibson (1966, 1979), in his ecological approach to perception, provided psychology with a way of describing the environmental contribution to experience. Energy arriving at perceptual systems is rich in higher order invariant structure bearing a regular relation to properties of the environment. Invariant structure has the potential to inform experience, to give it a particular pattern of changing organization over time. Yet, from a constructivist perspective, information is not by itself a sufficient condition for experience.

---

[1]Discussion of "individual" psychological phenomena is not meant to suggest that these phenomena are in any way asocial. Indeed the remainder of this chapter can be read as an extended argument for the intersubjective nature of the individual. Similarly, the terms *mind, cognitive system,* and so on are used throughout this chapter with the full recognition that mind is embodied and that explanation will require an account not just of mind but of the mind/brain system.

Experience not only has form, it has meaning. The construction of experience requires the detection and attribution of meaning to information from the environment. Detection and meaning attribution are dependent on the development of conceptual structures and processes in which information from and about the environment is actively gathered, assimilated to appropriate concepts, and thereby interpreted.

Perceiving, in other words, is a process in which experience is co-constructed in the interaction between an environment that provides structure over time in the stimulus flux and a mind that provides knowledge and the functioning of knowing processes. The cognitive processes through which structures relevant to incoming stimulus information are accessed, through which that information is assimilated to the cognitive system, are acts of meaning attribution. The cognitive system is a device for the generation of meaning.

There is, in passing, an important point that should be made here concerning the special nature of the perception of social events as the co-construction of social experience. This point depends on a fundamental and obvious but not always remarked fact about the social surround, taken ecologically. When another human being is present, the structures of energy to perceptual systems that unfold over time are informative of a wide range of personal characteristics of the other (his or her emotional state, intentions, attentional direction, etc.) that are unique to a social presence (i.e., that are not in the surround when one is alone). If, as is often the case, that social other happens to be engaged in a dyadic interaction with still a third person, there are even higher order invariants in energy flux unfolding over even longer intervals of time potentially available to the perceiver. These invariants will be informative concerning properties such as power, respect, affection or relative expertise that are unique to a dyadic or higher order social presence.

If, by chance, one finds oneself observing the unfolding of small group processes over even longer periods of time, still higher order invariants will exist in energy flux informative of group characteristics such as coalition, intragroup competition or cooperation, and fluctuations in leadership. Finally, as radical as this may sound, at the highest levels over the longest intervals of time, invariants in the energy flux can, I believe, be found that are informative about and therefore support the perception of aspects of the highest levels of social structure such as the workings of a profession, a political institution, or even of culture itself.

The key idea here is time. Perception is the attribution of meaning to information detected over time. Information specifying the properties of the social environment that afford interactions (and "interaction" is a concept to which I return shortly) is invariant and can be extracted by the perceiver only over time; and the more complex the social unit (from a single other to culture itself), the longer the time frame over which patterned invariance exists and over which information must be detected. To put it graphically, a snapshot can tell you rather a lot about another person, less about a dyadic interaction, very much less about the workings of a group (e.g., a family) and little about the workings of a profession or a culture.

SEMIOTIC ACTIVITY, SOCIAL MEANINGS, AND ACCULTURATION

In addition to experiencing the world, human beings also generate verbal and imaginal symbols to stand for it. Semiotic activity, the mental activity of symbol generation, has both representational and cultural functions. Representationally, symbols stand for something other than themselves. Through symbols, we can bring to awareness objects and events not currently present to the senses. Culturally, symbols embody the historically derived system of social meanings held in common by members of the broader society. Much of human ability to communicate interpersonally, to negotiate shared meaning, and to acculturate the young depends on the fact that we possess shared systems of symbols.

Like experience, symbols have form and meaning. The form of a spoken word, for example, is auditory and phonemic; of a written word, visual and orthographic. The semiotic act of generating a verbal symbol involves retrieving stored phonemic or orthographic information and assimilating it to the same or closely related conceptual structures that provide the basis for the meaning of the objects and events for which the symbol stands.

Meaning, in other words, does not inhere in the form of the symbol. Meaning is given to form in the act of generating symbols, just as it is in the co-construction of experience, by a mental act of assimilation. In fact, it is presumably just because the products of semiotic activity can be given most of the meaning of the objects and events they stand for that they are able to function as symbols. The word "chair," for example, shares much of the meaning that is attributed to the class of objects on which we routinely sit.

What critically differentiates symbolic discourse from experience, however, is its uniquely individual yet transpersonal nature. When an individual engages in the semiotic act of symbol generation, not only the meaning but also the form of the symbol can be generated from within. By contrast, in the co-construction of experience, while the meaning is provided by the perceiver, form is provided by the environment. This is a simple point, but its force is far reaching. It is part of the explanation for why human beings can, on a beautiful sunny day, imagine or tell themselves or others that it is raining while they are unable to go to the window, look out, and see the rain. It is also the reason why human beings can formulate personal beliefs, symbolic representations about the nature of physical and interpersonal reality, that may or may not be veridical (more about that in a moment).

Yet semiotic activity is not solely or even primarily an individual process. Although experience, even social experience, has only a personal existence, symbolic discourse exists transpersonally. Indeed, the human infant is born into a sociocultural world defined in large part by a system of historically developed social meanings embedded in already existing forms of symbolic discourse. As Vygotsky (1956) pointed out long ago, the child experiences the world in the context of communicative speech/action transactions.

Encountering cups in a variety of contexts, a little girl may be told by her mother, her father, or her siblings: "Hold the cup," "Let's put milk in the cup," "Don't drop the cup," "The cup will break," "The cup is empty," or "Give me the cup" as the cup is handed back and forth, filled by one and emptied by the other, turned upside down by one, righted by the other, dropped by one, retrieved by the other, and so on. In Vygotsky's view, the common lexical item "cup" serves as a nexus around which the child abstracts and generalizes experiences with others and with sets of objects in the world. The development of abstract, categorical concepts, in other words—in fact the very transition from the sensorimotor thought of the infant to the properly conceptual thought of the preschooler—occurs, for Vygotsky, in and through the internalization of speech.

More importantly, however, as Vygotsky constantly stressed, the word "cup" is itself embedded in discourse that conveys cultural meaning. This discourse, in turn, depends on the fact that the lexical items that facilitate the child's synthesis of experience already preexist the child in socially developed systems of meanings and articulated beliefs. These meaning systems, sociocultural *ideologies,* exist in social structures at all levels of complexity (friendship pairs, families, peer groups, schools, religious groups, subcultures, and societies).

In a patriarchal society, for example, the sentences a child hears and the books a child reads will reflect and foster gender distinctions. Relative to female nouns and pronouns, male nouns and pronouns might, for instance, be paired more frequently with action and mastery verbs (running, jumping, exploring, fixing). A child growing up in such a society and developing concepts of "male" and "female" through experience with men and women synthesized in the context of gendered discourse will automatically come to possess a meaning system that reflects the cultural values implicit in this discourse. The elaboration of that meaning system begins, for Vygotsky, with the transition from sensorimotor to abstract thought. This transition, which occurs through the internalization of a social semiotic system, is truly a process of acculturation. As a consequence, sociality and historicity are embedded in the very core of human conceptualization (see, Wozniak, 1987, for a somewhat longer discussion of this issue).

ACTION, INTERACTION, AND INTERSUBJECTIVITY

Finally, in addition to experiencing and generating symbolic discourse, human beings act on the world. *Action* here refers to a system of hierarchically patterned sequences of movement organized in relation to a system of goals and supported by the affordances of the environment. The schemes underlying action and the goals toward which action is organized furnish hierarchical systems of expectations against which the success of the action can be evaluated. The meaning of any action therefore includes the specification of end states and expectations, knowledge of the general structure or scheme for that action, and some specification of the range of variation in the action necessary and permissible under different environmental conditions.

Within the broad category of action, one particular class of actions stands out as unique: the category of interactions. Interactions differ from other actions in the nature of the expectational control that the cognitive system exerts as the interaction unfolds. When I reach out to pick up a glass (an action), to act successfully, I must feed forward expectations about such things as how long it will take my hand to make contact with the glass, the relative weight and solidity of the glass, the relative lack of attraction between the glass and the table, and so forth. These expectations, which are part of the normal functioning of the cognitive system and are therefore not in awareness, serve to regulate my reaching action, to serve as parameters against which the results of my action will be evaluated.

When I reach out to shake someone's hand, however, it can no longer be a case of acting only in terms of my own expectations. My action must now take into account my knowledge of the expectations that the other has concerning my action and, indeed, even my knowledge of the other's expectations about my expectations for my action. Successful interaction, in other words, depends on a mutuality of expectation — on what is, fundamentally, intersubjectivity.

By *intersubjectivity,* I mean the reciprocity of intention between knowing subject and known object that obtains when the known object happens itself to be a knowing, thinking, feeling subject. This is, it seems to me, the very essence of human sociality and as such it appears to have important consequences for any theory of human cognition. As 20 years of infancy research have persuasively documented, babies appear to be born into the world with a cognitive system preadapted to mutuality of expectation, to intersubjectivity, and to interaction.

If so, this suggests that the typical (and, indeed, Piagetian) assumption that babies are born into the world preadapted for acting on objects and become socialized by learning how to interact with that special category of strangely variable and unpredictable objects called people, must be abandoned. Instead, we must start from the radically different premise that babies are born into the world with a cognitive system preadapted to the mutuality of expectation that defines intersubjectivity and that what they must learn is that actions on objects are a special case, a case in which you don't have to concern yourself with what the objects think you happen to be doing.

Human intelligence, in other words, even as biologically motivated, must be organized in its function and in its development toward the acquisition of cultural meanings and toward the child's elaboration with others of shared reality in conjoint activity around objects. The child develops, in short, through a constant striving to become a person, like-minded and companionate with other people.

KNOWLEDGE AND ENVIRONMENT

Although both have so far figured prominently in this discussion, knowledge and environment are complicated constructs, and far more could be said of them than I can possibly say here. Nonetheless, there is one distinction concerning environment and one concerning knowledge that must be drawn before I turn to a discussion of the family as a specific context for acculturation.

With respect to environment, a distinction of critical importance for our purposes is that between the physical and the social. This distinction, as implied earlier, rests on our inferences concerning the presence or absence in environmental objects and events of mental states – of subjectivity. Although we have direct experience only of our own subjectivity, there are objects such as other people, and at least some animals in our environment, to which we seem irresistibly predisposed to attribute a subjectivity of their own. Such objects (or more properly *subjects*), and the events involving those subjective objects, constitute the social environment.

By contrast, there is a much larger class of objects and events to which we, as adults in this culture at least, do not attribute subjectivity. These objects, such as chairs, and events, such as the rising of the sun, constitute our physical environment. It should be clear from the nature of this discussion that the social/physical distinction, although principled, is by no means hard and fast. What is a physical object in one culture or for one person at a given point in time may be part of the social environment for another culture or for that same person under different circumstances of meaning attribution.

Knowledge, as it is used here, may be thought of as a structural mental code embodying information about the environment. Knowledge is both given in the human biological endowment and extracted from experience.

Although it is possible to distinguish among a number of broad classes of knowledge (cf. Piaget & Inhelder, 1969, and Wozniak, 1983, for somewhat more extensive discussions, especially for the distinction between logicomathematical knowledge and content knowledge), I briefly focus here on the nature of two types of content knowledge, psychological and social, as they relate to the problem of the sociality of cognition.

Psychological knowledge is knowledge of the subjective states of those objects and events to which we do attribute subjectivity, including ourselves. Psychological knowledge is derived both from symbolic discourse with others, about and from consistencies over time encountered in the symbolic discourse and actions of others, and from the patterns we encounter in our own subjective states of experience of, symbolic discourse about, and action in the environment. Psychological knowledge is also, therefore, knowledge of our own characteristics and consistency as selves operating in a physical and social world.

Social knowledge is knowledge of the relational events that characterize the interactions of others as they form groups (e.g., friendship pairs, families, classrooms, professions, subcultures, and even entire societies). Social knowledge is derived both from symbolic discourse with others about interaction and from consistencies over time in the interactions into which we and others enter.

As human beings develop and increase the range and depth of their psychological and social experience and action, their knowledge of the social and physical environment and of themselves and others as experiencers, symbolizers, and actors, undergoes continuous refinement. One would imagine that, on almost any sophisticated account, it would be presumed that these changes exert a powerful influence on the progressively changing social and physical environments to which the developing individual has access, and that the structures and processes of the environment would, in turn, be assumed to collaborate with the cognitive structures and processes that the individual brings to these environments to co-construct experience, semiotic activity and action as transactions between the individual and the environment.

FAMILIES AS SPECIFIC SOCIAL CONTEXTS FOR DEVELOPMENT

This brings me to the family as a specific social context for development. This is a topic, needless to say, whose surface I can only scratch; but that, at least, I do in two ways. First, I ask what sort of sense it can make to talk about the family as a social structure; and second, and quite briefly, I describe two research methodologies that have been developed at Bryn

Mawr (one in collaboration with Steven M. Alessandri, a second in collaboration with Patricia Cavanaugh Kelly) that are designed to provide techniques for identifying relevant variables of social structure in the family.

As I hope has been evident from what has already been said, social structure, from this perspective, is characterized at all levels by two clearly distinguishable classes of patterned invariances. One class belongs to the semiotic domain, to the domain of social meanings. It consists, for example, of the systems of beliefs, the ideologies, that are held by a group. The other belongs to the domain of social action, or, more properly, interaction. It consists, for example, of the action routines, rituals, and styles of interpersonal interaction that the group has worked out over time.

Families may be characterized as social contexts affording certain kinds of interactions and not others (see, Reed, chapter 2, this volume, for a discussion of social affordances) and providing instigation for development in certain directions and not in others (see, Bronfenbrenner, chapter 1, this volume, for a discussion of "developmentally instigative characteristics"). The social affordances and developmental instigations families provide reflect both their ideology, most especially but not exclusively the ideology embodied in their interpersonal belief systems, and their styles of interaction.

FAMILY BELIEF SYSTEMS AND INTERACTIONAL STYLES: A PROGRAM OF RESEARCH

Because our family research is still in its infancy, our focus to date has been largely on the family as an environment. The question we are asking is how can psychologically important structural characteristics that differentiate among families as contexts for development be reliably and validly assessed.

Without doubt, as Bronfenbrenner (chapter 1) so persuasively argued, research that is to have any hope of leading to a deeper understanding in this area must focus on the nature of the psychological transactions that result as a conjoint function of individual children developing within specific families. This in turn will require a rich specification of patterns of coherence among person and family variables, patterns of coherence among ideological and interactional variables characterizing the macrosystems of which families are a part, and of processes that link the individual to the nested social systems in which he or she participates. But we must walk before we run — and developing techniques for making meaningful distinctions among families on the basis of the patterns in which psychologically critical variables cluster seems a very crucial first step.

I conclude this chapter, then, by briefly describing the techniques that we have developed for studying systems of interpersonal beliefs and styles of interaction within families. The belief work, carried out in collaboration with Steven Alessandri (Alessandri & Wozniak, 1987, 1989a, 1989b, 1991) has resulted in a number of intriguing developmental findings. For now, however, I concentrate almost solely on the method employed in this research, mentioning just two or three results that bear directly on the method as method.

The technique we have used involves interviewing preadolescents and adolescents about their self-beliefs about the beliefs they hold regarding their mothers' and fathers' respective beliefs concerning them. To achieve this, the child is interviewed three times, once focusing on each parent and once regarding self-beliefs. At each interview, 15 short vignettes that present situations that the child might encounter at home or at school are read and the child is asked to tell the interviewer what his or her mom (or dad as the case might be) would predict he or she would do in this situation and why.

Two of the vignettes, for example, are as follows: (a) "Imagine that one of your friends who lives nearby is out of school sick for 2 days and the teacher gives the class a handout to study. Do you think your mom would predict that you would or would not think on your own to ask the teacher for an extra copy for your sick friend? Why?" (b) "Imagine that in class today, your teacher explained some complicated principles. Only 5 of 20 kids understood the teacher's explanation. Would your dad predict that you would be one of the 5 kids who understood or one of the 15 who needed more time? Why?" Mothers and fathers are also interviewed with the 15 vignettes and asked to make predictions about their child's behavior based on the parents' own beliefs.

Although this procedure generates a huge amount of data that can be examined from a variety of perspectives, at the moment we are focusing particularly on parental agreement, the child's accuracy in predicting the mother's and father's respective beliefs, and maternal and paternal respective congruence with the child's self-beliefs.

Data reported in our first three articles were all from Italian-American Catholics from a relatively delimited area of South Philadelphia. In our fourth paper, we presented results obtained with West Philadelphia Black, single-parent families with children in Catholic schools and children's teachers. In passing, I should point out that this is an attempt ultimately to provide the data for a macrosystems analysis of the sort Bronfenbrenner (chapter 1) requested and is in my view an absolutely essential requirement for family research. Indeed, we are committed never again to doing a study with a convenience sample of middle-class, White, suburban subjects of unknown, heterogeneous ethnicity or religious background.

Of relevance to the method as method are three findings from our first two studies. The first is that our 48 Italian-American families varied widely in overall agreement levels. When, for example, we calculated a mean agreement score across the 5 agreement variables for each family, families were found to vary from a low of 47.4% to a high of 81.3%. Furthermore, and of great importance, when we reinterviewed the families after a lapse of 2 years, the correlation between mean agreement levels at Time 1 and Time 2 was a remarkable .75, indicating the extent to which agreement levels in this domain appear to be a stable characteristic of the family.

The problem with this analysis, however, is that it fails to live up to the spirit of a pattern analysis of belief systems. Although it is nice to know that average agreement levels vary and seem to remain stable, it isn't *average* agreement levels, but the *pattern* of agreement that should be the focus of our attention. Thus, for example, we should be asking, family by family, whether high parental agreement tends to cohere with high accuracy in the child's prediction of what the parents will say or whether a child's being substantially more accurate in predicting what the mother says than what the father says tends to cohere with low parental agreement.

There are many ways to do this analysis, all of them somewhat arbitrary. One version that I computed on the data from our 48 Italian-American families is presented in Table 3.1.

Separating families who were high (73% or better), medium (from 54%–72%), or low (53% or less) in parental agreement, I looked to see, family by family, how child accuracy patterns cohere within parental agreement categories. Thus, for example, of the 14 families high in parental agreement, 5 were also high in the child's accuracy for predicting what both mothers and fathers would have to say; whereas in only 1 family with high parental agreement was there a large disparity between the child's accuracy for mother and that for father (HL). Among the 12 families low in parental agreement, only 1 had a child who was highly accurate in predicting what both parents would say, whereas 5 families were also low in child accuracy

TABLE 3.1

Distribution of Families as a Function of Patterns of Parental Agreement and Children's Accuracy in Predicting Parental Beliefs

| | Child's Accuracy in Predicting Mother/Father | | | | | | | | |
| | [H = High, M = Moderate, L = Low, Mother/Father] | | | | | | | | |
Parental Agreement	HH	HM	HL	MH	MM	ML	LH	LM	LL
High (73% +) N = 14	5		1	2	4	2			
Mod (54%–72%) N = 22	4				4	6	1	4	3
Low (53% −) N = 12	1	1		1	2	1		1	5

for both parents and no family showed a large discrepancy between the child's accuracy for the mother and that for the father.

Other patterns are obvious in the table and need not be mentioned here. Rather, I would simply suggest that families can be clearly distinguished in terms of the patterns in which agreement concerning the personal charac- teristics of the child cohere. Furthermore, this sort of analysis could be done for each family member (thus, the mother, for example, could be asked what she thinks her spouse and children think about her) and the complete system of agreement in all of its various reciprocal modes could be examined. Given the likelihood that this aspect of family ideology is potentially of great import, such an analysis should be pursued.

FAMILY INTERACTIONAL STYLES

The interactional styles research, which began with a dissertation carried out by Patricia Cavanaugh Kelly, has also generated a great deal of data; but, again, I want to focus on method, reporting only two single method- related results.

The technique we use involves inviting families (mother, father, and all of the children—in the Kelly dissertation, children ranged in age from 1 to 17 and family size varied from 3 to 8 members) into the laboratory for a two-part session. In Part 1, family members are gathered around a table and asked to involve everyone in making a dish garden from assorted materials (a shallow metal pan, plants, soil, stones, moss, etc.). Instructions stress the idea that the garden should reflect the contributions of the entire family. In Part 2, after a break, family members return to the table to find pieces of Legos and Ramagon and are told to build anything they wish. This time, however, parent–child hierarchy is stressed as the experimenter indicates that this is a construction task with mom and dad acting as supervisor and foreman to decide what to build, how it will be built, and who will build it.

This research, too, generates data that can be viewed from a variety of perspectives, but at the moment we are focusing on how the family interacts in organizing itself during the first 5 minutes of the dish garden and construction tasks respectively, and on whether the family adjusts its interactional style as a function of the differing organizational task demands of the two contexts.

We began our analysis by coding the 24 different characteristics of the families' self-organizing interactions listed in Table 3.2; but as we pursued this work, we noticed that these characteristics seemed to cohere in definite patterns.

Based on this observation, we developed a technique (see Kelly, 1990, for a detailed discussion) that involves evaluating each family's deviation from

TABLE 3.2
Characteristics of Family Interactional Style

1. Latency to action.	Immediate, delayed
2. Successful calls for planning	Father, mother, neither
3. Unsuccessful calls for planning	Father, mother, neither
4. Partitions roles or materials	Father, mother, neither
5. Controls materials flow and use	Father, mother, neither
6. Organizes spatial positions at table	Father, mother, neither
7. Overall activity directed predominantly by	Father, mother, neither
8. Unsuccessful attempts to direct	Father, mother, neither
9. Father explicitly supports mother	Yes, no
10. Mother explicitly supports father	Yes, no
11. Father consults mother	Yes, no
12. Mother consults father	Yes, no
13. Minimal parental interaction	Yes, no
14. Sibling rivalry	Yes, no
15. Children direct attention/questions to	Father, mother, neither
16. Children attempt to instruct or direct	Father, mother, neither
17. Mother's attention to children's ideas	Sensitive, insensitive
18. Father's attention to children's ideas	Sensitive, insensitive
19. Characteristic use of inclusive language	Yes, no
20. Frequent use of inhibiting language	Father, mother, neither
21. Mother's physical involvement	High, moderate, low
22. Father's physical involvement	High, moderate, low
23. Children's physical involvement	High, moderate, low
24. Family members' overall comfort level	High, not high

three prototypical patterns in which the 24 characteristics were found to cluster and assigning the family to one of three taxonomic categories based on which of the prototypes generated the closest match to their own particular pattern. Very roughly speaking, the three classes of patterns are differentiated in terms of whether the father, the mother, or neither parent is a dominant force in the organizing interactions.

Suffice it to say that, with 30 families, this technique classified all families, 11 of whom showed Pattern A (egalitarian relationship between parents, no sibling rivalry, no latency to action, no calls for planning, and high sensitivity to children's ideas, among other things), 6 of whom showed Pattern B (heavily father organized, long latency to action with fathers calling for planning, insensitivity on the father's but not necessarily the mother's part to children's ideas, and, almost invariably, the presence of sibling rivalry), and 13 of whom showed Pattern C (mother organized, mothers calling for planning, mothers controlling access to materials and typically assigning roles, insensitivity on mothers' part to children's ideas).

Of the 11 Pattern A (egalitarian) families on the dish garden, 6 remained A on the construction task, three adopted B (father organized), and two C (mother organized). Of the 6 families classified as Pattern B (father organized) on the dish garden, all 6 remained B on the construction task.

Finally, of the 13 families coded C (mother organized) on the dish garden, 7 remained C on the construction task, 3 adopted Pattern A, and 3 adopted Pattern B.

Although 7 of the 9 possible patterns (AA, AB, AC, etc.) were obtained, for a majority (19 of 30) of the families, there was surprising consistency across contexts. In addition, the profiles by pattern for most families were quite sharp (e.g., A families typically shared only a small number of characteristics with B or C families, etc.). Taken together with the fact that every family gave the overwhelming impression that the need to organize to accomplish the tasks immediately elicited the engagement of family interactional routines and rituals leads us to think that organizational style, assessed as a pattern among clustered variables, will prove to be a valuable way to characterize individual differences among families as social contexts for development.

CONCLUSION

Each member of a family experiences and acts on the world and generates symbols to stand for it. As individuals, their experiences and actions and the symbols they generate are transactions that reflect the joint contributions of the situations they find themselves in and the knowledge and values they bring to making sense of those situations. All human beings, however, live a collective as well as an individual existence. As members of groups, from dyads through families to cultures, individuals are inherently social.

Arriving at birth with a cognitive system adequate to the mutuality of expectation, infants are designed for the intersubjectivity that is prerequisite to dialogue, interaction, shared experience, and acculturation. As children develop, they are immersed in a sea of social events. Affectionate glances, arguments, daily rituals, all of the family's varied interactional patterns unfold over time to provide a context for the child's construction of social experience and joint participation.

At the same time, however, the child is also surrounded by and involved in a constant stream of symbolic discourse. Mothers, fathers, and siblings talk about the world as they act in and experience it. As the child develops the abstract conceptual system that will function as the source of future meaning attribution, experience of the world from which conceptual invariances are extracted is both mediated by interactions between and with others and synthesized through accompanying discourse. The basic structures of the web of conceptual connections that will underlie a lifetime of meaning making are spun as the child participates in the family.

As a social system, families are characterized by interactional routines and rituals, on the one hand, and symbolically articulated systems of beliefs on the other. To understand the developmentally instigative and acculturating functions of the family, functions that assist the child in becoming a like-minded member of the broader culture, it is necessary to focus on the family as both an interactional and an ideological system.

REFERENCES

Alessandri, S., & Wozniak, R. H. (1987). The child's awareness of parental beliefs concerning the child: a developmental study. *Child Development, 58,* 316-323.

Alessandri, S., & Wozniak, R. H. (1989a). Continuity and change in intra-familial agreement in beliefs concerning the adolescent: A follow-up study. *Child Development, 60,* 335-339.

Alessandri, S., & Wozniak, R. H. (1989b). Perception of the family environment and intrafamilial agreement in belief concerning the adolescent. *Journal of Early Adolescence, 9,* 67-81.

Alessandri, S., & Wozniak, R. H. (1991). The child's awareness of adult beliefs concerning the child: the effects of gender and subculture. *Journal of Youth and Adolescence, 20,* 1-12.

Gibson, J. J. (1966). *Senses considered as perceptual systems.* Boston: Houghton Mifflin.

Gibson, J. J. (1979). *Ecological approach to visual perception.* Boston: Houghton-Mifflin.

James, W. (1890). *Principles of psychology.* New York: Holt.

Kelly, P. M. C. (1990). *Organizational style and flexibility and its relationship to perception of family environment.* Unpublished doctoral dissertation, Bryn Mawr College, Bryn Mawr, PA.

Piaget, J., & Inhelder, B. (1969). *The psychology of the child.* New York: Basic Books.

Vygotsky, L. S. (1956). *Izbrannye psikhologischeskie issledovaniia* [Selected psychological investigations]. Moskva: RSFSR Akademia pedagogicheskii nauk.

Wozniak, R. H. (1975). Dialecticism and structuralism: The philosophical foundations of Soviet psychology and Piagetian cognitive developmental theory. In K. F. Riegel & G. C. Rosenwald (Eds.), *Structure and transformation: Developmental and historical aspects* (pp. 25-45). New York: Wiley.

Wozniak, R. H. (1981). The future of constructivist psychology. Reflections on Piaget. *Teachers College Record, 83,* 197-199.

Wozniak, R. H. (1983). Is a genetic epistemology of psychology possible? *Cahiers de la fondation archives Jean Piaget, 4,* 323-347.

Wozniak, R. H. (1985). Notes toward a co-constructive theory of the emotion/cognition relationship. In D. Bearison & H. Zimiles (Eds.), *Thought and emotion: Developmental issues* (pp. 39-64). Hillsdale, NJ: Lawrence Erlbaum Associates.

Wozniak, R. H. (1987). Developmental method, zones of development, and theories of the environment. In. L. Liben (Ed.), *Development and learning: Conflict or congruence?* (pp. 225-235). Hillsdale, NJ: Lawrence Erlbaum Associates.

Wozniak, R. H. (1992). Co-constructive, intersubjective realism: metatheory in developmental psychology. In W. Kurtines, M. Azmitia, & J. L. Gewirtz (Eds). *The role of values in psychology and human development* (pp. 89-104). New York: Wiley.

4

The Dynamics of Competence: How Context Contributes Directly to Skill

Kurt W. Fischer
Harvard University

Daniel H. Bullock
Boston University

Elaine J. Rotenberg
Denver, Colorado

Pamela Raya
Harvard University

In psychological development, person and context collaborate to produce action and thought. Although this statement or something close to it is now generally accepted by many developmental scholars, the full implications of the contributions of context are still not widely appreciated. Context does not merely influence behavior. It is literally part of the behavior, participating with the person to produce an action or thought.

Psychological systems in general arise from the collaboration of person and context. Most theories of psychological systems treat the person as the source of the systems and relegate the context to a minor role. An especially clear case of this mistake is the concept of competence, which characterizes a person's best knowledge — the upper limit of what he or she can say or do. A person is typically said to *possess* a certain competence, independent of its use in any context.

In this chapter we show that competence is an emergent characteristic of a person-in-a-context, not of the person alone. Competence arises from the collaboration between person and context, with competence changing when context changes. People are especially important in this collaboration, molding the context to support particular kinds of actions and thoughts in those they interact with. The effects of this sort of social support are dramatic, producing sharp shifts in competence level in individual children. Competence rises abruptly with the provision of support and drops dramatically when the support is removed.

Theories of mind have generally suffered from the fundamental mistake of focusing explanation primarily on either the organism or the environment as the primary source of knowledge or intelligence (Fischer & Bullock,

93

1984). Theories of competence have been fundamentally flawed by their focus on the organism and their failure to recognize the contributions of context to competence. We suggest a different approach that grounds competence in the concept of skill, starting with the assumption that all behavior arises from collaboration of person and context. The dynamics of changes in competence are explained by analysis of developmental levels of skills as well as a neural network model.

THE FAILURE OF COMPETENCE THEORIES

Cognitive scientists and psychometricians often speak of a person's competence, or ability, as if the person possessed a fixed capacity analogous to the amount of liquid that can be placed in a glass. Whatever context the child is in, the competence remains the same, according to this view. Variations in performance across context and age provide a serious problem for such theories.

The most extreme versions of such competence theories have proved untenable. Chomsky (1965) treated the child's language competence as fixed from early infancy through the operation of an innate language acquisition device. To explain the vast developmental changes that researchers have documented in language and cognition, he and his students impute biological constraints to the child that somehow interfere with the Chomskian competence, preventing it from becoming fully evident in behavior until later years. Building on this analysis, neonativists have repeatedly searched for some early behavior that relates to a "competence" and then neglected to analyze how the purported competence develops or how it is affected by context (Fischer & Bidell, 1991).

Another example of an extreme competence theory is Piaget's hypothesized epistemic subject, defined as a knower uninfluenced by context, analogous to a moving object in a perfect vacuum, where there is no resistance from other objects, events, or energy fields. Although Piaget (1936/1952) was one of the early voices calling for an approach integrating organismic and environmental influences, he built a theory that focused primarily on the child and neglected the environment and the bothersome developmental decalage that it produced (Beilin, 1971; Broughton, 1981; Piaget, 1971). In the last years of his life, however, Piaget recognized the problems with his earlier view and outlined a different view giving a more important role to context (Piaget 1981-1983/1987).

As developmentalists, most of us have taken a path similar to Piaget's, rejecting extreme competence theories. In their place, competence/performance models have been proposed, providing more moderate characterizations of competence (e.g., Flavell & Wohlwill, 1969; Klahr &

Wallace, 1976; Overton & Newman, 1982; Pascual-Leone, 1970). For a given domain and age, the child is considered to have a fixed competence, as reflected in his or her highest stage of performance. Variation below this highest stage occurs commonly and is attributed to factors like effort and task difficulty that impede demonstration of the true competence. As in the extreme competence theories, the person's competence is fixed at any one time, like the capacity of a glass to hold water. But unlike in the extreme theories, a set of processes are specified by which the competence eventuates in performance—ways that the person activates and utilizes the competence. Just as the glass can be half empty, people may only use a portion of their competence at any moment. When all the performance factors are controlled, people will show their true competence, the real upper limit on their performance.

Like their predecessors, these theories fail because they segregate the organism from the environment, locating most organismic factors in competence and most environmental ones in performance. This fundamental error not only fails to recognize the collaboration of person with context, but it also insulates the theory from test. The performance factors in the theory interfere both with the expression of competence and with the testing of the theory of competence. When findings do not support a prediction, they are interpreted as reflecting some performance factor rather than requiring a revision of the theory of competence. Like the Ptolemaic view that the stars and planets circle the earth, the competence theory is saved by post hoc epicycles in the performance component to maintain the perfect spheres of competence. The framework proposed in this chapter eliminates the segregation of organism from environment and makes competence a directly observable characteristic of individual people-in-context.

TAKING CONTEXT SERIOUSLY: THE ECOLOGY OF MIND

In recent years, there have been many calls for giving environment or context a more active role in explaining cognition and development. Bronfenbrenner (1979), Neisser (1976), J. J. Gibson (1979), and others have called for an ecological approach. For cognitive development, the works of Vygotsky and Gibson have been especially powerful in leading investigators to analyze the contribution of environment. Vygotsky (1978) focused on the social environment—how other people contribute to children's cognitive development and how children internalize these social influences. Gibson (1979) emphasized that the perceptual inputs for people in specific environments, called affordances, are richly structured and that people can detect and use them without the need for complex internal, mental construction.

Many voices argue currently that context is actually a part of people's action, perception, thought, and knowledge (e.g., Cole & Scribner, 1974; Magnusson, 1988; Rogoff & Lave, 1984; chapters by Bronfenbrenner, Meacham, Reed, Rogoff, Wozniak, this volume).

These views require a radical restructuring of developmental theories. It is not enough to recognize the importance of experience in cognitive functioning. Of course, people need to experience a specific context to master skills in it or to detect affordances in it. A mechanic who has mastered the repair of a Toyota four-cylinder engine will typically have difficulty when first faced with the fancy engine of a Porsche. Likewise, a person who has grown up in Peoria will often have difficulty making sense of a myth told by African hunter–gatherers. Examples like the auto mechanic and the person from Peoria are frequently cited to support contextualism, but they are not convincing to skeptics because they are too obvious, showing only a global effect of experience. Virtually any framework that allows for the effects of experience will predict effects like these, including competence/performance theories.

What is needed instead is analysis of the dynamic effects of context on skill. For competence in development, this analysis predicts that *context affects the developmental level or stage of a person's competence even when the effects of experience and domain are controlled for.* We describe research that shows powerful effects in which for a narrowly specified domain, a person's developmental level varies dramatically as a function of contextual support. This effect is so powerful that a person's competence or ability can no longer be treated as a fixed characteristic of the person independent of context.

SKILL: COLLABORATION BETWEEN PERSON AND CONTEXT

The concept of *skill* is a good starting point for the integration of person with context (Bruner, 1982; Fischer, 1980). In ordinary English usage, it implies both person and context simultaneously. People have a skill for riding a bicycle, a skill for listening to their friends, a skill for repairing Toyota engines, a skill for doing analysis of variance. A person cannot have a skill independent of a context. Skill requires a *collaboration* between person and context.

This conception means that skills vary not only between people but also across contexts for a given person (Fischer & Farrar, 1987). When a man borrows someone else's bicycle and rides it or rides his familiar bicycle on an unfamiliar kind of terrain (say, across a grassy field instead of on a road or sidewalk), he must adapt his skill to the context of the new bicycle or terrain. He cannot immediately ride skillfully by using the skill he possesses from before. He initially rides awkwardly, working to adapt the old skill to the new bicycle or terrain. Similarly, when a woman attempts to perform analysis of variance with a difference computer program or when she tries to analyze the data in a study with an unfamiliar design, she has to work to adapt her skill. It can take days or weeks of hard work to generalize the skill to the new context.

Notice that the skill concept includes the person as well as the context. It is as much a mistake to leave out the person as to leave out the context (Fischer & Bullock, 1984). Skills are characteristics of persons-in-contexts.

The concept of skill provides a foundation for building a theory of how person and environment collaborate to produce competence. Skill replaces the organismic definition of competence with the radical idea that capacities literally arise from the collaboration of person with context. A major goal of theory and research then becomes finding principles that specify how person and context collaborate to produce competences. Empirically, competence is defined most simply as an upper limit on the developmental level of behavior. Our research shows that behavior shows not one upper limit but different limits as a function of context.

HOW CONTEXTUAL SUPPORT DIRECTLY AFFECTS DEVELOPMENTAL LEVEL

A person does not have a single developmental level, even when assessment is limited to a specific domain. Level varies systematically both across people and across contexts within the domain. For example, within a few minutes a 7-year-old child will demonstrate, in Piagetian terminology, concrete operational thinking as his or her best performance in one context and then preoperational thinking as his or her best performance in a slightly different context.

The domains in our research were highly specific. In one series of studies, we assessed individual children acting out and telling pretend stories in which they made realistic dolls act nice and/or mean with each other. All assessment contexts involved the same setting, toys, and contents, the same experimenter, and similar procedures. Another domain involved individual children sorting blocks into boxes forming classification matrices based on color, shape, and size, again with each context involving the same setting, toys, contents, experimenter, and procedures. Yet another domain (described in a later section) involved adolescents and adults explaining how they made decisions about complex knowledge dilemmas.

Within each domain, the contexts varied primarily in terms of the degree and type of social support that the experimenter provided for the task. In low support contexts, he or she simply asked a child to act out some mean and nice stories or to sort some blocks into boxes. In high support contexts, he or she provided explicit support for a particular behavior — for example, modeling a specific story or a way of sorting blocks.

The understanding of mean and nice social interactions was measured on the multistep developmental sequence shown in Table 4.1, which captures development between approximately 2 and 15 years of age. For example, for Step 3, the story involved one-dimensional social influence or reciprocity: One doll acted mean (or nice) to a second, and the second one acted mean (or nice) in return because of the first one's meanness (or niceness). The steps in Table 4.1 were specified in terms of the cognitive-developmental levels and transformations of skill theory, which was used to predict the sequence (Fischer, Hand, Watson, Van Parys, & Tucker, 1984; Hand, 1982; Rotenberg, 1988). The sequence was tested via the statistics of scalogram analysis, and in several studies it formed a virtually perfect Guttman scale.

Despite the narrowness of the domain, the individual child's competence varied dramatically with assessment context. Competence was defined as the upper limit on the child's performance, his or her highest step. In one type of context, as shown in Fig. 4.1, a typical 7-year-old produced stories at the upper limit of Step 3, as well as at lower steps. In another type of context, that same child produced a story at the upper limit of Step 6, as well as at lower steps. For both types of contexts, the data fit the basic empirical criterion for competence: Behavior often varied below the highest step (3 and 6, respectively), but it did not exceed that step.

We have replicated this phenomenon across a score of studies of stories and classification involving hundreds of middle-class U.S. girls and boys between 3 and 18 years of age (Elmendorf, in press; Fischer & Elmendorf, 1986; Fischer et al., 1984; Fischer, Shaver, & Carnochan, 1990; Lamborn & Fischer, 1988; Rose, 1990; Woo, 1990). The stories have included not only the domain of nice and mean interactions, but also various other social

Level	Step	
Rp1	1	
	2	
Rp2	3	FUNCTIONAL LEVEL (low support)
	4	
	5	
Rp3	6	OPTIMAL LEVEL (high support)
	7	
Rp4/A1	8	
A2	9	

FIG. 4.1   Developmental range of a 7-year-old.

domains, including social roles (such as doctor–patient, mother–father- –child, boy–girl, and child–adult), attributions about aggression, and perspective taking. The phenomenon has also replicated for several non-story tasks, including classification of blocks.

In the classification research, a developmental scale for classification that was generally similar to that in Table 4.1 was used with children between 1 and 7 years of age (Fischer & Bidell, 1991; Fischer & Roberts, 1991). When children were repeatedly tested in low and high support contexts over a 2-month period, they showed different competences (upper limits), with the low support context consistently evoking a competence several steps lower than the high support context.

In summary, the research showed that in diverse domains, children demonstrated two very different competences, which we have called their *functional* and *optimal* levels. These two competences were tied to different kinds of social-contextual support: Low support contexts allowing rela-tively spontaneous behavior produced functional-level competence, whereas high support contexts priming more complex behavior produced optimal-level competence. The interval between the two levels is called a child's developmental range (Lamborn & Fischer, 1988).

Spontaneous Contexts and Functional Level

In several kinds of spontaneous contexts, children showed the same upper limit – their functional level. For the mean and nice story tasks, individual children acted out or told stories spontaneously in two different contexts after they had seen an adult act out a series of stories about mean and nice interactions. In one context, called *free play,* the adult asked the child to make up some stories of her own while the adult went away to do something else for several minutes. In the other context, called *best story,* the adult returned and asked the child to show the best story she could.

Children's upper limit was the same in both spontaneous contexts. During free play, they produced several stories that ranged from the upper limit down to lower steps in the sequence. The 7-year-old in Fig. 4.1 showed at least one story at Step 3 and several other stories at Steps 1 and/or 2. In the best-story context, children produced a single story, and it was almost always at the highest step shown in free play. For the 7-year-old in Fig. 4.1, the best story was at Step 3.

To test whether the children were indeed showing a true upper limit, we introduced several procedures that could reasonably be expected to induce higher performance. The best-story context itself was one such check, and it supported the competence hypothesis: When asked to give the best story they could, 80%–100% of the children produced the same highest step as in free play, and most of the remaining children were within one step of that

TABLE 4.1
A Developmental Sequence for Understanding Mean and Nice Social Interactions

Level	Step	Skill	Examples
Rp1: Single representations	1	*Active agent:* A person performs at least one behavior fitting a social-interaction category of mean or nice.	Child pretends that one doll hits another doll ("mean") or gives another doll candy ("nice").
	2	*Behavioral category:* A person performs at least two behaviors fitting an interaction category of mean or nice.	Child has one doll act nice to another doll, giving it candy and saying, "I like you." The second doll can be passive.
Rp2: Representational mappings	3	*One-dimensional social influence:* The mean behaviors of one person produce reciprocal mean behaviors in a second person. The same contingency can occur for nice behaviors.	Child has one doll say mean things and hit another doll, who responds by hitting and stating dislike for the first one. The second one's behavior is clearly produced by the first one's behavior.
	4	*One-dimensional social influence with three characters behaving in similar ways:* Same as Step 3, but with three people interacting reciprocally in a mean way (or a nice way).	With three dolls, child has one tease the others, while a second one hits the others. The third doll rejects both of the first two because they are mean.
	5*	*One-dimensional social influence with three characters behaving in opposite ways:* The nice behaviors of one person and the mean behaviors of a second person produce reciprocal nice and mean behaviors in the third person.	With three dolls, child has one act friendly to others, while a second one hits others. The third doll responds nicely to the first doll and meanly to the second.
Rp3: Representational systems	6	*Two-dimensional social influence:* Two people interact in ways fitting opposite categories, such that the first one acts both nice and mean, and the second one responds with reciprocal behaviors in the same categories.	Child has one doll initiate friendship with a second doll but in a mean way. The second one, confused about the discrepancy, declines the friendship because of the meanness. The first then apologizes and makes another friendly gesture, which the second one responds to accordingly.

7	*Two-dimensional social influence with three characters:* Same as Step 6 but with three people interacting reciprocally according to opposite categories.	With three dolls, child has one doll act friendly to a second one, while a third initiates play in a mean way. The second doll acts friendly to the first one and rejects the third, pointing out the latter's meanness. The third then apologizes for being mean, while the first one does something new that is mean. The second doll accepts the third one's apology and rejects the first one, pointing out the change in his or her behavior.
Rp4/A1: Single abstractions		
8	*Single abstraction integrating opposite behaviors:* Two instances of interactions involving opposite behaviors take place as in Step 6, and the relations between the two interactions are explained in terms of some general abstraction, such as that intentions matter more than actions.	With three characters, child has one act friendly to a second, while a third initiates play in a mean way. The second character responds to each accordingly, but then learns that the nice one had mean intentions while the mean one had nice intentions. The second character then changes his or her behavior to each to match their intentions and explains that he or she cares more about people's intentions than their actions.
A2: Abstract mappings		
9	*Relation of two abstractions integrating opposite behaviors:* Two instances of interactions involving opposite behaviors are explained in terms of the relation of two abstractions, such as intention and responsibility: People who have a deceitful intention can be forgiven if they take responsibility in a way that undoes the deceit.	With three dolls, child has two of them act nice on the surface to a third, both with the intention of deceiving him or her into doing their homework. When the deceit is discovered by the third character, the first one takes responsibility for the deceit by admitting the intention and re-establishing his or her honesty. But the second one does not show such responsibility. The third character forgives the first one, but not the second, because he or she cares about people taking responsibility for their deceitful intention and undoing the deceit.

*Step 5 is transitional between Levels Rp2 and Rp3. Apparently it can be mastered at Level Rp2, but it is much easier to do at Level Rp3.

limit. When there was a difference between the two contexts, best story was usually one step lower than free play. This difference is predictable from measurement error, because the child had only one chance to show the highest step in the best-story context but multiple chances in the free-play context.

Other checks of the common limit in the two contexts included practice with the stories and instruction. Under both circumstances, the phenomenon replicated, with the same highest step continuing to obtain for both free play and best story. When practice or instruction produced a change in functional level in free play, it typically produced the same change in best story. Overall, however, the effects of practice and instruction were only modest. Average functional level improved at most one step when children were given both instruction and practice (Rotenberg, 1988).

Taken alone, these results would seem to support a simple competence view, because free-play and best-story contexts produced the same upper limit even with repeated assessment. However, the results for the second type of assessment context were dramatically different: The children's competence increased substantially in high support contexts.

Supportive Contexts and Optimal Level

The type of context that evoked a higher level involved immediate contextual support for performance: An adult presented key information to the child about a story, and then the child acted out or told a story based on that information. Across two different contexts providing such contextual support, children showed the same optimal level. In one, called *elicited imitation,* the adult acted out and explained the story in detail and then asked the child to make up a similar story. In the other, called *memory prompt,* the adult reminded the child of the gist and key elements of an earlier story and then asked the child to show that story. Both of these contexts prompted key elements in the story.

Children showed the same upper limit in both contexts—their optimal level. In both elicited-imitation and memory-prompt contexts, they correctly produced all stories presented up to the upper limit and failed all stories beyond the limit. For the 7-year-old in Fig. 4.1, the limit was Step 6—a jump of three steps above the functional level. This level is called optimal because it is hypothesized to reflect the best performance that children can produce on their own. We have argued elsewhere that it also shows stagelike discontinuities in development, whereas the functional level shows nonstagelike continuous change (Fischer & Pipp, 1984). But that issue is not essential to this argument.

Children showed consistent optimal levels across repeated trials. In studies where children practiced the stories repeatedly, there was only a modest increase in step, averaging at most one step in Table 4.1 (Rotenberg, 1988). Individual differences were consistent from trial to trial. Instruction also caused a small increase in performance beyond that of practice, and it was similarly reliable. The occurrence of optimal level was thus a stable, replicable phenomenon in individual children.

Figure 4.2 shows results of one of the studies of practice and instruction, in which children performed under four contexts — two supportive contexts (elicited imitation and memory prompt) and two spontaneous contexts (free play and best story; Rotenberg, 1988). Eight 7-year-olds, instructed in how to recall the gist of the story to help their performance, were tested on the stories for Steps 3, 5, 6, and 7 in Table 4.1. They were assessed three times with the elicited-imitation, free-play, and best-story conditions and once with the memory-prompt condition. In the latter, memory prompts were given for each story, with the prompt providing the gist of the story, including a few key actions and objects. In Fig. 4.2 the upper limit is shown for the third elicited-imitation assessment, the second and third free-play and best-story assessments, and the single memory-prompt assessment.

The highest steps elicited by the two supportive contexts were virtually identical, and those elicited by the two spontaneous contexts were lower and virtually identical. In elicited imitation, the stories were at Step 6. In free play and best story, they dropped precipitously to Step 3. Then, the memory prompts were given, and the stories again rose to Step 6, which was identical

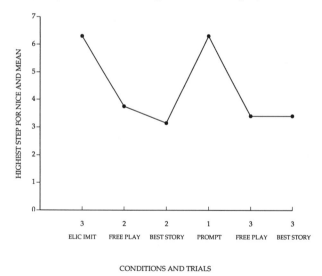

FIG. 4.2   Reliability of highest step for understanding nice and mean under high and low support conditions with repeated assessments (Note: Elicited imitation and prompt conditions provided high support. Free play and best story conditions provided low support. Numbers on x-axis indicate the repetition of the condition that is graphed).

to the results for elicited imitation. Free-play and best-story contexts were repeated, and the stories again fell to Step 3. Every child showed the same general pattern of change, with some variation in the individual child's optimal and functional levels.

Clearly, the optimal- and functional-level results are highly replicable. In these studies children showed distinct competences for spontaneous and supportive contexts. Their competences arose from the dynamic interplay of person with context, changing in a matter of minutes as the context changed. A child participates in one context, producing a specific level, and then the child changes to participate in a different context, producing a different specific level. Return to the first context produces a return to the initial level, and so forth. This kind of effect can be repeated trial after trial for each individual child.

DEVELOPMENTAL RANGE—WHERE COMPETENCES GROW

We propose that functional and optimal levels define the developmental range of a domain for a child—from skills that the child can produce easily on his or her own to skills that the child can produce only with strong contextual support (Bidell & Fischer, 1991). It is primarily within this range that short-term growth in skill occurs and that practice, instruction, and contextual variation have their effects.

Researchers or educators wanting to assess a child's understanding need to think in terms of a range, not a point on a scale. And they need to always consider context as an integral part of any competence they assess. Context includes not only the dimension of social support but also issues of domain. Children's functional and optimal levels vary substantially across domains. Failure to consider range and context leads to major errors of assessment.

The developmental range is related to Vygotsky's (1978) concept of the zone of proximal development as well as the associated concept of scaffolding (Bruner, 1982; Wood, 1980). Like developmental range, these Vygotskian concepts emphasize that the child's actions vary over a range closely tied to development and are strongly affected by the behaviors of other people.

There is at least one important difference between developmental range and zone of proximal development, however. In most of the studies of the zone, the adult actually intervenes in the task and performs part of it for the child. In our research, on the contrary, the adult does not directly intervene in the performance of the task. It is no surprise that a child and an adult together can perform a task better than a child alone. It is more surprising that the mere provision of social contextual support strongly affects the child's solo performance. In the supportive context, an adult prompts a skill in the child and then does nothing more: The child has no direct aid from the adult. But even with the adult not doing any of the task, the child and the supportive context collaborate to produce optimal performance. The child truly demonstrates a competence to act on his or her own with support.

In addition, the research results show what appears to be a contradiction of the Vygotskian analysis. The zone of proximal development involves the child's gradual internalization of interactions between two people, one of whom is an adult or an accomplished peer (Vygotsky, 1978). As the child becomes adult, he or she becomes able to control the structures individually, without scaffolding. Thus, the zone gradually decreases or even disappears with age. On the other hand, the developmental range does not shrink with age but grows larger, as shown in Fig. 4.3 for the mean and nice stories (Hand, 1982). In infancy and early childhood, children's functional level seems to be close to their optimal level, at least for familiar domains (Fischer & Hogan, 1989; Watson & Fischer, 1980). Starting at about 3½ years, the gap between functional and optimal level becomes strong, and thereafter it seems to grow ever larger with age.

CONTEXTUAL SUPPORT OF HIGHER REASONING: REFLECTIVE JUDGMENT

The developmental range does not end with childhood but extends into adulthood. A study of the developmental range for reflective judgment

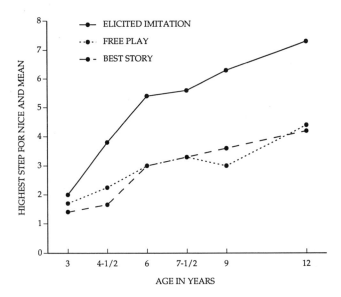

FIG. 4.3   Highest step for understanding nice and mean under three conditions as a function of age.

shows that developmental range grows larger at least through the late 20s, as people construct high-level abstract reasoning about the bases of knowledge. Optimal and functional levels occur at these ages too, and the distance between them grows with age.

Reflective judgment is reasoning about the bases for knowing, especially when dealing with conflicting arguments about a complex issue. Kitchener and King (1981) devised an interview for assessing reflective judgment by asking people to deal with dilemmas in which at least two opposing opinions are stated about an issue. For example, one of the dilemmas deals with the health effects of chemical additives to food: Do these additives promote health or cause disease?

Longitudinal research has shown that people's judgments develop through the seven stages shown in Table 4.2. Children start out with the view that knowing is a concrete state based on direct experience. At the middle stages, they come to understand that knowledge depends on one's viewpoint and is therefore uncertain. In the later stages, they move beyond the focus on uncertainty and consider the justification and evidence for a conclusion and the process of inquiry by which it was reached. Kitchener and Fischer (1990) presented a skill analysis of the stages of reflective judgment.

To assess optimal and functional levels of reflective judgment, we asked students to reason about knowledge dilemmas in two contexts (Kitchener, Lynch, Fischer, & Wood, in press). The low support context was the traditional Reflective Judgment Interview (RJI), in which the person is presented with a series of dilemmas and for each dilemma is asked to state a position and to explain the bases for it. The high support context was a new assessment interview, the Prototypic Reflective Judgment Interview (Kitchener & Fischer, 1990). People were presented with the same dilemmas as in the RJI, but contextual support was provided by presentation of a prototypic answer for each stage of each dilemma. (These prototypes were based on answers given by people in earlier studies using the RJI.) After a student read one of the prototypes, he or she was asked to explain it in his or her own words.

Subjects were 104 students between 14 and 28 years of age, half male and half female. Students were tested individually in two sessions, with each session including first the spontaneous context (RJI) and then the supportive context (Prototypic Reflective Judgment Interview). After the first session, students were also given a series of questions and guidelines to help them think about drawing conclusions about complex issues before the second session; these materials did not include direct statements about the actual dilemmas.

The results showed a clear separation of functional and optimal levels, with students performing approximately a stage higher in the supportive

TABLE 4.2
Stages of Development of Reflective Judgment

Skill Level	*Stage of Reflective Judgement*
Level Rp1: Single representations	Stage 1: Single category for knowing: To know means to observe directly without evaluation.
Level Rp2: Representational mappings	Stage 2: Two categories for knowing: People can be right about what they know, or they can be wrong.
Level Rp3: Representational systems	Stage 3: Three categories for knowing: People can be right about what they know, or they can be wrong, or knowledge may be incomplete or temporarily unavailable. The status of knowledge may differ in different areas.
Level Rp4/A1: Systems of representational systems, which are single abstractions	Stage 4: Knowledge is uncertain: The fact that knowledge is unknown in several instances leads to understanding knowledge as an abstract process that is uncertain.
Level A2: Abstract mappings	Stage 5: Knowledge is relative to a context or viewpoint; it is subject to interpretation. Thus it is uncertain in science, history, philosophy, etc. Conclusions must be justified.
Level A3: Abstract systems	Stage 6: Knowledge is uncertain and subject to interpretation, but it is possible to abstract some justified conclusions across domains or viewpoints. Knowledge is an outcome of these processes.
Level A4: Systems of abstract systems, which are principles	Stage 7: Knowledge occurs probabilistically via inquiry, which unifies concepts of knowledge. Knowledge can be reached with various degrees of certainty depending on justifications and evidence.

Note. Descriptions are adapted from Kitchener and Fischer (1990) and Kitchener and King (1981).

context than in the spontaneous one. These results held over both sessions. That is, producing higher stage responses in the supportive context in the first session and having 2 weeks to think about the dilemmas did not reduce the difference between optimal and functional levels, although there was a small overall increase in level between sessions.

Consistent with the previous finding that developmental range increased with age in childhood, the distance between functional and optimal levels of reflective judgment grew with age during adolescence and adulthood too. In the teenage years, the mean difference was about .6 stages, but by the late 20s it had grown to twice as much, 1.2 stages. The increasing size of the developmental range with age thus seems to extend well beyond the years of childhood into at least the years of early adulthood.

The reflective-judgment results thus illustrate the generality of the developmental range across domains and ages. People show one developmental level — one competence — when they act in a spontaneous context and a much higher developmental level — a different competence — when they act in a socially supportive context. The difference is remarkably robust. Not only does it occur across many domains, but practice and simple instruction do not eliminate it.

DYNAMICS OF COMPETENCE IN A NEURAL NETWORK IN CONTEXT

The robustness and generality of the developmental range suggest that it is a basic characteristic of human cognition, a property of the way the human nervous system operates in context. To begin to understand the neural foundations for developmental range, we looked to modern neural network theory, especially models of parallel, distributed networks that involve a collaboration between top-down processes in the network itself and bottom-up processes from input to the network. Adaptive resonance theory (ART) has these properties and has been used with success to model many cognitive processes (Bullock, Carpenter, & Grossberg, 1991; Grossberg, 1980). ART networks have the capacity to learn and to function in many ways like intelligent organisms. As parallel distributed networks, they use a set of input to make generalizations about the form of that input, often producing surprises not built into the original network. Building on these properties, they achieve great power through specifying particular, diverse network architectures like those of human neural systems.

Developmental Range in Neural Networks

Within adaptive resonance theory, neural networks have exactly the dynamic properties we anticipated: They generate not merely one competence but a range of competences affected powerfully by input from the context in which the network is functioning. Especially relevant to this developmental range is the role of contextual input in stimulating complex neural activity that is sustainable through short-term memory processes.

The networks contain short-term memory components that can be activated without being directly encoded into long-term memory. Indeed, complex neural systems exhibiting short-term memory, long-term memory, and differentiation of the two would seem inevitably to produce a property like developmental range. When the short-term memory components are activated by context, they allow the consequences of the transient contextual input to persist without any input from long-term memory components. For a significant interval after the contextual input, the network exhibits this competence, but the ability is fragile because it depends on the induced short-term memory components, which are not subject to long-term memory encoding at the current level of network maturity. Therefore, after intervening activities push the system into some other state, the network cannot autonomously re-enter the state originally induced by the context. The competence associated with having entered the contextually induced state is real, but the state itself cannot be regenerated by the network alone without appropriate contextual input.

In general, when bottom–up input (like that coming from context) and top–down input (like that coming from individual goals or plans) show an appropriate match, they produce resonance in the circuit. When the match is absent because of the absence of one or the other input, the network can still function, but it functions differently, in a less complex way. Thus a single network can show one organization when it is functioning without matching inputs and a more complex organization when it is functioning with both contextual input and matching top–down input, such as that from short-term memory.

The structure of this network is illustrated in a highly schematic way in Fig 4.4. The output process involving network sites R_1 and R_2 produces a simple activity state at an early stage of development when it is activated by signals along pathways S_1 and S_2. As development proceeds, this process is reorganized by hierarchical inputs from sites C_1 and C_2 to sites R_1 and R_2 along pathways S_3 and S_4. When sites C_1 and C_2 are activated even briefly, they can maintain their active state by virtue of the excitatory feedback loop

FIG. 4.4 A neural network that shows the phenomena of developmental range.
Key: Circles mark neural network sites, and arrows mark activation pathways.
C and R designate hierarchally organized sites, with C providing input to R.
The + sign indicates excitatory feedback loops, which sustain short-term memory for a site.
S designates pathways of activation from one neural site to another.
I marks input from the context.
M designates memory pathways.
The diagram shows only the part of the network central to the text.
The open circle at the top and activation pathways S_1 and S_2 show links to other parts of the network.

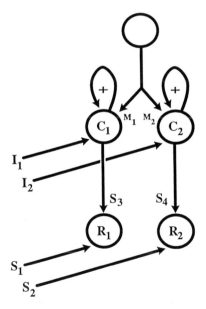

(shown with the + sign to indicate its excitatory nature). That is, when contextual inputs I_1 and I_2 activate C_1 and C_2, the pattern can be maintained in reverberatory short-term memory and continue to enable reorganized processing through sites R_1 and R_2—optimal level behavior.

However, when the system is reset by, for example, a change in context, the loop will be interrupted, and the reorganized processing will cease. Now all that the system can sustain is the simpler activity produced by signals S_1 and S_2—functional level behavior. To overcome this functional-level limit, the system must be able to generate the more complex activity through sites C_1 and C_2 on its own without contextual inputs I_1 and I_2. This development occurs when the long-term memory pathways M_1 and M_2 to sites C_1 and C_2 become functional. As further development and learning bring these long-term memory pathways into operation, a child can permanently encode the pattern induced at C_1 and C_2 in long-term memory. As a result, the child becomes able to endogenously regenerate the induced state at a later time in the absence of immediate contextual support. Now, what was previously optimal level becomes functional level: Behavior that previously depended on contextual support can now be produced spontaneously.

The partial independence of short- and long-term memory processes is only one part of the general complexity and diversity of animal nervous systems. A central nervous system (CNS) is made of many components in composite structure, including diverse neural circuits and diverse inputs to those circuits. The components are not only parallel and distributed but often distinct in structure. Advanced brains are built up from many separate local circuits that operate in partial independence of other local circuits. Although all regions of the CNS are ultimately linked, partial independence is assured by variability in linkage strengths, occurrence of both cooperative (mutually excitatory) and competitive (mutually inhibitory) interactions, radical differences among networks in sensitivities to inputs of various types, and highly diverse inputs from the environment and the body. In addition, partial independence is also assured by developmental delays in effective interaction between many component networks (Fischer & Rose, in press; Thatcher, 1991, in press), as in the delay in development of the M components in Fig. 4.4. Given all the complexity and independence of components, it is inevitable that among the system's multiple activity states, some will be dependent on specific contexts. In addition, some of these context-dependent states will eventually develop so that a child can generate them autonomously.

Advantages of Multiple Levels of Competence

In time, children typically develop the capacity to evoke the complex activity at sites C_1 and C_2 on their own through long-term memory sites M_1

and M_2. That is, after some key experiences, a child becomes capable of autonomously generating the developmentally advanced performance earlier exhibited only transiently—a capacity that Bullock, Carpenter, and Grossberg (1991) called autonomous supercession of (endogenous) control. This capacity has major advantages, of course, but there also seem to be good reasons that its development is delayed.

The advantages of autonomous control are clear. It is advantageous to be able to re-enter a state that generates an adaptive behavior without strong dependence on exogenous input such as social contextual support. Instead of a lengthy process of search for the supportive context to produce the behavior, the organism can directly generate the desirable behavior. Such re-entry to desirable states is a theme in both Piagetian theory, with its emphasis on circular reactions and the regeneration of sensorimotor states (Piaget, 1936/1952; see also Kaufmann, 1980), and conditioning theory, with its emphasis on the regeneration of positively reinforcing states (Skinner, 1969). In fact, there are many different kinds of autonomous supercession of control within and across species (Bullock, 1981; Bullock et al., 1991; Fischer & Bullock, 1984). Because of the emphasis on autonomous control, neural network theories of perceptual and motor skill learning have focused on showing how more endogenously activated input pathways to component networks can gracefully supercede more exogenously activated input pathways, as illustrated with the supercession of control by long-term memory in Fig. 4.4. (Note that in neural network models the supercession effect is graded rather than all-or-none.)

Despite all these obvious advantages, children do not develop autonomous control quickly in all domains. Instead, they develop it slowly and hierarchically, with vast arenas of behavior requiring social contextual support for years before children gain autonomous control over them. Of course, it is these delays that produce the developmental range, the difference between optimal and functional levels. This aspect of developmental range has not been a major subject of research in neural network theory or in other parts of cognitive science.

The key questions are: What does an organism have to gain by delaying the time that a level of supercession of control matures, and how is the delay achieved? Of these two aspects of the problem, how the delay could be achieved is easier to answer. The full functioning of neural connections can be readily delayed by many processes, including slow myelination of pathways. For example, if learned supercession of control depends, as in Fig. 4.4, on the correlated activation of sites C_1 and C_2 with long-term memory pathways M_1 and M_2, which project to C_1 and C_2 from remote brain regions, then supercession can be prevented by delayed myelination of pathways M_1 and M_2 prior to that time. Without myelin, signals will be transmitted slowly and with great attenuation along M_1 and M_2. The result will be negligible long-term memory encoding of C_1 and C_2 activations, even if the cells that give rise to pathways M_1 and M_2 show functional connections within the local circuit to C_1 and C_2. In fact, myelination is a slow developmental process in human beings (Yakovlev & Lecours, 1967), and there are many other processes as well that delay the full functioning of neural connections (Thatcher, in press).

Questions about the adaptive value of such delays have seldom been asked by developmentalists. They seem to assume that developmental delays are explained in terms of intrinsic maturational factors, such as the inherent dependence of upper levels of a hierarchy on prior development of lower levels. We have argued since the early 1980s that timing of developmental transitions arises from a set of dynamically interacting factors, not merely from intrinsic maturation (Fischer, 1980; Fischer & Bullock, 1981).

The advantages of delaying autonomous supercession of control, we hypothesize, center on the relation between levels of organization in a hierarchy. When a higher level assumes control, there is truncation of the search process at the lower level—that is, reduction in the scope of search for adaptive combinations for generalization at the lower level. Consequently, delaying supercession of control by level n + 1 prolongs the search for new adaptive combinations at level n.

Delaying the control of level n + 1 not only allows time to find adaptive combinations at level n, but it reduces the risk of finding inadequate combinations there. The form that activity takes in a neural network depends very much on the input it experiences—its sampling base. With insufficient experience at level n, poor generalizations can be formed there. Delays in supercession of control to a higher level will avoid powerful generalizations drawn from insufficient sampling.

A self-organizing hierarchy can produce compact representations together with great generative power, but this potential requires that its generalizations be well suited to its task environments. The effectiveness of its generalizations are directly related to the thoroughness of its sampling of task environments. Indeed, Elman (1992) showed this limitation in a parallel, distributed network that learned to speak based on experience. For the network to learn adequate generalizations about lower levels of speech production, it required extensive experience at a lower level before moving to a higher level. When the network was not required to function at a lower level first, it missed important generalizations. There is a selective benefit to prolonging lower level sampling well beyond the minimum that is strictly necessary for construction of skills to begin at the next level.

Even while there is a disadvantage to truncating lower level sampling too early, there is also an advantage to being able to activate higher level generalizations that have been successful. The developmental-range phenomenon provides a way of having both advantages at the same time by separating the two levels. A child can sustain higher level generalizations when the context induces them, but the child can simultaneously delay higher level control in order to have extensive opportunity for learning important generalizations at the lower level. This kind of process has been outlined not only for development but also for multiple memory systems in primates (Levine & Prueitt, 1989; Mishkin, Malamut, & Bachevalier, 1984) and for alternative substrates for learning in neural networks (Grossberg, 1978).

The coexistence of lower level and higher level functioning in the developmental range essentially separates sampling and generalization processes. The collapsing of these separated processes would pose serious problems for a developing organism dependent on learning. Some neural network theories, such as back propagation models (McClelland & Rumelhart, 1986), have architectures that virtually collapse sampling and generalization, and as a result the networks must learn very slowly in order to prevent premature, poor quality generalizations (Bullock & Grossberg, 1990; Grossberg, 1987; see also Prince & Pinker, 1988).

The separation of competences evident in the phenomena of developmental range thus make sense in terms of how neural networks function and in terms of the demands of adaptation to a complex environment.

SUMMARY AND CONCLUSIONS: THE DYNAMICS OF COMPETENCE

Across domains and ages, context contributes directly to competence. That is, skill level is a characteristic not only of a person but also of a context. People do not have competences independent of context.

The phenomenon of developmental range shows one way that this person–environment collaboration works. Immediate context contributes directly to skill, affecting the developmental level of a child's behavior. By evoking specific skill components, context induces a particular skill. This effect is powerful, with performance varying from moment to moment up and down a developmental scale as a function of degree of contextual support for high-level functioning. When the support changes, the child's level changes.

Traditional conceptions of competence and performance fail because they treat competence as a fixed characteristic of the child, analogous to a bottle with a fixed capacity. Performance factors are seen as somehow interfering with this capacity. The concept of skill overcomes these limitations by providing a dynamic framework for analyzing variations in behavior with context.

Our research shows that children do indeed have stable levels of competences when domain and degree of support are held constant across assessment contexts. In optimal contexts — with high support, familiar tasks, and motivation to perform — children show a true upper limit on performance, called their optimal level. In spontaneous contexts — with minimal support — children show a much lower upper limit, their functional level. The optimal level develops in a stagelike way, while the functional level develops slowly and gradually.

Neural networks based in adaptive resonance theory show the same separation of levels of functioning. When contextual support induces an optimal-level organization, short-term feedback can sustain that level until the circuit is disrupted. Without contextual support, the network functions at a simpler, functional level. This property of separation of levels allows children to function at a high level when the context demands it while at the same time keeping lower levels of functioning open to new learning from experience. In this kind of system, there is no single fixed competence like that of a glass but a dynamic range of competences reflecting the complexity of human behavior and experience.

ACKNOWLEDGMENTS

The work in this chapter was supported by grants from the MacArthur Network on Early Childhood, the Spencer Foundation, and Harvard University. We would like to express appreciation to Gail Goodman, Helen Hand, Karen Kitchener, Michael Mascolo, Malcolm Watson, and Robert Wozniak for their contributions to the ideas and research reported here.

REFERENCES

Beilin, H. (1971). Developmental stages and developmental processes. In D. R. Green, M. P. Ford, & G. B. Flamer (Eds.), *Measurement and Piaget.* New York: McGraw-Hill.

Bidell, T. R., & Fischer, K. W. (1991). Beyond the stage debate: Action, structure, and variability in Piagetian theory and research. In R. Sternberg & C. Berg (Eds.), *Intellectual development* (pp. 100–140). New York: Cambridge University Press.

Bronfenbrenner, U. (1979). *The ecology of human development: Experiments by nature and design.* Cambridge, MA: Harvard University Press.

Broughton, J. M. (1981). Piaget's structural developmental psychology, III. Function and the problem of knowledge. *Human Development, 24,* 257–285.

Bruner, J. S. (1982). The organization of action and the nature of adult-infant transaction. In M. Cranach & R. Harre (Eds.), *The analysis of action* (pp. 280–296). New York: Cambridge University Press.

Bullock, D. (1981). On the current and potential scope of generative theories of cognitive development. In K. W. Fischer (Ed.), *Cognitive development. New Directions for Child Development* (Vol. 12, pp. 93–109). San Francisco: Jossey-Bass.

Bullock, D., Carpenter, G. A., & Grossberg, S. (1991). Self-organizing neural network architectures for adaptive pattern recognition and robotics. In P. Antognetti & V.

Milutinovic (Eds.), *Neural networks: Concepts, applications, and implementations* (Vol. 1, pp. 33–53). Englewood Cliffs, NJ: Prentice-Hall.

Bullock, D., & Grossberg, S. (1990). Motor skill development and neural networks for position code invariance under speed and compliance rescaling. In H. Bloch & B. I. Bertenthal (Eds.), *Sensory-motor organizations and development in infancy and early childhood* (pp. 1–22). Dordrecht: Kluwer Academic.

Chomsky, N. (1965). *Aspects of the theory of syntax.* Cambridge: MIT Press.

Cole, M., & Scribner, S. (1974). *Culture and thought: A psychological introduction.* New York: Wiley.

Elman, J. (1992). Incremental learning, or the importance of starting small. In *Proceedings of the Thirteenth Annual Conference of the Cognitive Science Society.* Hillsdale, NJ: Lawrence Erlbaum Associates.

Elmendorf, D. (in press). Development of distortions in children's understanding of intentions behind physically harmful acts. Unpublished doctoral dissertation, University of Denver. *Dissertation Abstracts International.*

Fischer, K. W. (1980). A theory of cognitive development: The control and construction of hierarchies of skills. *Psychological Review, 87,* 477–531.

Fischer, K. W., & Bidell, T. R. (1991). Constraining nativist inferences about cognitive capacities. In S. Carey & R. Gelman (Eds.), *The epigenesis of mind: Essays on biology and knowledge* (pp. 199–235). Hillsdale, NJ: Lawrence Erlbaum Associates.

Fischer, K. W., & Bullock, D. (1981). Patterns of data: Sequence, synchrony, and constraint in cognitive development. In K. W. Fischer (Ed.), *Cognitive development. New Directions for Child Development* (Vol. 12, pp. 69–78). San Francisco: Jossey-Bass.

Fischer, K. W., & Bullock, D. (1984). Cognitive development in school-age children: Conclusions and new directions. In W. A. Collins (Ed.), *The years from six to twelve: Cognitive development during middle childhood* (pp. 70–146). Washington, DC: National Academy Press.

Fischer, K. W., & Elmendorf, D. (1986). Becoming a different person: Transformations in personality and social behavior. In M. Perlmutter (Ed.), *Minnesota Symposium on Child Psychology, Vol. 18: Cognitive perspectives on children's social and behavioral development* (pp. 137–178). Hillsdale, NJ: Lawrence Erlbaum Associates.

Fischer, K. W., & Farrar, M. J. (1987). Generalizations about generalization: How a theory of skill development explains both generality and specificity. *International Journal of Psychology, 22,* 643–677.

Fischer, K. W., Hand, H. H., Watson, M. W., Van Parys, M., & Tucker, J. (1984). Putting the child into socialization: The development of social categories in preschool children. In L. Katz (Ed.), *Current topics in early childhood education* (Vol. 5, pp. 27–72). Norwood, NJ: Ablex.

Fischer, K. W., & Hogan, A. (1989). The big picture for infant development: Levels and variations. In J. Lockman & N. Hazen (Eds.), *Action in social context: Perspectives on early development* (pp. 275–305). New York: Plenum.

Fischer, K. W., & Pipp, S. L. (1984). Processes of cognitive development: Optimal level and skill acquisition. In R. J. Sternberg (Ed.), *Mechanisms of cognitive development* (pp. 45–80). New York: Freeman.

Fischer, K. W., & Roberts, R. J., Jr. (1991). *The development of classification skills in the preschool years: Developmental level and errors.* Cambridge, MA: Cognitive Development Laboratory Report, Harvard University.

Fischer, K. W., & Rose, S. P. (in press). Development of coordination of components in brain and behavior: A framework for theory and research. In G. Dawson & K. W. Fischer (Eds.), *Human behavior and the developing brain.* New York: Guilford Press.

Fischer, K. W., Shaver, P., & Carnochan (1990). How emotions develop and how they organize development. *Cognition and Emotion, 4,* 81–127.

Flavell, J. H., & Wohlwill, J. F. (1969). Formal and functional aspects of cognitive development. In D. Elkind & J. H. Flavell (Eds.), *Studies in cognitive development*. London: Oxford University Press.

Gibson, J. J. (1979). *The new ecological approach to visual perception*. Boston: Houghton-Mifflin.

Grossberg, S. (1978). A theory of human memory: Self-organization and performance of sensory-motor codes, maps, and plans. In R. Rosen & F. Snell (Eds.), *Progress in theoretical biology* (Vol. 5, pp. 233–374). New York: Academic Press.

Grossberg, S. (1980). How does a brain build a cognitive code? *Psychological Review, 87*, 1–51.

Grossberg, S. (1987). Competitive learning: From interactive activation to adaptive resonance. *Cognitive Science, 11*, 23–63.

Hand, H. H. (1982). The development of concepts of social interaction: Children's understanding of nice and mean. *Dissertation Abstracts International, 42*(11), 4578B. (University Microfilms No. DA8209747)

Kaufmann, G. (1980). *Imagery, language, and cognition*. Oslo: Universitetsforlaget.

Kitchener, K. S., & Fischer, K. W. (1990). A skill approach to the development of reflective thinking. In D. Kuhn (Ed.), *Developmental perspectives on teaching and learning thinking skills. Contributions to human development* (Vol. 21, No. 4, pp. 48–62). Basel, Switzerland: S. Karger.

Kitchener, K. S., & King, P. M. (1981). Reflective judgement: Concepts of justification and their relation to age and education. *Journal of Applied Developmental Psychology, 2*, 89–116.

Kitchener, K. S., Lynch, C., Fischer, K. W., & Wood, P. (in press). Developmental range of reflective judgement. *Developmental Psychology*.

Klahr, D., & Wallace, J. G. (1976). *Cognitive development: An information-processing view*. Hillsdale, NJ: Lawrence Erlbaum Associates.

Lamborn, S. D., & Fischer, K. W. (1988). Optimal and functional levels in cognitive development: The individual's developmental range. *Newsletter of the International Society for the Study of Behavioral Development, 2*(14), 1–4.

Levine, D. S., & Prueitt, P. S. (1989). Modeling some effects of frontal lobe damage: novelty and perseveration. *Neural Networks, 2*, 103–116.

Magnusson, D. (1988). *Individual development from an interactional perspective: A longitudinal study*. Hillsdale, NJ: Lawrence Erlbaum Associates.

McClelland, J. L., & Rumelhart, D. E. (Eds.). (1986). *Parallel distributed processing*. Cambridge, MA: MIT Press.

Mishkin, M., Malamut, B., Bachevalier, J. (1984). Memories and habits: Two neural systems. In G. Lynch, J. McGaugh, & N. Weinberger (Eds.), *Neurobiology of learning and memory* (pp. 65–77). New York: Guilford.

Neisser, U. (1976). *Cognition and reality*. New York: Freeman.

Overton, W. F., & Newman, J. L. (1982). Cognitive development: A competence-activation/utilization approach. In T. M. Field, A. Huston, H. C. Quay, L. Troll, & G. E. Finley (Eds.), *Review of human development*. New York: Wiley.

Pascual-Leone, J. (1970). A mathematical model for the transition rule in Piaget's developmental stages. *Acta Psychologica, 32*, 301–345.

Piaget, J. (1952). *The origins of intelligence in children* (M. Cook, Trans.). New York: International Universities Press. (Original work published 1936)

Piaget, J. (1971). The theory of stages in cognitive development. In D. R. Green, M. P. Ford, & G. B. Flamer (Eds.), *Measurement and Piaget*. New York: McGraw-Hill.

Piaget, J. (1987). *Possibility and necessity* (2 vols., H. Feider, Trans.). Minneapolis, MN: University of Minnesota Press. (Original work published 1981 and 1983).

Prince, A., & Pinker, S. (1988). Rules and connections in human language. *Trends in Neuroscience, 11*, 195–202.

Rogoff, B., & Lave, J. (Eds.). (1984). *Everyday cognition: Its development in social context.* Cambridge, MA: Harvard University Press.

Rose, S. P. (1990). *Levels and variations in measures of perspective-taking.* Unpublished doctoral dissertation, University of Denver, Denver, CO.

Rotenberg, E. J. (1988). *The effects of development, self-instruction, and environmental structure on understanding social interactions.* Unpublished doctoral dissertation, University of Denver, Denver, CO.

Skinner, B. F. (1969). *Contingencies of reinforcement: A theoretical analysis.* New York: Appleton-Century-Crofts.

Thatcher, R. W. (1991). Maturation of the human frontal lobes: Physiological evidence for staging. *Developmental Neuropsychology, 7,* 397–419.

Thatcher, R. W. (in press). Cyclic cortical reorganization: Origins of human cognitive development. In G. Dawson & K. W. Fischer (Eds.), *Human behavior and the developing brain.* New York: Guilford.

Vygotsky, L. (1978). *Mind in society: The development of higher psychological processes* (M. Cole, V. John-Steiner, S. Scribner, & Ellen Souberman, Trans.). Cambridge, MA: Harvard University Press.

Watson, M. W., & Fischer, K. W. (1980). Development of social roles in elicited and spontaneous behavior during the preschool years. *Developmental Psychology, 16,* 484–494.

Woo, N. S. (1990). *The development of person categorization in Korean preschool children: Understanding and use of age and sex categories.* Unpublished doctoral dissertation, Harvard University, Cambridge, MA.

Wood, D. J. (1980). Teaching the young child: Some relationships between social interaction, language, and thought. In D. R. Olson (Ed.), *The social foundations of language and thought.* New York: Norton.

Yakovlev, P. I., & Lecours, A. R. (1967). The myelogenetic cycles of regional maturation of the brain. In A. Minkowsky (Ed.), *Regional development of the brain in early life* (pp. 3–70). Oxford: Blackwell.

II

CONTEXT AND THE ACQUISITION OF SOCIOCULTURAL KNOWLEDGE

5 Children's Guided Participation and Participatory Appropriation in Sociocultural Activity

Barbara Rogoff
University of Utah, and
University of California at Santa Cruz

Author Patricia MacLachlan discusses with her editor, Charlotte Zolotow, how she solves problems in writing:

> I try to anticipate the experience of the reader. I myself, of course, am the first reader, and I try to envision a small, objective, heartless Patty MacLachlan looking over my shoulder saying, "Aw, come on!" when I am clumsy or self-indulgent. But the small Patty MacLachlan somehow turns into a Charlotte Zolotow. Her voice has become ingrained in my consciousness; I can hear her.

> I've passed this on. My daughter Emily is becoming a wonderful, imaginative writer herself, and we spend a good deal of time discussing her work. "When I write a theme in class," she told me the other day, "I hear your voice in my ear." (MacLachlan 1989, pp. 740–741)

A young man who has little flying experience leans over to another passenger, who is an experienced flyer returning home:

> Excuse me. . . . I wonder where the baggage claim area will be. (Experienced passenger pauses, trying to think of the area of the airport where they will land, and to figure out why the young man would want to know.) After we go out the gate area, . . . it's down some stairs and to the right.

> Young man: Will it, uh, be marked by airplane?

> Experienced passenger: Yes. But don't worry—it won't be hard . . . (Young man displays a look of relief.)

> Experienced passenger: Just follow everybody else on the plane.

> Young man (with a sheepish grin of realization): Oh! Sure.

The sociocultural context of cognitive development involves individuals solving problems with each other, working at times in a solitary fashion and at times side by side or face to face, in activities that tie to cultural institutions inherited from previous generations and transformed to fit current needs and to anticipate future needs.

In this chapter, I explicate the concepts of *guided participation* and *appropriation* that I have used to examine how individual cognitive development fits in sociocultural context in a process of *apprenticeship* (Rogoff, 1990). In guided participation children take part in the skilled activities of their community, engaging with other children and adults in routine and tacit collaboration (whether in social interaction or in otherwise socially structured activities) in which children appropriate from their ongoing involvements the skills and understanding that they use in their later efforts.

I begin by discussing how the work of some key intellectual ancestors — Vygotsky, Gibson, Piaget, and Dewey — fits together and provides a basis for a sociocultural theory of development. Vygotsky, Gibson, Piaget, and Dewey share an emphasis on the importance of mutuality of individual and environment in cognitive development — an emphasis that has yet to be understood in mainstream developmental psychology. Vygotsky and Piaget share an emphasis on understanding human processes through studying *development* — an approach to scholarly inquiry that contrasts with the study of static forms of thought without concern for their transformations. Gibson and Vygotsky (and Vygotsky's colleague Leont'ev) share a conception of thinking as *process:* actively remembering, planning, contemplating, perceiving, rather than the acquisition and possession of memories, plans, cognitions, and percepts. Dewey and Vygotsky (and their colleagues) set out to explain the sociocultural context of thinking; it is not surprising that their views provide the richest accounts of this aspect of cognitive development. Piaget also addressed the question of the role of social interaction in cognitive development, and adds some important points. These aspects of the four theories have been especially influential in the development of my ideas of guided participation and appropriation.

After discussing the contributions of Vygotsky, Gibson, Piaget, and Dewey to my version of a developing sociocultural theory, I describe my use of the concepts of apprenticeship, guided participation, and appropriation to account for how individuals develop in sociocultural activity.

INSEPARABLE ROLES OF ORGANISM AND ENVIRONMENT IN ACTIVITY

It has been common in developmental psychology to limit attention to either the individual or to the environment (e.g., examining how adults teach children or how children construct reality, with the emphasis on separate individuals or independent environmental elements as the basic units of analysis). Even when both individual and environment are considered, they are often regarded as separate entities, rather than being mutually defined and interdependent in ways that preclude their separation as units or elements (Rogoff, 1982). This predilection within developmental studies has led to some interesting assimilations of Piagetian and Vygotskian approaches. Piagetian theory had to struggle for years with controversy regarding whether it fit on one side or the other of the nature–nurture debate (Bovet, Parrat-Dayan, & Voneche, 1989), although it fits neither, but rather recasts the issue to point out the mutuality of organism and environment in development. Vygotskian theory has similarly been assimilated to stimulus–response or social learning approaches, which it does not fit; rather, it reorganizes the conception of individual–environment relations to recognize their mutuality within sociocultural processes.

Vygotsky, Gibson, Piaget, and Dewey all stressed that the individual is not an independent or separate entity but is inherently bound to the environment. Dewey and Bentley (1949) stressed the integrity of whole events that cannot be reduced to the interaction of separate elements. (See Pepper, 1942, and Rogoff, 1982, for discussion of the assumptions and implications of contextual world views and contextual event approaches.)

The ecological theory of Gibson and colleagues stresses animal–environment mutuality in which the characteristics of animal and environment are defined and develop in relation to one another (Johnston & Turvey, 1980; Michaels & Carello, 1981; Reed & Jones, 1977). The concept of affordance describes what the environment offers or means to an animal; the complementary concept of effectivity describes the purposive potentials of the animal (Gibson, 1982; Turvey & Shaw, 1977).

For Gibson, as for Dewey, Vygotsky, and Leont'ev, the world is one of meaning, with objects and events defined with reference to the organism's purposes (Gibson) and in the context of sociohistorical purposes and practices (Vygotsky and Leont'ev).

Piaget (1952) described relativity between organism and environment in his discussion of assimilation and accommodation; in a 1977 printing of an earlier essay, Piaget (1977a) claimed that the individual and society cannot be separated: "What is primary is not . . . the individual, nor the collection of individuals, but the relation between individuals, a relation that endlessly modifies the individual consciousnesses themselves" (p. 146).

Vygotsky's emphasis on the interrelated roles of the individual and the social world in microgenetic, ontogenetic, sociocultural, and phylogenetic development (Scribner, 1985; Wertsch, 1985) embeds individual and environment together in successively larger time frames. Likewise, Vygotsky's interest in the mutuality of individual and sociocultural environment is apparent in his concern with finding a unit of analysis that preserves the inner workings of larger events of interest, rather than separating an event into elements that no longer function as does the living unit (Cole, 1985; Leont'ev, 1981; Wertsch, 1985; Zinchenko, 1985). Leont'ev's (1981) elaboration of Vygotsky's concept of activity refers to a molar unit of analysis that involves both the individual and the social context in a "process of reciprocal transformations between subject and object poles" (p. 46).

The focus of Gibson, Vygotsky and Leont'ev, and Dewey on whole events as the unit of analysis contrasts with the more traditional psychological approach, using the individual as unit of analysis. It has profound implications for how we understand individual psychological processes as well as for how we integrate individual processes with interpersonal and cultural processes.

Event/Activity as Unit of Analysis

If we consider the activity or event as the unit of analysis, with active and dynamic contributions from individuals, their social partners, and historical traditions and materials and their transformations, we can think about the mutually defining roles of each. None exists separately. However, the parts making a whole can be considered separately as foreground without losing track of their inherent interdependence in the whole. Their structure can be described without assuming that the structure of each is independent of the others. By analogy, the organs in an organism work together with an inherent interdependence, but if we are interested in foregrounding one organ to examine its functioning more closely, we can describe the structure and the functioning of the heart or the skin or whatever, remembering that by itself the organ would not have that structure or functioning. Similarly, we may consider individual thinking or cultural functioning as foreground without assuming that they are actually separate elements.

An important perspective that results from using the dynamic event/activity as unit of analysis is a shift from considering cognition as a collection of mental possessions (such as thoughts, schemas, memories, scripts, and plans) to regarding cognition as the active process of solving mental and other problems (e.g., by thinking, recounting, remembering, organizing, planning, and contemplating), generally in the service of intelligent action. These are points essential to Gibson's (1979) approach, foundational to Leont'ev (1981) and treated by Vygotsky, and key in my concepts of appropriation and guided participation (Rogoff, 1990).

Instead of studying a person's possession of a capacity or a bit of knowledge, the focus is on the active changes involved in an unfolding event or activity in which people participate singly or in groups. Events and activities are inherently dynamic, rather than consisting of static conditions with time added to them as a separate element. Change and development, rather than static characteristics or elements, are assumed to be basic. (These views of time are important to Dewey's, Gibson's, and Pepper's approaches.) Understanding processes becomes essential.

Mental processes such as remembering, planning, contemplating, calculating, or narrating a story generally occur in the service of accomplishing something, and cannot be dissected away from the goal to be accomplished and the practical and interpersonal (as well as intrapersonal) actions used.

An important feature of problem solving in a contextual event or activity approach is its embedding of individual activity in specific sociocultural contexts. In the next section, I discuss views of individual cognitive activity as this activity relates to interpersonal and sociohistorical contexts.

THE RELATION OF INDIVIDUAL AND SOCIAL WORLD

Piaget, Vygotsky, and Dewey all discussed the role of social interaction as a context for advances in thinking. However, the role of social interaction was never central to Piaget's theory, and where it was treated it was not tied with sociocultural processes. In contrast, for Vygotsky and Dewey, social interaction is essential to children's learning and cognitive development as children work with more skilled partners in sociocultural activity. Vygotsky stressed that cognitive processes such as voluntary attention, mediated memory, and language are themselves sociocultural phenomena. Thus, for Vygotsky, cognitive development is a sociocultural process involving development of skill with cultural tools through participation and communication with more skilled partners, whereas for Piaget, cognitive development is an individual process that may be influenced by social interaction. For Dewey and Vygotsky, the social world is central to development, whereas for Piaget it is an influence on individual development.

Centrality of the Social World

There are deep differences in how Piaget, on the one hand, and Vygotsky and Dewey, on the other, view the centrality of the social world. In some of his early writing, Piaget focused directly on the social context of cognitive development. He argued that the development of the child is an adaptation as much to the social as to the physical milieu: "Social life is a necessary condition for the development of logic. We thus believe that social life transforms the individual's very nature" (Piaget, 1928/1977b, p. 239). However, Piaget's theory touched only occasionally on social relations, and his research did not investigate the social context of cognitive development (see Doise, 1985; Forman & Kraker, 1985). The question of social context appears to have been an issue that forced itself upon him, rather than being a central tenet of his theory. In a 1927 speech, he admitted that "one cannot speak of the child without asking whether logic is a social thing and in what sense. I have been bothered by this question; I have sought to put it aside; it has always returned" (Piaget, 1928/1977b, p. 204).

Furthermore, Piaget's speculations on the social world were largely limited to the interpersonal context providing for cognitive conflict, without substantial consideration of the cultural and historical context of the intellectual problems and solutions involved in cognitive development. Although Piaget acknowledged that the hypothetico-deductive thought of adolescents is of social origin (Piaget, 1977a, p. 158), this was as close as he came to considering the societal context of thinking.

Vygotsky's theory was built on the premise that individual mental development must be understood with reference to the sociocultural milieu in which the child is embedded. Vygotsky (1978) suggested that rather than deriving explanations of psychological activity from the individual's characteristics plus secondary social influences, psychologists should focus on the social unit of activity and regard individual higher cognitive functioning as derived from that (Wertsch, 1985).

Bakhurst (1988) argued that the tenets of activity theory as proposed by Vygotsky and argued philosophically by Ilyenkov require a radical shift in world view from the predominant Cartesian philosophy, which stresses the individual. The shift makes individual thinking a function of social activity in which the individual internalizes the ways of thinking and acting that have developed in sociocultural history; mind is "in society": "The study of mind, of culture, and of language (in all its diversity) are internally related: that is, it will be *impossible* to render any one of these domains intelligible without essential reference to the others" (Bakhurst, 1988, p. 39).

For Vygotsky (1978, 1987), children's cognitive development must be understood not only as taking place with social support in interaction with others, but as involving the development of skill with societally developed tools—especially language—for mediating intellectual activity. The sociohistorical context is considered by Vygotsky to become accessible to the individual through interaction with other members of the society who are more conversant with the society's intellectual skills and tools, in joint problem solving in the *zone of proximal development*—the region of sensitivity to guidance where the child is not quite able to manage the problem independently. Dewey's (1916) account is similar to Vygotsky's:

> Every individual has grown up, and always must grow up, in a social medium. His responses grow intelligent, or gain meaning, simply because he lives and acts in a medium of accepted meanings and values. . . . Through social intercourse, through sharing of the activities embodying beliefs, he gradually

acquires a mind of his own. The conception of mind as a purely isolated possession of the self is at the very antipodes of the truth. The self *achieves* mind in the degree in which knowledge of things is incarnate in the life about him; the self is not a separate mind building up knowledge anew on its own account. (p. 344)

Thus, although Piaget focused on the individual, sometimes interacting with others on logical problems with social origin, Vygotsky and Dewey focused on children participating with other people in a social order. Their views of social interaction differed in accord with the phenomena they sought to explain.

Explanations of Cognitive Development Through Social Interaction

Whereas Vygotsky and Dewey placed social interaction as the immediate context in which children participate in skilled cultural practices with guidance, Piaget's view of social interaction does not situate it in the context of sociocultural activity. Thus, Vygotsky's and Dewey's views seem more adequate to an overall conception of individual development in sociocultural context. Adding social and cultural levels of explanation secondary to a "basic" individual level, as would be necessary for the Piagetian position to encompass development in sociocultural context, is an unwieldy alternative that does not lead to the same seamless involvement of individuals in sociocultural activity that is offered by Vygotsky and Dewey and their colleagues and followers. In accord with the differences in centrality of the social world, the views of Vygotsky and Dewey differ from those of Piaget with regard to the nature of shared thinking.

Cooperation and Collective Thinking Processes.   Vygotsky, Dewey, and Piaget share an emphasis on the importance of interacting partners sharing a common frame of reference. However, they differ in viewing shared thinking as a collective process versus as an individual process influenced by conflicting views presented by others. In Vygotsky's and Dewey's perspectives, people share in joint endeavors, thinking in common, whereas in Piaget's view, individuals work with independence and equality on each other's ideas.

In Piaget's theory, social influence is expected to foster change through the induction of cognitive conflict and the logical operations carried out by children attempting to reconcile their differing views to achieve equilibrium in their understanding. The model of most effective social interaction is thus cooperation between equals attempting to understand each others' views through reciprocal consideration of their alternative views in logical discussions (Piaget, 1963/1977c). Piaget (1977) laid out three conditions under which equilibrium is achieved in intellectual exchange: (a) The partners need a common scale of intellectual values allowing them to understand terms and ideas in the same sense, in order to translate the differing conceptions of one partner to those of the other; (b) each partner must conserve his or her propositions such that they do not contradict themselves, and must search for agreement on propositions or find facts justifying the difference in points of view; (c) there must be a reciprocity between partners in which the propositions of the partners are treated interchangeably. Piaget emphasized cognitive conflict as the working out of differences of opinion through coming to understand each other's perspective and logically comparing the value of the two perspectives. Piaget's notion of cooperation involves a meeting of minds of two separate individuals, each operating on the other's ideas using the back-and-forth of discussion for each to advance their own development. Piagetian discussion is the product of two individuals considering alternatives provided socially, rather than the construction of a joint understanding between partners.

In a Vygotskian view, children are assumed to be involved in collaboration in which shared thinking produced *in the interaction* (rather than by the individuals) provides the opportunity to be involved in joint decision-making processes with experts, which the child may internalize for later use. The individual makes use of the joint decision-making process itself to extend understanding and skills, internalizing the social process as it is carried out externally in joint problem solving.

Forman (1987) discussed this distinction in collaborative problem solving in Piaget's and Vygotsky's theories. In Piaget's theory, collaborative problem solving is explained by deriving both cognitive and social processes from the same central intrapsychological process, whereas in Vygotsky's theory, the correspondence between cognitive and social processes is due to the derivation of individual cognitive processes from joint cognitive processes in social interaction. Forman contrasted Vygotskian intersubjectivity as a process that takes place between people and Piagetian perspective-taking as an individual process working on socially provided information.

Dewey's view resembles Vygotsky's in emphasizing that thinking occurs in communities:

> The social environment . . . is truly educative in its effects in the degree in which an individual shares or participates in some conjoint activity. By doing his share in the associated activity, the individual appropriates the purpose which actuates it, becomes familiar with its methods and subject matters, acquires needed skill, and is saturated with its emotional spirit. (Dewey, 1916, p. 26)

This statement from Dewey is beautifully consistent with the concepts of guided participation and appropriation that I discuss in a few pages, following a brief consideration of Piaget's and Vygotsky's different emphases on relative skill and status of children's partners in shared thinking.

Equal Status Versus Skilled Guidance: Peer Versus Adult Partners. Piaget stressed the value of social interaction between equals allowing for resolution of cognitive conflict, whereas Vygotsky focused on the guidance provided by collaboration with a more skilled partner supporting children's developing expertise. The differences in the role relations and mechanisms stressed by Vygotsky and Piaget may relate to differences in what aspects of human development they were attempting to explain: The development of skills in the use of cultural tools (especially language) and abstract thought as historical products, on the one hand, and shifts in perspective in logical/scientific concepts as evidence of developmental transitions in rational thought, on the other. (See Rogoff, 1990, and Tudge & Rogoff, 1989, for more detailed comparison of Vygotsky and Piaget.)

Piaget, in his stress on reciprocal consideration of ideas, argued for the importance of equal status and peer interaction. Piaget (1926) felt that children's discussions with adults are unlikely to lead to cognitive restructuring because of the unequal power relations between adults and children. An asymmetric interaction in which an adult has the power disrupts the condition of reciprocity for achieving equilibrium in thinking (Piaget, 1977a, p. 165), and simply leads young children to abandon their own ideas for those presented without examining or verifying the ideas.

Although Piaget argued that children's interaction with adults does not promote their cognitive development, his focus was on the use of adult authority. He allowed for the possibility that adults may be able to interact with children in a cooperative fashion that permits the sort of reciprocity required for children to advance to a new level of equilibrium (Piaget, 1928/1977b).

For Vygotsky, ideal partners are not equal, but the inequality is in skills and understanding rather than in power. For this reason either adults or peers can bring about cognitive growth, but for cognitive development to occur in the course of interacting with a peer, the partner should be "more capable" (Vygotsky, 1978).

The differing aspects of development of interest to Piaget and Vygotsky would likely involve different social interactional processes. The resolution of cognitive conflict may be necessary for a child to discard an existing logicomathematical conviction to consider one that is qualitatively different, to achieve a Piagetian shift in perspective. The sort of cognitive conflict that Piaget posited to occur between peers who have different answers to the same question may contribute to making a person aware that there are alternatives and to directing the individual to accept another view through presentation and consideration of alternatives.

In contrast, interaction with a more skilled partner may be necessary to provide practice in symbolic and practical skills and access to information required to become proficient with the culturally provided tools for thinking (especially language) studied by Vygotsky. The partner must be someone who knows more about the tools than does the child.

Focusing on the relative advantages of interaction with experts (in peer tutoring) and equals (in peer collaboration), Damon (1984) suggested that interaction with experts may be useful in the acquisition of information or skills that are within students' reach, whereas peer collaboration with free and reciprocal exchange of ideas among equals encourages children to wrestle with intellectual challenges in difficult new principles.

Investigations of the relative advantages of peer versus adult–child interaction in laboratory planning and categorizing tasks consistently show greater advances following collaboration with adults than with peers for school-age children (Ellis & Rogoff, 1982, 1986; Radziszewska & Rogoff, 1988, in press). For younger children, the evidence is less consistent (Rogoff, 1990). We are currently investigating whether the advantage for older children of working with an adult rather than with a peer changes when children engage in similar cognitive tasks situated outside the laboratory, in a domain in which children feel especially at home—computer games (Tudge & Rogoff, 1989).

At the same time, it is clear that children can serve as important facilitators of each other's cognitive development. A number of studies deriving from the Piagetian tradition have demonstrated that peer interaction can foster advances in cognitive development (Bearison, 1991; Doise & Mackie, 1981; Mugny & Doise, 1978; Perret-Clermont & Nicolet, 1988; Sigel & Cocking, 1977).

Research is sparse examining the roles of peers versus adults in Piagetian shifts of perspective. In the area of moral reasoning, the work of Kruger and Tomasello (1986; Kruger, 1988) supports the idea that children are more free to examine the logic of arguments when interacting with peers than with adults, and that discussion with peers leads to more progress in moral reasoning. However, in Piagetian operational tasks (conservation of area and volume), collaboration with adults involved as much transactional discussion of ideas and progress in conservation as did collaboration with peers (Radziszewska & Miller, in preparation).

The research to date largely compares one-on-one interaction of children with either peer or adult partners in constrained situations designed by others (who happen themselves to be adults). If we are to consider the role of interaction with adults and peers in children's cognitive development, it will be valuable to widen our field of vision to include the broader sociocultural context in which peer and adult–child interaction occurs. Although dyadic interaction within constrained tasks does occur in a variety of situations, it is important to recognize that much of children's interactions occurs in the context of systematic relationships among people varying in age, status, and expertise—consider families and classrooms (Rogoff, Mistry, Göncü, & Mosier, in press). Some efforts in this direction are available in research demonstrating the value of cooperative classroom learning, in which peers work together effectively on academic tasks when the social structure of the classroom supports peer collaboration (Cooper, Marquis, & Edward, 1986; Damon, 1984; Slavin, 1987).

In using the model of apprenticeship, discussed in the next section, I argue that guided participation should be conceived as the individual's involvement in a social system involving both more skilled partners and peers of varying levels of skill and status, as apprentices guide and challenge each other with the supervision and model of experts in common sociocultural activity.

APPRENTICESHIP, GUIDED PARTICIPATION, AND APPROPRIATION

Apprenticeship in Thinking (Rogoff, 1990) developed the concept of guided participation that I had introduced earlier (Rogoff & Gardner, 1984), and introduced the concept of appropriation. Apprenticeship, guided participation, and appropriation have an important relation to each other that helps explicate my version of a sociocultural account of cognitive development.

A sociocultural perspective draws attention to how individual efforts, interpersonal involvements, and culturally organized activities constitute each other. In fact, without an understanding of such mutually constituting processes, the approach is at times assimilated to other approaches that examine only a part of the package. For example, it is incomplete to focus only on the relation of individual development and social interaction without concern for the cultural activity in which individual and interpersonal actions take place. And it is incomplete to assume that development occurs in one plane and not in others (e.g., that children but not their partners or their cultural communities develop) or that influence can be ascribed in one direction or another or relative contributions be counted (e.g., parent to child or child to parent; culture to individual). The three concepts—apprenticeship, guided participation, and appropriation—refer to inseparable processes that occur at different levels of sociocultural activity—cultural, interpersonal, and personal.

The metaphor of *apprenticeship* provides a model at the level of community activity, involving active individuals participating with others in culturally organized activity that has as part of its purpose development by the less experienced participants. To speak of apprenticeship it is necessary to be concerned with apprenticeship in WHAT, and to attend to how the activity at hand relates to other aspects of the culture in which it is embedded—economic, political, moral, and material.

The concept of *guided participation* refers to the process and system of involvement of individuals with other individuals, as they communicate and collaborate in carrying out culturally valued activity. This includes not only the face-to-face interaction that has been the subject of much research, but also the side-by-side joint participation that is frequent in everyday life and the more distal arrangements of people's activities that do not require co-presence. Consider the guided participation that occurs in the collaboration and negotiation of children and parents as parents make and limit opportunities in making daycare decisions or saving chores until toddlers are asleep and as children choose (or choose not to) be involved in watching TV, doing chores, playing with matches, and engaging in a variety of activities negotiated with others.

The concept of *appropriation* refers to how individuals change through their involvement in one or another activity, becoming prepared for subsequent involvement in other, related activities. Although Piaget assumed that cognitive development was all-of-a-piece, with general conceptual changes across widely different domains, considerable research of the last few decades has pointed to the fact that cognitive development is not unitary but tied to specific domains, contexts, or tasks (see Rogoff, 1982). Granting that cognitive development is not unitary, we are left with the question of how individuals' involvement in particular activities relates to their efforts in subsequent activities. The unitary version of cognitive development was an oversimplification; the current challenge is to unravel the threads that tie development in one situation to the next. With guided participation as the interpersonal process in which people are involved in sociocultural activity, appropriation is the personal process in which, through engagement in an activity at one time, individuals change so that they handle other situations in accord with development in previous situations.

Each of these concepts is explored in greater depth here, with examples of each to help tie them together.

Apprenticeship

A metaphor that has appealed to many scholars interested in considering the mutual embeddedness of the individual and the sociocultural world is that of apprenticeship—in which novices become more skilled through participation with other people in culturally organized activities (Bruner, 1983; Dewey, 1916; Goody, 1989; John-Steiner, 1985; Lave, 1988; Rogoff, 1990). The notion of apprenticeship focuses attention on the active role of children in organizing development, the active support and use of other people in social interaction and arrangements of tasks and activities, and the socioculturally ordered nature of the institutional contexts, technologies, and goals of cognitive activities.

Research that focuses on the sociocultural context of thinking, as in the metaphor of apprenticeship, focuses on social structure of intellectual activity (e.g., in schooling, work), as well as on the cultural tools used in cognitive problem solving. For example, it encourages the recognition that planning involves cultural tools such as maps, pencils, and linguistic and mathematical systems, as well as cultural values and situational constraints and resources influencing what means are valued for solving problems (e.g., improvisation or planning all moves in advance of action). A sociocultural view examines the definition of a problem as having cultural origins in institutions and value systems.

An Example.   We are currently examining the sociocultural context of planning as Girl Scouts manage the sales and delivery of Girl Scout cookies, using the apprenticeship model to investigate the organization of the process (Rogoff, Lacasa, Baker, & Goldsmith, in preparation). The individual girls carry a great deal of responsibility for planning routes; keeping track of sales, cookies, and money; and managing their time, in the context of collaboration with other scouts, siblings, parents, customers, and adult troop leaders. Many of the other children and adults have been involved in sales before, so that there are multiple sources of information and assistance available to the individual girls. Further, the collective experience of planning cookie sales is carried forward in the cultural context of institutional supports and constraints provided by traditions and practices of the Girl Scout organization, which provides training to troop leaders and many organizational supports to the individual girls. For example, the cookie order form is color coded in a way that facilitates keeping track of the different kinds of cookie (e.g., thin mints are ordered in the green column), with organization and information to facilitate the calculation of amounts of money, the information to be presented to customers, and the keeping track of key dates.

Our view of the planning process is expanded, with attention drawn to the importance of improvisation and the successful adaptation to circumstances, as we examine planning in what resembles an apprenticeship system, with girls collaborating with and competing with peers, guiding and being guided by peers and adults, and working within and modifying traditions and institutional constraints and supports. Such a view of cognitive activity as occurring within interpersonal and institutional contexts could be undertaken for many other problem solving situations in which children engage — including those occurring in school and in laboratories. It is facilitated, however, by examining the functioning of institutions and cultural systems that one does not take for granted. Systems in which one is completely immersed are difficult even to detect. Analysis of the sociocultural context of social and individual activity is difficult for researchers embedded in educational situations or research traditions that are often seen as the way things must be rather than just one way that things happen to be.

Guided Participation

In the concept of guided participation (Rogoff, 1990; Rogoff & Gardner, 1984), I stress the mutual roles of individuals and their social partners, participating in socioculturally structured collective activity. The everyday involvement of people in shared endeavors in turn constitutes and transforms cultural practices with each successive generation.

The concept of guided participation incorporates guidance in the sense of direction of the shared endeavor, whether in the arrangements of the activity or in tacit or explicit, face-to-face or side-by-side communication. It involves participation that may be peripheral or central; what is key is participation in meaning — not necessarily in shared action of the moment. A child who is actively observing and following the decisions made by another person is participating whether or not he or she contributes directly to decisions as they are made. A child who is working alone on a report is participating in a cultural activity with guidance provided by the child with the teacher, classmates, family members, librarian, and authors, as they set the assignment and choice of materials and approach to be used.

The concept of guided participation is a way of looking at a system of interpersonal involvements and arrangements, not an operational definition that one might use to identify some and not other interactions. The perspective of guided participation focuses attention on the system of interpersonal engagements and arrangements involved in participation in activities (promoting some involvements and restricting others), which is managed collaboratively by individuals and their social partners in face-to-face or other interaction as well as in adjustment of arrangements for each others' and their own activities. Within the perspective offered by the concept of guided participation, it is possible to characterize the nature of guidance and the nature of participation (and variations in different participants' contributions and in the circumstances related to varying forms of guidance and participation). However, the concept of guided participation does not define when a particular situation is or is not "guided participation." Rather it provides a *perspective* on how to look at variations in means of interpersonal engagements and arrangements as they fit in sociocultural contexts, to understand processes of learning and development.

In guided participation, the notions of active participation and communication are central. Novices are active in their attempts to make sense of activities and may be primarily responsible for putting themselves in the position to learn. At the same time, their more mature partners can often more easily find effective ways to achieve shared thinking that stretch the less skilled partner's understanding. The process of communication requires people to seek a common ground of understanding from which to proceed, with extensions from the common ground requiring adjustments or growth in understanding. This is the basis of intersubjectivity. As Dewey (1916) said:

> There is more than a verbal tie between the words common, community, and communication. [People] live in a community in virtue of the things which they have in common; and communication is the way in which they come to possess things in common. (p. 5)

> One shares in what another has thought and felt and in so far, meagerly or amply, has his attitude modified. (p. 6)

Skilled partners may support a novice's efforts by structuring subgoals of an endeavor to focus the novice on a manageable aspect of the activity (Saxe, Gearhart, & Guberman, 1984). Over the course of participation with more skilled partners, individuals may come to take increasingly central and responsible roles in shared endeavors.

The notion of guided participation emphasizes that children and their social partners collaborate in determining the arrangements for children's daily routines, tasks, circumstances, and partners — both within and outside of explicit social interaction.

Guided participation in sociocultural activity involves more than dyads and includes engagement with people at similar levels of responsibility for an activity as well as with people more or less centrally involved. Often a group of novices (peers) serve as resources to each other in exploring an activity and aiding and challenging each other. Among themselves, novices are likely to differ usefully in expertise, as are experts, who are still developing breadth and depth of skill and understanding in the process of carrying out the activity and guiding others in it.

> The one who communicates [is not] left unaffected. . . . [An] experience has to be formulated in order to be communicated. To formulate requires getting outside of it, seeing it as another would see it, considering what points of contact it has with the life of another so that it may be got into such form that he can appreciate its meaning. (Dewey, 1916, p. 6)

Hence the apprenticeship model and the concept of guided participation stress active learners in a community of people who support, challenge, and guide novices as they participate in skilled, valued cultural activity.

This perspective, although it is likely consistent with the basic notions of Vygotsky's theory, emphasizes tacit as well as explicit communication and arrangements between children and their companions. This differs from the orientation in Vygotsky's work that stresses academic/"scientific" concepts and "higher" cognitive processes as the goal of cognitive development and the greatest tools of thought. It also draws attention to the role of children's efforts to arrange for participation and observation of the skilled activities of their community. In these ways, the concept of guided participation is intended to encompass scenarios of cognitive development that may be of less centrality in the Vygotskian account — especially the arrangements and interactions of children in cultural communities that do not aim for school-based intellectual processes (see Rogoff, Mosier, Mistry, & Göncü, in press) as well as the arrangements and interactions of middle-class children in their routine involvement in everyday cognitive activities at home and in their neighborhoods.

An Example. In the context of adult–child and peer collaboration in imaginary errand planning, Radziszewska and Rogoff (1988, 1991) examined the nature of guided participation in collaborative problem solving and children's later efforts in the same task. In imaginary errand planning, 10-year-old children exhibit less sophisticated planning than adults, which we expected to relate to the forms of guided participation of children interacting with adult versus peer partners in this task.

Dyads were given a map of an imaginary downtown and two lists of errands (see Fig. 5.1) and were asked to plan a trip to get materials for a school play. Each partner had a list with five items to be picked up, but the partners needed to coordinate their planning of the route so the school driver could make an efficient trip (to save gasoline). An optimal route involved incorporating stores that had to be visited (to get items that were available from only one store), and deciding which of two alternatives would be more efficient to include for items available from two stores (e.g., paintbrushes available from the paint shop or the shopping center). The map was the same for each trip and the optimal route was similar, but the lists of items varied on each trip. Partners planned two trips together; then each planned a trip independently.

The collaborative planning of adult–child dyads was more efficient than that of peer dyads, who focused on one decision at a time (Radziszewska & Rogoff, 1988). Peers usually identified the store closest to the current location and checked to see if it was on either list, yielding much less efficient routes. Adult–child dyads planned longer sequences of moves,

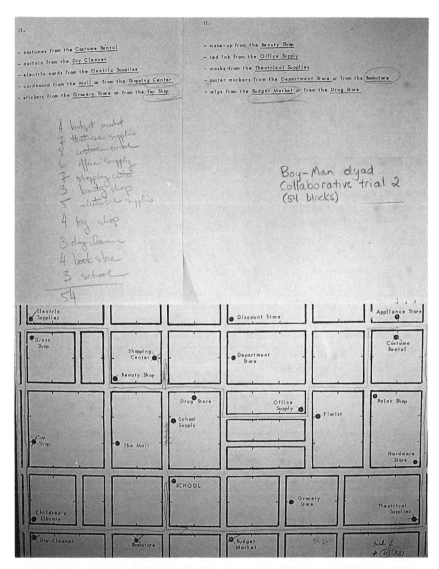

FIG. 5.1 List of errands and map for imaginary errand planning, as used by a father–son dyad on their second collaborative trial, with a near optimal route.

were twice as likely to explore the layout before making moves — often marking the choice and no-choice stores with different colors and symbols to facilitate planning — and were far more likely to state planning strategies.

During collaboration with adults, children usually participated in the sophisticated strategies organized by the adults. Although statements of strategy and thinking-aloud of decisions were contributed primarily by adults, the children participated in managing the sophisticated decisions. There were suggestions that children who produced more efficient imaginary errand routes after collaborating with adults had had more opportunity to share in decision making than those who performed poorly after collaborating with adults. In contrast, the interaction between peers was characterized by less sharing of decision making, less sophisticated planning, and less communication of strategies.

Even when peer partners were trained in errand planning prior to their collaboration with target children and the planning efficiency of dyads containing trained peers and adults did not differ, children who had collaborated with adults were more efficient in independent planning than were children who had worked with either trained or untrained peers, who did not differ significantly (Radziszewska & Rogoff, 1991).

These findings seem to result from striking differences in the nature of the guided participation of the children who worked with adults compared with those who worked with trained peers. During collaborative planning, the adults more frequently communicated the optimal strategy and there was frequent thinking aloud of decisions in the adult–child dyads. Practically all of the children working with adults were active participants in decision making (making or elaborating on decisions), whereas fewer than half of the children working with trained peers were active participants. Children who worked with untrained peers often collaborated, but without one partner skilled in errand planning, such involvement was least effective for the target children's learning. The interactions of the children with peers likely contributed to their understanding of the errand planning task and of processes of collaboration although in ways other than those which were the focus of these studies.

The notion of guided participation is meant to draw attention to how interactions such as those with adults as well as those with peers (and the arrangements by others such as the experimenter) are all part of a larger system of interpersonal engagements and arrangements fitting in sociocultural activity.

Appropriation

Whereas the metaphor of apprenticeship calls attention to the sociocultural organization of cognitive activity, and guided participation refers to interpersonal interaction and arrangements, appropriation is the process by which individuals transform their skills and understanding through their participation. Appropriation occurs in the context of engagement (often with others) in sociocultural activity, but focuses on the personal processes of transformation that are part of an individual's participation.

Appropriation Versus Internalization.   I have argued that the process by which children gain from their involvement with others in sociocultural activity is *appropriation* rather than *internalization* (Rogoff, 1990). The idea of internalization has been used in a variety of theories to account for how children make use of social interaction, but generally with the processes of internalization unspecified. It is left that children make the external internal, somehow. In my view, however, it is not difficult to explain how children appropriate from their participation in shared activity because they must already be functioning in the social activity in order to be making their contributions. To emphasize this point, I at times refer to my notion of appropriation as *participatory appropriation.* Rather than viewing the process as one of internalization in which something rather static is taken across a boundary from the external to the internal, I see the child's active participation itself as being the process by which the child gains in skill and understanding of the activity. As Wertsch and Stone (1979, p. 21) said, "the process *is* the product." Or in Dewey's (1916) words,

> The living creature is a part of the world, sharing its vicissitudes and fortunes, and making itself secure in its precarious dependence only as it intellectually identifies itself with the things about it, and, forecasting the future consequences of what is going on, shapes its own activities accordingly. If the living, experiencing being is an intimate participant in the activities of the world to which it belongs, then knowledge is a mode of participation, valuable in the degree in which it is effective. It cannot be the idle view of an unconcerned spectator. (p. 393)

By adopting the participatory appropriation view of how development and learning occur, we shift to a perspective in which children and their social partners are interdependent, their roles are active and dynamically changing, and the specific processes by which they communicate and share in decision making are the substance of cognitive development.

My contrast involving the term *internalization* here is limited to the usage that it often has in information processing and learning accounts, where the term implies a separation between the person and the social context and assumptions that learning and thinking involve the acquisition and retrieval of static concepts, memories, and so on.

There are authors who use the term *internalization* in ways resembling how I use the term *participatory appropriation.* Translations of Vygotsky often use the term *internalization;* I assume that my use of appropriation is similar to his concept, at least in emphasizing the inherent transformation involved in the process. Similarly, Berger and Luckmann (1966) provided a consistent account using the term *internalization* (along with externalization). Forman (1989) summarized their approach:

Berger and Luckmann argued that there are three components to the social construction of reality: externalization, objectivation, and internalization. All three components are necessary to their theory and together they explain how social institutions, technologies and knowledge are created, maintained, legitimated, and transmitted through social interaction. They proposed that knowledge begins as a natural by-product of the externalization of human activity. As people try to interact over time with each other, an implicit mutual understanding develops between them. Soon, however, this tacit knowledge becomes objectified in explicit concepts and rules to which language and other sign systems can refer. The final step in the process occurs when this knowledge needs to be internalized by people who were not part of its creation. (p. 57)

I first noticed the term *appropriation* in Bakhtin's (1981) writing, as I was searching for a way to express the difference between my views and the version of internalization involving importing objects across boundaries from external to internal:

The word in language is half someone else's. It becomes "one's own" only when the speaker populates it with his own intention, his own accent, when he appropriates the word, adapting it to his own semantic and expressive intention. Prior to this moment of appropriation, the word does not exist in a neutral and impersonal language (it is not, after all, out of a dictionary that the speaker gets his words!), but rather it exists in other people's mouths, in other people's contexts, serving other people's intentions: it is from there that one must take the word, and make it one's own. (pp. 293–294)

Bakhtin's account resembles the use of the notion of appropriation in art history. Haverkamp-Begemann (1988)[1] noted that creative copies of other artists' work have served an important role in artists' training and inspiration across the centuries.

Each individual reaction to an older work of art represents a synthesis of the artists' intentions: to record, to interpret, to criticize and to learn. Each copy constitutes a dialogue between the interpreter and the interpreted; this dialogue fosters new solutions to problems shared by the two artists and creates new ideas. (p. 13)

My "appropriation" of the term from Bakhtin of course transforms the meaning to my own use. I use the term *appropriation* to refer to the change resulting from a person's *own participation* in an activity—as they make a process their own, changing how they may treat future situations that they see as related (a phenomenon of great importance, discussed later). This

---

[1]My thanks to Hal Fishbein for the Haverkamp-Begemann (1988) reference noted here.

differs from other uses in considering the person's own participation in sociocultural activity rather than some external model or experience to be appropriation.

The term *appropriation* is defined as "taking for one's own use." In my view, however, it is not one person taking from another (yours becomes mine), but rather one or more people taking from their common activity (ours becomes mine or ours1 becomes ours2, where ours2 involves an overlapping group with ours1 or the same group of people at a later time in another situation).

People make a process their own through their (necessarily creative) efforts to understand and contribute to social activity, which by its very nature involves bridging between several ways of understanding a situation. Communication and shared endeavors always involve adjustments between participants to stretch their common knowledge to fit with new perspectives. Such stretching to fit several views together *is* development, and occurs in the process of communication and shared efforts. Appropriation is each participant's own change in understanding and skill in participation.

The term *appropriation* appears elsewhere as well, such as in the quote from Dewey (1916) referred to earlier, and in Perret-Clermont, Brun, Saada, and Schubauer-Leoni (1984). Some uses are quite different than mine. For example, Harre (1983) used the term *appropriation,* but treated it as a process that precedes transformation. In my view, appropriation *is* a process of transformation and cannot be treated as separate.

Newman, Griffin, and Cole (1989) also used the term *appropriation,* noting Leont'ev as their source. Their use appears to differ a little from mine, as they referred to appropriation of cultural resources and tools (such as systems of language) through involvement in culturally organized activities in which the tool plays a role. The sense is close, but it seems to differ in that their *appropriation* is the use of external tools, whereas my *participatory appropriation* involves individuals changing through their own adjustments and understanding of the sociocultural activity.

The purpose of my emphasis on participatory appropriation rather than internalization is to distinguish two conceptual systems: A system using the concept of participatory appropriation views development as an active process of peoples' participation in cultural activities. The system using the concept of internalization views development in terms of the static and wholly internal acquisition of pieces of knowledge (either by solitary construction or by internalization of separate, external pieces of knowledge). These are, I believe, quite different theoretical views.

Assumptions About Time.   An important difference between the participatory appropriation model and the internalization model is in assumptions about the place of time. In the internalization model, time is cut into segments involving past, present, and future. These are separate and yield problems of accounting for the relation of the past and the present or the present and the future, which are solved by assuming that the individual stores memories of the past that are somehow retrieved and used in the present, and that the individual makes plans in the present and (if they are stored effectively) executes them in the future. Notice that the links between these separate time segments are bridged in somewhat mysterious ways, to bring information or skills stored at one point in time to use in another. It involves a storage model of mind, with static elements, and the need for a homunculus or mysterious executive process to bring the elements stored at one point in time to implement at another point in time (Baker-Sennett, Matusov, & Rogoff, in press). This is the same homunculus or mysterious executive process that is required to bring external pieces of knowledge or skill inside the person in the internalization model, where learning is the acquisition and accumulation of mental objects.

In the participatory appropriation model, time is an inherent aspect of events and is not divided into separate units of past, present, and future.[2] Any event in the present is an extension of previous events and is directed toward goals that have not yet been accomplished. As such, the present contains past and future and cannot be separated from them. Pepper gave the example that the meaning of a word in a sentence ("the present") brings with it the previous meanings of that word in other sentences and of other words already expressed in that sentence (the past in the present). The meaning of the particular word is also directed toward the overall idea to which the word contributes but which is not yet fully expressed (the future in the present).

When a person acts in the present on the basis of previous experience, their past is present. It is not merely a stored memory called up in the present; it is contributing to the event at hand by having prepared it. The present event is different than it would have been if previous events had not occurred; this does not require a storage model of past events.

A physical example may help: The size, shape, and strength of a child's leg at age 6 is a function of growth and use that has occurred previously; the child's leg has *changed* over development — it is not a summation of stored units of growth or of exercise. The past is not *stored* in the leg; the leg has developed, changed to be as it is currently. There is no need to separate past and present or future, or to conceive of the development in terms of the acquisition of stored units. Development is clearly a process spanning time, dynamic, with change throughout rather than accumulation of new items.

---

[2]My discussion here is greatly influenced by assumptions regarding time in Gibson's theory and in Pepper's account of a contextual world hypothesis. I am endebted to Beth Shapiro for discussion of Gibson's view, and to Christine Mosier for pointing out the importance of this view in distinguishing internalization and appropriation.

In this view, participatory appropriation is an aspect of ongoing events. A person who participates in events changes in ways that make a difference in subsequent events. Participatory appropriation is ongoing development as the person participates in events, with changes based on previous events being simply present in current events. This contrasts with the internalization model in which one would look for exposure to external knowledge or skills, followed by internalization, followed by evidence of internalization as the person retrieves the acquired knowledge or skill independently.

In some efforts to understand internalization, time is used as a tool for examining the internalization of social events, but still with the assumptions of separation between internal and external, of boundaries between past, present, and future, and of development as acquisition of static pieces of information or skill. Sequential analyses of social interaction, for instance, may examine change over time by breaking an event into smaller units (either with units of time or with moves made by one person or the other), but often define the contributions of each partner separately, to look at the impact of one upon the other. For example, a study may examine maternal assistance and child learning by choosing categories of maternal behavior (e.g., questions, directives, praise) and categories of child behavior (e.g., errors, correct response, off-task behavior), and examining the contingencies between them.

This sequential strategy, I argue, is still consistent with the internalization model, in which time is separate from the events, the external and internal events are arbitrarily separated, and development is seen as accumulation. The contrasting participatory appropriation model focuses instead on events as dynamically changing, with people participating with others in whole events (where one could examine each person's contribution but not define them separately), and development is seen as transformation.

Mutually Constituting Processes.   Inherent to the participatory appropriation view is the mutual constitution of personal, interpersonal, and cultural processes, with development occurring at all planes in sociocultural activity. The contrast in the internalization view is an assumption that the individual is the primary unit of analysis, with statically conceived interpersonal and cultural influences added onto basic individual processes. In the internalization model, the individual is either a passive recipient of external social or cultural influence—a receptacle for the accumulation of knowledge and skill—or else an active seeker of passive external social and cultural knowledge and skill. The participatory appropriation model views personal, interpersonal, and cultural processes all as active, in the process of transformation in sociocultural activity, and constituting each other.

Figure 5.2 sketches the differences between some models of internalization as social influence (both in simple and sequential versions) and of participatory appropriation.

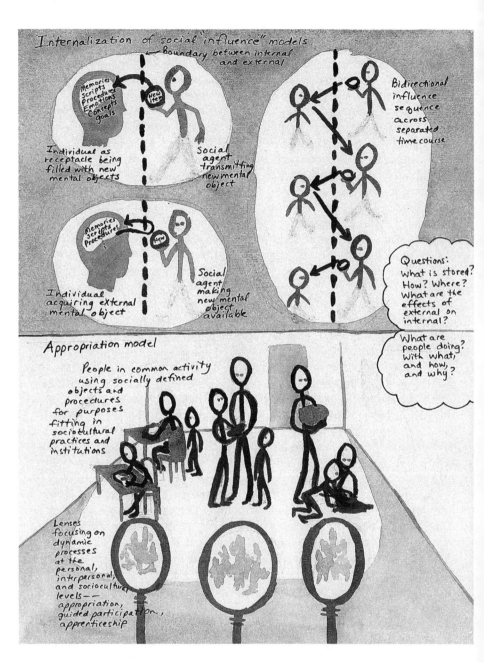

FIG. 5.2 A sketch comparing models: Internalization of social "influence" versus participatory appropriation.

If we can view cognitive development as a process of participatory appropriation, then the questions we are to investigate change their shape. Instead of searching for a separate mechanism for internalizing static and "context-free" knowledge from outside to inside, we begin to examine in closer focus the actual processes by which children participate with other people in cultural activity, and the ways in which they transform their understanding in the context of their activities. This becomes the basis of our understanding of development, rather than simply the surface that we must get past. It leads us to closer examination of processes in the context of people's activities. How and in what way do people participate in sociocultural activity, and how does their participation change from relatively peripheral (cf. Lave, 1988), observing and carrying out secondary roles, to sometimes central responsibility for carrying out activities?

Viewing development as participatory appropriation recasts the question of transfer of knowledge. Transfer is clearly not automatic; nor is it a characteristic of a piece of knowledge or a kind of task. Treatment of one situation as being like another must have to do with the individual construing the purpose or the meaning of one situation as allowing or calling for its treatment as similar to another. Hence, the process is inherently *creative,* with individuals actively seeking meaning and making links between situations on the basis of their understanding of the previous and current situations.

> In real knowledge there is a particularizing and a generalizing function working together. . . . Anything which is *to be* known, whose meaning has still to be made out, offers itself as particular. But what is already known, if it has been worked over with a view to making it applicable to intellectually mastering new particulars, is general in function. Its function of introducing connection into what is otherwise unconnected constitutes its generality. Any fact is general if we use it to give meaning to the elements of a new experience. (Dewey, 1916, p. 399)

Appropriation is not a purely solitary process, of course. It occurs as individuals, often with others, and always in the context of sociocultural activity, puzzle out how to manage a new situation on the basis of their own and their shared history, to reach their own and their shared goals, through emotional, nonverbal, and verbal communication indicating what kind of a situation this is. This is the case in research on problem isomorphs, in which transfer is most likely to occur if the Experimenter points out that a new problem is similar to a previously solved one. It occurs throughout everyday communication from emotional cues indicating that this situation is dangerous or fun to explicit statements of similarity ("Division is like multiplication except backwards") to the routine choice of familiar words to get an idea across (e.g., referring to an electric socket as "hot" in speaking with a preschool age child). Wozniak (personal communication, 1989) pointed out that in the Vygotskian view,

> spoken lexical items occurring in different practical and linguistic contexts ["Here's a cup," "Don't drop the cup," "The cup is glass," "The cup is empty," etc.] serve as a nexus around which the child abstracts and generalizes experience with objects and events, and . . . since these lexical items pre-exist the child in a communally held system of meanings, the internalization of speech as a generalizing, abstracting, but socially-elaborated semiotic system embeds sociality and historicity at the very core of human abstract conceptualization.

Introducing the concept of participatory appropriation does not answer all the questions through suggesting that it occurs through individuals' active involvement in sociocultural activity, with the adjustments necessary for communication and participation themselves constituting development. But orienting the question this way, I believe, demystifies the process. Rather than searching for the nature of internalization as a conduit from external bits of knowledge or skills to an internal repository, the viewpoint leading from adopting the notion of participatory appropriation allows us to examine cognitive development as children are engaged with others in the activities of their culture. It allows us to look closely at children's efforts and those of their companions and the structure of their institutions to give answers grounded in the particularities of those efforts, opportunities, and constraints.

An Example.   In the research on children's imaginary errand planning (Radziszewska & Rogoff, 1988), collaboration with an adult provided an opportunity for children to participate in more skilled planning, which enhanced their later planning. Evidence of children's participatory appropriation of sophisticated planning strategies from their collaboration with adults appears in some specific features of their planning that they carried forward from the collaborative sessions to later planning.

In the collaborative trips involving adults, the partners frequently marked up the lists of errands in ways that facilitated their distinguishing destinations that they had to visit from those for which they had to choose one of two destinations (so that they could first plan a route involving the obligatory destinations to choose the best of the options for the choice items). This was generally an idea contributed by adult partners, with the children participating in its use. Evidence of participatory appropriation is that following this involvement in the marking strategy, almost all the children from adult–child pairs started the individual trial by searching for and marking the choice and the no-choice stores on the map in ways closely resembling those used in the collaborations with adults. In contrast, almost none of the children from peer dyads marked the stores in advance of making moves.

A case in which a child appropriated a marking strategy from participation in its use with his father is presented in Fig. 5.1 and 5.3. During the collaborative trips, one of which is presented in Fig. 5.1, the father and son decided which of the optional stores to visit, circling them on the list, and made a list of the stores to visit with an accounting of the blocks required to get to each. The father held clear leadership, with the son taking an active secondary role.

The father began by looking for the no-choice stores from his list on the map and marking them on the map; the son spontaneously assisted his father in searching and marking, with increasing responsibility when they worked on the son's list. When they finished marking the no-choice stores, the father commented "She's got us going all over the place," and studied the map. The son proposed the first move, but the father interrupted him, saying "First, we ought to see now what is the most direct route to all of those stores." The son repeated his own suggestion, but the father began tracing a preliminary route connecting the no-choice stores with his finger. The son carefully observed his father's actions, trying to make suggestions. But the father held him back, "wait a minute," seeming to want to consolidate the strategy before involving his son in the decision-making process. When the father started to make preliminary decisions among the choice stores, the son tried to participate, and the father at first slowed his involvement ("wait a minute"). By the time they reached the choice stores on the son's list, the son was increasingly involved in decision making and also helped to mark the preliminary choices of alternative stores on the map. The father drew the final route on the map, occasionally presenting the son with a choice of two alternative routes to the same destination, and counting blocks to compare the length of the alternative subroutes. After each move, the father recorded on his list the number of blocks that were included in the move.

On the second collaborative trip, shown in Fig. 5.1, the father and son followed the same basic procedure, but the son also participated in drawing a portion of the route, and the father increased his thinking aloud and justification of his choices (e.g., "Drug Store is right on the way"; "Here we have to double-back, otherwise we would have to go all the way around").

When the son later planned routes on his own, he systematically implemented the same steps that he had done with his father earlier. Figure 5.3 shows his independent use of the strategy of marking the map to choose between the alternative optional stores and checking the distances by listing the stores and the number of blocks between them.

This case illustrates the concept of participatory appropriation in its

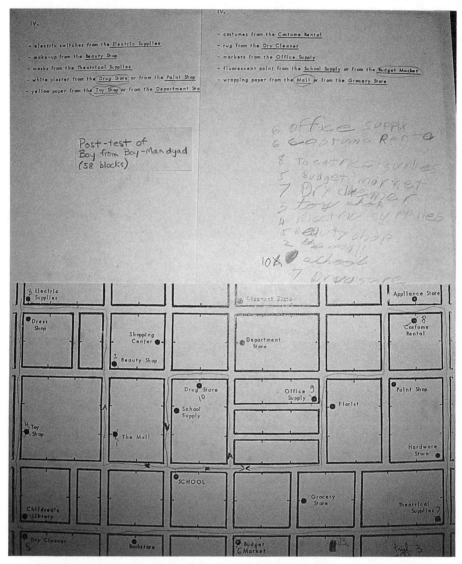

FIG. 5.3   Lists and maps used in the posttest by the son whose collaboration was shown in Fig. 5.1. Note the similarity with the collaborative planning of Fig. 5.1 in strategy for managing the decisions, and the near-optimal route.

emphasis on the child's involvement in the process during the collaboration. Alternative accounts might call the child's learning a product of imitation of the adult model or internalization of a process that was external, but both of these would overlook the child's active role during the collaboration. The child's role during collaboration was neither a passive taking over of an adult model's activity nor an importation of external activity inside the child. It involved intersubjective engagement in the shared problem solving process, through which the child's approach to such problems changed in a process of appropriation.

SUMMARY

The concepts of apprenticeship, guided participation, and participatory appropriation build on the sociohistorical perspective, adding emphasis on the tacit and routine interactions and arrangements in which children participate and on the active process by which children contribute to and appropriate from their involvement in sociocultural activity, in which they thereby constitute both cognitive development and sociocultural activity.

I suggest that children's social interactions and involvement in activities are dynamic and inseparable from the cultural context, in which children engage in shared thinking as well as comparison of ideas with companions varying in skill in relationships varying in the symmetry of status. These variations in the skills and status of partners are likely to be important to the full richness of understanding that children develop of skilled cultural activity. Children appropriate from their guided participation in sociocultural systems of activity involving guidance, challenge, and opportunities for leadership in interactions with other people.

Viewing development as a process of apprenticeship allows us to see the ways in which individual, interpersonal, and cultural processes constitute each other. An apprenticeship involves active individuals working with others in systems involving direct interaction and social arrangements of situations making use of solitary and joint efforts using objects and systems of thought and practices that are socioculturally constituted; their participation in such endeavors simultaneously constitutes institutional community cultural activity.

The apprenticeship model is often applied to systems of practice that are valued by the reader. For example, children's literacy develops through participation in a community of readers and writers, and skill in weaving develops through participation in weaving with more skilled weavers using the tools and skills of weaving in the context of this economic activity. However, the apprenticeship model can also be applied to understanding the development of practices that the reader may prefer to prevent, such as learning to participate as victim and perpetrator in abusive relationships or learning to handle life's problems through aggression or drugs. The same ideas of apprenticeship, guided participation, and participatory appropriation can be applied to these local goals to achieve a greater understanding of the processes involved.

The goal for future work is to examine the conditions in which and processes by which children and other newcomers to sociocultural activities share in collective activity and change in the process.

ACKNOWLEDGMENT

The comments of Rob Wozniak and Kurt Fischer and discussion with Pilar Lacasa, Jackie Baker, Christine Mosier, Eugene Matusov, Denise Goldsmith, Nancy Bell, Batya Elbaum, Barbara Radziszewska, and Paul Klaczynski were very useful in the preparation of this chapter. I am grateful for the support of the University of Utah and the time to write and the support provided by the Center for Advanced Study in the Behavioral Sciences where I was a Fellow for 1988-1989, with funding from the Spencer Foundation, the National Science Foundation (#BNS87-00864), and a Faculty Fellow Award from the University of Utah. The research reported here is supported by the National Institute of Child Health and Human Development (#16793) and the Spencer Foundation.

REFERENCES

Baker-Sennett, J., Matusov, E., & Rogoff, B. (in press). Planning as developmental process. In H. Reese (Ed.), *Advances in child development* (Vol. 24). New York: Academic Press.
Bakhtin, M. M. (1981). *The dialogical imagination* (M. Holquist, Ed.). Austin: University of Texas Press.
Bakhurst, D. (1988). Activity, consciousness and communication. *Newsletter of the Laboratory for Comparative Human Cognition, 10,* 31-39.
Bearison, D. J. (1991). Interactional contexts of cognitive development: Piagetian approaches to sociogenesis. In L. T. Landsmann (Ed.), *Culture, schooling and psychological development* (pp. 56-70). Norwood, NJ: Ablex.
Berger, P. L., & Luckmann, T. (1966). *The social construction of reality.* New York: Doubleday.
Bovet, M., Parrat-Dayan, S., & Voneche, J. (1989). Cognitive development and interaction. In M. Bornstein & J. S. Bruner (Eds.), *Interaction in human development* (pp. 41-58). Hillsdale, NJ: Lawrence Erlbaum Associates.
Bruner, J. S. (1983). *Child's talk: Learning to use language.* New York: Norton.
Cole, M. (1985). The zone of proximal development: Where culture and cognition create each other. In J. V. Wertsch (Ed.), *Culture, communication, and cognition: Vygotskian perspectives* (pp. 146-161). Cambridge: Cambridge University Press.
Cooper, C. R., Marquis, A., & Edward, D. (1986). Four perspectives on peer learning among elementary school children. In E. C. Mueller & C. R. Cooper (Eds.), *Process and outcome in peer relationships* (pp. 269-300). Orlando, FL: Academic Press.
Damon, W. (1984). Peer education: The untapped potential. *Journal of Applied Developmental Psychology, 5,* 331-343.
Dewey, J. (1916). *Democracy and education: An introduction to the philosophy of education.* New York: Macmillan.
Dewey, J., & Bentley, A. F. (1949). *Knowing and the known.* Boston: Beacon Press.
Doise, W. (1985). Social regulations in cognitive development. In R. A. Hinde, A.-N. Perret-Clermont, & J. Stevenson-Hinde (Eds.), *Social relationships and cognitive development* (pp. 294-308). Oxford: Clarendon Press.

Doise, W., & Mackie, D. (1981). On the social nature of cognition. In J. P. Forgas (Ed.), *Social cognition: Perspectives on everyday understanding* (pp. 53–83). London: Academic Press.

Ellis, S., & Rogoff, B. (1982). The strategies and efficacy of child versus adult teachers. *Child Development, 53,* 730–735.

Ellis, S., & Rogoff, B. (1986). Problem solving in children's management of instruction. In E. Mueller & C. Cooper (Eds.), *Process and outcome in peer relationships* (pp. 301–325). Orlando, FL: Academic Press.

Forman, E. A. (1987). Learning through peer interaction: A Vygotskian perspective. *Genetic Epistemologist, 15,* 6–15.

Forman, E. A. (1989). The role of peer interaction in the social construction of mathematical knowledge. *International Journal of Educational Research, 13,* 55–70.

Forman, E. A., & Kraker, M. J. (1985). The social origins of logic: The contributions of Piaget and Vygotsky. In M. W. Berkowitz (Ed.), *Peer conflict and psychological growth* (pp. 23–39). San Francisco: Jossey-Bass.

Gibson, E. J. (1982). The concept of affordances in development: The renascence of functionalism. In W. A. Collins (Ed.), *Minnesota Symposia on Child Psychology, Vol. 15: The concept of development* (pp. 55–81). Hillsdale, NJ: Lawrence Erlbaum Associates.

Gibson, J. J. (1979). *The ecological approach to visual perception.* Boston: Houghton Mifflin.

Goody, E. N. (1989). Learning, apprenticeship and the division of labor. In M. W. Coy (Ed.), *Apprenticeship: From theory to method and back again* (pp. 233–256). Albany, NY: State University of New York Press.

Harre, R. (1983). *Personal being.* Oxford: Basil Blackwell.

Haverkamp-Begemann, E. (1988). *Creative copies.* London: Sotheby's Publications.

John-Steiner, V. (1985). *Notebooks of the mind: Explorations of thinking.* Albuquerque: University of New Mexico Press.

Johnston, T. D., & Turvey, M. T. (1980). A sketch of an ecological metatheory for theories of learning. In G. H. Bower (Ed.), *The psychology of learning and motivation* (Vol. 14, pp. 147–205). New York: Academic Press.

Kruger, A. C. (1988, March). *The effect of peer and adult-child transactive discussions on moral reasoning.* Paper presented at the meeting of the conference on Human Development, Charleston, SC.

Kruger, A. C., & Tomasello, M. (1986). Transactive discussions with peers and adults. *Developmental Psychology, 22,* 681–685.

Lave, J. (1988, May). *The culture of acquisition and the practice of understanding* (Report No. IRL 88–0007). Palo Alto, CA: Institute for Research on Learning.

Leont'ev, A. N. (1981). The problem of activity in psychology. In J. V. Wertsch (Ed.), *The concept of activity in Soviet psychology* (pp. 37–71). Armonk, NY: Sharpe.

MacLachlan, P. (1989). Dialogue between Charlotte Zolotow and Patricia MacLachlan. *Horn Book, 65,* 740–741.

Michaels, C. F., & Carello, C. (1981). *Direct perception.* Englewood Cliffs, NJ: Prentice-Hall.

Mugny, G., & Doise, W. (1978). Socio-cognitive conflict and structure of individual and collective performances. *European Journal of Social Psychology, 8,* 181–192.

Newman, D., Griffin, P., & Cole, M. (1989). *The construction zone: Working for cognitive change in school.* Cambridge: Cambridge University Press.

Pepper, S. C. (1942). *World hypotheses: A study in evidence.* Berkeley, CA: University of California Press.

Perret-Clermont, A.-N., Brun, J., Saada, E. H., & Schubauer-Leoni, M.-L. (1984). Psychological processes, operatory level and the acquisition of knowledge. *Interactions didactiques* (No. 2 bis). Universities of Geneva and of Neuchatel.

Perret-Clermont, A.-N., & Nicolet, M. (1988). *Interagir et connaitre.* Cousset, Switzerland: DelVal.

Piaget, J. (1926). *The language and thought of the child*. New York: Harcourt, Brace.

Piaget, J. (1952). *The origins of intelligence in children*. New York: Norton.

Piaget, J. (1977a). Les operations logiques et la vie sociale. In *Etudes sociologiques*. (pp. 143–171). Geneva, Switzerland: Librairie Droz.

Piaget, J. (1977b). Logique genetique et sociologie. In *Etudes sociologiques* (pp. 203–239). Geneva, Switzerland: Librairie Droz. (Reprinted from *Revue Philosophique de la France et de l'Etranger, 53*(3,4), 1928, pp. 161–205.)

Piaget, J. (1977c). Problemes de la psycho-sociologie de l'enfance. In *Etudes sociologiques* (pp. 320–356). Geneva, Switzerland: Librairie Droz. (Reprinted from *Traite de sociologie*, G. Gurvitch, Paris: PUF, 1963, pp. 229–254.)

Radziszewska, B., & Miller, K. (in preparation). *Sociocognitive processes in adult-child and peer collaboration on conservation of area and volume tasks.*

Radziszewska, B., & Rogoff, B. (1988). Influence of adult and peer collaborators on children's planning skills. *Developmental Psychology, 24,* 840–848.

Radziszewska, B., & Rogoff, B. (1991). Children's guided participation in planning errands with skilled adult or peer partners. *Developmental Psychology, 27,* 381–389.

Reed, E. S., & Jones, R. K. (1977). Towards a definition of living systems: A theory of ecological support for behavior. *Acta Biotheoretica, 26,* 153–163.

Rogoff, B. (1982). Integrating context and cognitive development. In M. E. Lamb & A. L. Brown (Eds.), *Advances in developmental psychology* (Vol. 2, pp. 125–170). Hillsdale, NJ: Lawrence Erlbaum Associates.

Rogoff, B. (1990). *Apprenticeship in thinking: Cognitive development in sociocultural activity.* New York: Oxford University Press.

Rogoff, B., & Gardner, W. P. (1984). Guidance in cognitive development: An examination of mother-child instruction. In B. Rogoff & J. Lave (Eds.), *Everyday cognition: Its development in social context* (pp. 95–116). Cambridge, MA: Harvard University Press.

Rogoff, B., Lacasa, P., Baker, J., & Goldsmith, D. (in preparation). *A sociocultural analysis of children's planning.*

Rogoff, B., Mistry, J., Göncü, A., & Mosier, C. (in press). Cultural variation in role relations of toddlers and their families. In M. Bornstein (Ed.), *Cultural approaches to parenting.* (pp. 173–183). Hillsdale, NJ: Lawrence Erlbaum Associates.

Rogoff, B., Mosier, C., Mistry, J., & Göncü, A. (in press). Toddlers' guided participation with their caregivers in cultural activity. In E. Forman, N. Minick, & A. Stone (Eds.), *The institutional and social context of mind.* New York: Oxford University Press.

Saxe, G. B., Gearhart, M., & Guberman, S. B. (1984). The social organization of early number development. In B. Rogoff & J. V. Wertsch (Eds.), *Children's learning in the "zone of proximal development"* (pp. 19–30). San Francisco: Jossey-Bass.

Scribner, S. (1985). Vygotsky's uses of history. In J. V. Wertsch (Ed.), *Culture, communication, and cognition: Vygotskian perspectives* (pp. 119–145). Cambridge: Cambridge University Press.

Sigel, I. E., & Cocking, R. R. (1977). Cognition and communication: A dialectic paradigm for development. In M. Lewis & L. A. Rosenblum (Eds.), *Interaction, conversation, and the development of language: The origins of behavior* (Vol. 5, pp. 207–226). New York: Wiley.

Slavin, R. E. (1987). Developmental and motivational perspectives on cooperative learning: A reconciliation. *Child Development, 58,* 1161–1167.

Tudge, J. R. H., & Rogoff, B. (1989). Peer influences on cognitive development: Piagetian and Vygotskian perspectives. In M. Bornstein & J. Bruner (Eds.), *Interaction in human development* (pp. 17–40). Hillsdale, NJ: Lawrence Erlbaum Associates.

Turvey, M. T., & Shaw, R. E. (1977). The primacy of perceiving: An ecological reformulation of perception for understanding memory. In L. G. Nilsson (Ed.), *Perspectives on memory research: Essays in honor of Uppsala University's 500th Anniversary* (pp. 167–222). Hillsdale, NJ: Lawrence Erlbaum Associates.

Vygotsky, L. S. (1978). *Mind in society: The development of higher psychological processes.* Cambridge, MA: Harvard University Press.

Vygotsky, L. S. (1987). *Thinking and speech.* In R. W. Rieber & A. S. Carton (Eds., N. Minick, Trans.), *The collected works of L. S. Vygotsky* (pp. 37–285). New York: Plenum.

Wertsch, J. V. (1985). *Vygotsky and the social formation of mind.* Cambridge, MA: Harvard University Press.

Wertsch, J. V., & Stone, C. A. (1979, February). *A social interactional analysis of learning disabilities remediation.* Paper presented at the International Conference of the Association for Children with Learning Disabilities, San Francisco.

Zinchenko, V. P. (1985). Vygotsky's ideas about units for the analysis of mind. In J. V. Wertsch (Ed.), *Culture, communication and cognition: Vygotskian perspectives* (pp. 94–118). Cambridge, MA: Cambridge University Press.

Mediating the Environment: Communicating, Appropriating, and Developing Graphic Representations of Place[1]

6

Roger M. Downs
Lynn S. Liben
The Pennsylvania State University

AN OVERVIEW

This volume is driven by the proposition that development takes place in context, and therefore that we will never truly understand development if we ignore the environment. In this chapter, we accept, extend, and reinterpret this proposition by beginning with a literal reading of the phrase, "takes place in context."

Among the meanings of context is "place." Events and actions occur in places; places are distinctive parts of the earth's surface that have been created by and therefore have meaning to the people who live in them. Thus, we want to emphasize the importance of understanding the spatial environment, and hence places, as a context for the development and activation of cognitive skills. This meaning, although underrepresented in the current literature is, by itself, an obvious interpretation of context.

---

[1]This chapter began as a formal discussion of Barbara Rogoff's address to the 19th Annual Symposium of the Jean Piaget Society (Philadelphia, June 1989). The final text of our chapter (September 1990) was based on the written version of Rogoff's chapter available at that time, and incorporated responses to the helpful suggestions made by the editors on our earlier written draft.

As befits a discussion of the dynamics of sociocultural development, we discovered at the time that the volume went to press that Rogoff's final work had evolved further. Although the general thrust of her argument, most of the empirical illustrations, and much of the text remained unchanged, some text was redrafted. For those "direct" quotations of text that were not retained verbatim in the current volume, we have simply cited Rogoff's unpublished 1989 paper (available from us on request).

Of greater significance to this chapter is a second meaning of context: that which precedes a passage and influences its meaning and effect. Although this meaning of context is most commonly encountered in the interpretation of prose text, it need not be limited to that medium. The context for place is often stated by means of graphic representations of place: maps, aerial photographs, satellite images, cross sections, scale models, diagrams, drawings, landscape paintings, and so on. Graphic representations of place, especially maps, literally stand "in place" of the spatial environment and are themselves the "shaping context" for significant aspects of behavior (events and actions) that occur in those places.

Central to this interpretation of context is the recognition that maps are not simply miniaturizations of the world, but rather are complex symbolic statements about it. Maps are symbolic models of the world. As such, maps communicate what a culture considers to be important about its environment in all aspects, spatial and social; maps highlight certain details, ignore others; maps not only provide ways of archiving information and wayfinding, but they foster new ways of "seeing" the world and detecting relationships within it (Downs, 1981a).

By reviewing some of the varied functions of maps and illustrating the diverse range of map forms, we argue here that graphic representations of place must be appreciated as tools that are cultural inventions like others (e.g., language) discussed by Rogoff elsewhere in this volume.

Further, we use these functions and illustrations to demonstrate the nontransparent nature of maps. Maps are neither automatically nor immediately comprehensible to either children or adults. They are symbols, in large measure arbitrary and conventional. As a consequence, societies must find mechanisms for transmitting an understanding of these symbolic tools. We speculate on this transmission process by linking it to Rogoff's example of cultural transmission in spatial route planning.

Our focus on the striking cultural differences in the form and perhaps function of maps as symbolic tools is consistent with Vygotsky's emphasis on cultural variability in developmental processes. Although evidence for this variability is often taken as providing a contrast to, or even as conflicting with Piaget's emphasis on developmental universality, we believe that the two theoretical approaches are instead complementary and therefore compatible.

We discuss the complementary contributions of the Vygotskian and Piagetian traditions with respect to understanding developmental phenomena that may be arrayed along a dimension ranging from universal to unique. What we take from a Vygotskian approach is the recognition that different cultures may evolve different surface forms for the graphic representation of place, and may use different mechanisms to transmit those forms across generations. What we take from a Piagetian account is the possibility of characterizing the development of an understanding of graphic forms as a predictable, ordered, progressive, and necessary sequence.

In applying a developmental perspective to graphic representations of place, we discuss development at two levels. At one — the societal level — we consider historical changes in representational techniques that are specific to a given cultural context and differentiate such technical changes from the more universal properties of maps. At the second level — the individual — we consider the relation between developmental changes in the child (e.g., developing logical, cognitive, and spatial concepts) and the ability to create and assimilate (or, in Rogoff's language, to "appropriate") the graphic representations of place offered by the culture. In both cases, we consider the subtle interplay between the externally motivated social transmission and the internally regulated cognitive development of the skills necessary to understand graphic representations of place.

In the concluding section, we argue that the field can gain from a two-pronged approach to development, one (exemplified by Vygotsky and Rogoff) that focuses on societal variations and societal processes, and the second (exemplified by Piaget) that focuses on universals by controlling for or minimizing the effects of cultural variation.

THE PLACE OF CONTEXT IN DEVELOPMENT: MIND IN SOCIETY AND SPACE

Environment as Society and Space

This volume is addressed to the role of the environment in development. Rogoff (this volume), for example, provides an excellent introduction to some of the environmental factors that shape the course of cognitive development. As befits the idea of *environ*-ment as a sociocultural milieu (the social world), attention is paid to the social processes that *surround* the child: social interaction and roles (adult–child and child–child dyads, for example), social interaction practices (the distinctions among tutoring, apprenticeship, and guided participation), and social interaction dynamics (cooperation, collaboration, conflict, and reciprocity). Cognitive development is thus set within a sociocultural context; the child is immersed in society.

The power of linking development to the environment is clear. Mind is "in society." And yet, there is relatively little attention paid in this interpretation to what is usually meant by the "environment" either in everyday terms (as in "environmental awareness") or in academic terms (as in "man–environment studies"). This oversight is reminiscent of the one that Wohlwill (1973) discussed at the meetings of the Environmental Design

Research Association almost 20 years ago in his paper, "The Environment is Not in the Head!" Wohlwill's point was that behavior occurs in the *physical* environment of the world, not just in the phenomenological psyche of the subject. He concluded his argument with a suggestion: "As psychologists, we cannot fail to deal with the mind. As environmental psychologists, however, I suggest that we at least provide our model of the mind with a window to the outside world" (p. 180).

By obvious and necessary extension, we would claim that as developmental psychologists, we must situate our model of the developing mind in the environment, and recognize that the "environment" encompasses more than "society." Society is itself in space. Thus, the child develops in environmental contexts that simultaneously have social and spatial dimensions. There is both a social and a spatial world outside. Just as the individual and the environment are inseparable for understanding intellectual development, so too are society and space inseparable for understanding the role of the environment in intellectual development. Mind is "in society and in space."

These two aspects of the environment, society and space, interact with each other to affect the process of development by joint *mediation*. Thus, for example, access to the social aspects of the environment may be mediated by the physical aspects of the environment and vice versa. Places in different physical environments (low density rural areas vs. medium density suburban areas vs. high density urban neighborhoods) offer children very different patterns of spatial access and hence social interaction with peers, family members, and other adults. In turn, the child's opportunity to interact, to explore and experience places in the physical environment may itself be mediated by the social environment. The free range areas available to children for independent play vary according to the gender and/or age of the child, the availability of older siblings, and the child-rearing styles of the caretakers. But yet again, the "safe" places in which independent play (social interaction with peers) is permitted are also determined by the physical space of roads, traffic, crossing points, topography, parks, playgrounds, and so forth, as well as by the social space of class, race, ethnicity, gangs, and the like. Physical environments may be changed by social factors as well, as when unsafe areas are rehabilitated by social group pressure on the local government. Places beyond the limits of independent play may be added to the child's world through supervision by older children and adults. There is an inseparability and reciprocity between the shape of society and space.

Once having recast the idea of environment in this way, we can undertake the project that Rogoff (this volume, p. 127) advocates: understanding "the seamless involvement of individuals in sociocultural activity." In addition, therefore, to emphasizing the role of the environment in explaining cognitive development and insisting on the duality of society and space in the environment, we add the term *place*. Places are distinctive parts of the social and spatial environment that have meaning to the people who live in them. Development takes place literally in place.

The Mediation of the Environment Through Societally Developed Tools

There is another important way in which the effect of the environment on cognitive development is "mediated" and in which the mediation process itself undergoes developmental change at the sociocultural and individual levels. In part, children learn about and learn in environments as a function of the way in which the social and spatial environment is presented to them through societally developed media, that is, through cultural tools and the mechanisms developed for their transmission. In this sense, the social and spatial environment is *media*-ted.

An illustration of how this argument may be used comes from the studies discussed by Rogoff (this volume) on the development of spatial planning skills. Her analysis focuses on the process of social interaction, the *mechanism* for cultural transmission. She rightfully notes that her emphasis on social interaction ". . . largely ignores the nature of the cultural tools used in planning (such as maps and pencils) . . ." (Rogoff, 1989, p. 17). By implication, she recognizes the importance of those *cultural tools* as well. It is instructive, then, to examine such mundane objects — maps and pencils — as examples of the societally developed tools that are fundamental to the sociocultural transmission of ideas and skills.

Interestingly, Petroski (1990) wrote a sociocultural history of one of these objects. *The Pencil: A History of Design and Circumstance* relates the origins, design, and manufacturing of the pencil to its practical and symbolic role in political, social, and cultural life. In the light of our argument, this comment is particularly telling: "Although the pencil has been indispensable, or perhaps because of that, its function is beyond comment and directions for its use are unwritten. We all know from childhood what a pencil is and is for . . ." (Petroski, 1990, p. x). To a developmental theorist advocating the importance of sociocultural context, Petroski's statement should be a source of disquiet and opportunity. How can we focus attention on indispensable, mundane tools whose functions are obvious and whose mode of use apparently needs no explanation? To put it bluntly, when and how do children come to grasp the idea of a pencil?

Maps as Environmental Mediators

In this chapter, we consider these questions by discussing in more detail the other societally developed tool that Rogoff acknowledges: the map. As Fig.

5.1 and 5.3 in Rogoff's chapter demonstrate, a map can be indispensable to sociocultural activities. (See also Radziszewska & Rogoff, 1988, p. 842, for the original map from which these working copies were derived.)

Rogoff's study is predicated on a degree of map understanding that is extensive and largely tacit: Map understanding appears to be, as in Petroski's words about the pencil, "beyond comment." Three simple observations document the extent to which Rogoff assumes a tacit understanding of maps. First, children and adults are expected to understand the cartographic conventions that give form to the map: Pairs of closely spaced parallel lines indicate streets, whereas the larger rectangular shapes formed by the same lines indicate city blocks that contain buildings; routes can be depicted using continuous lines with directional arrow heads interspersed at suitable intervals (i.e., at or near key decision points); solid black dots with labels stand for the location of named places.

Second, giving the subjects red, blue, and standard pencils with erasers (Radziszewska & Rogoff, 1988) invites them to adapt the map to solve a problem: The presence of these tools invokes, in Petroski's words, "the unwritten directions for its use." The map is a worksheet that can be revised during the problem-solving process. Thus, differential map use skills are activated in the spatial planning process such that adult–child dyads: ". . . were twice as likely to explore the layout before making moves — often marking the choice and no-choice stores with different colors and symbols to facilitate planning. . ." (Rogoff, this volume, p. 137).

Third, there is a complex interaction between the physical map as presented, and the subject's presumed knowledge about the world that has been represented. In this case, the downtown area is imaginary and therefore the subjects must make inferences about that place based on most likely situations. For example, one must presume that travel is possible in either direction on the streets because one-way streets would have been specified with an appropriate symbol. One should assume that the black dots indicate only the approximate center of the location of the store, not its size, shape, layout, and so on. Therefore, stores located at street corners can be entered from either abutting street, thus permitting flexibility in achieving a minimum distance solution to the route planning task. Because the city is based on a rectangular gird, there may be several identical minimum distance routes between two places. This map–knowledge–inference interaction is subtle, hidden, and yet essential to the completion of the task. These are things that, in Petroski's words, "(w)e all know from childhood."

Given the age of the children involved in Rogoff's study (9-year-olds), it goes without saying that they understand that travel is restricted to movement along the streets because the task instructions state that the trip is to be made in a school car. But, to paraphrase Petroski's comment about the knowledge associated with the use of a pencil, when do children understand that a map stands for a place, real or imaginary? When do children know that you can find routes on a map? When do they know how to find shortest paths on a map? When do they realize the distinction between finding shortest paths on a map based on as-the-crow-flies versus route distance metrics? These understandings are in Petroski's words, parts of the function that are "beyond comment," at least in Rogoff's current study.

Such an analysis of presumptions provokes fascinating questions about the role of *media*-tors for the environment in sociocultural activity. Environmental contexts are often experienced by means of graphic representations of place: maps, aerial photographs, satellite images, cross sections, scale models, diagrams, flow charts, drawings, landscape paintings, and so on. Graphic representations of place literally stand in place of the environment and are the shaping context for significant aspects of behavior (events and actions) in places (Liben, 1991). In Rogoff's case, the map is the only way in which this imaginary environment could be encountered and together with the task instructions, the map is assumed to be an ecologically valid context for understanding social interaction behaviors.

As one of the ". . . societally developed tools for mediating intellectual activity. . ." (Rogoff, 1989, p. 6), the map is particularly interesting from two developmental perspectives. (For elaborations of these ideas, see Downs, 1985; Downs, Liben, & Daggs, 1988; Liben & Downs, 1989). First, maps form a powerful graphic symbol system. As such, we may ask: How do children develop an understanding of the system of maps and mapping? Unlike most other domains of symbolic functioning (such as language, reading, and mathematics), mapping in our culture is rarely, if ever, formally instructed at home or in school, at least in the pre-kindergarten years. As a consequence, we may have an opportunity to study the development of individual's symbolic functioning in a domain less "contaminated" by instruction at young ages.

At the same time, maps are pervasive across cultures and through time. Maps are *the* pre-eminent graphic symbol system for representing the experience of space and place. There has been an endless variety of forms and functions of maps. As social inventions, maps have changed through time and display significant formal variations across different cultural groups. As a result, maps provide an interesting context in which to study the development of the tools in a sociocultural perspective.

To illustrate these two developmental perspectives, we next discuss two additional case studies of spatial planning. By taking these examples from different sociocultural contexts, we hope to show the roles of maps (and other forms of graphic representation) as societally developed tools; to discuss their different surface forms and yet underlying structural similarities; and to identify the mechanisms for their transmission in a sociocultural context.

Development in Place: Voyaging in the Caroline Islands

Thomas Gladwin's (1970) classic study of ocean sailing in the South Pacific depicts a sociocultural context in which values (mastering the challenge of the sea), beliefs (a seascape full of myth and symbolism), knowledge (navigational lore), and tools (outrigger canoes) create a way of life that is distinctive and arcane to the Western mind. There is a "seamless involvement" of people in the activity of sailing. At the same time, the system of sailing is fascinating for what it reveals about the power of the "mind in society and in space."

Successful voyaging over hundreds of miles is accomplished by navigators skilled in a system that makes no use of Western navigational tools and techniques: a compass, map, chronometer, sextant, and so on. In their stead is a vast reservoir of memorized information that links the appropriate courses to be steered with such diverse environmental information as star positions, sun angles, ocean currents, wave patterns, cloud shapes and colors, and the flight paths of birds. Navigation depends on a process of dead reckoning. It is a system that necessarily places a premium on cognitive skills: memory, observation, and logic.

It is also a system that is tailored to the particulars of the social and spatial environment of each place. Although groups on islands as widely separated as the Marianas and the Marquesas island chains use the same navigational system, the base of environmental information is different in each case. As Gladwin (1970) and others (e.g., Lewis, 1972) made clear, each cultural group in each physical context has developed its own specific knowledge base.

We can, therefore, look at the development of the sociocultural tools in both the individual and the social contexts. At the individual level, mastery of navigation is attained only over periods of many years. Master navigators, few in number, are men distinguished by seniority, skill, and knowledge that has been honed by years of learning on land and sea. The learning system is one of apprenticeship; entry as an apprentice is achieved by sponsorship and initiation into a particular boat house.

Gladwin (1970) described the essence of the on-land learning system, depicted in Fig. 6.1.

Often they sit together in the canoe house, perhaps making little diagrams with pebbles on the mats which cover the sandy floor. The pebbles usually

FIG. 6.1   Sketch of Angora using pebbles arrays to teach new apprentices the star compass (from Gladwin, 1970, p. 129).

represent stars, but they are also used to illustrate islands, and how islands "move" as they pass the canoe on one side or the other. (p. 129)

Whether one calls the pattern of pebbles on the mat a map or a diagram or a model matters less than an acknowledgment that the representation of place is integral to the instruction process, a social tool that has developed within the sociocultural context.

The graphic representation has interesting formal and functional properties. It draws on readily available raw materials (pebbles, sticks, mats); it is flexible (pebbles can symbolize either stars or islands); it is adaptable (pebbles can be re-named to reflect stars visible at different times of the year); it is temporary and ephemeral, inviting restructuring and re-use.

Many of the formal and functional properties of these graphic representations are also shared by the stick charts that are used throughout the South Pacific. (For a discussion of stick charts, see Lewis, 1972, pp. 200–208.) Made from palm ribs, coconut fibers, and shells, stick charts depict essential spatial patterns in the environment. Lewis (1972) argued that: "The stick charts are not charts in the Western sense, but instructional and mnemonic devices concerned with swell patterns" (p. 201). *Mattang,* for example, represent islands with shells and use palm ribs to depict the ocean swell patterns associated with currents from different directions (see Fig. 6.2). The pattern of the ribs models the typical wave interference patterns that are generated as swells encounter islands. Mattang are used during the instructional process on land and are not taken on the canoes during voyages.

Ocean sailing is a sociocultural activity that has developed its own ensemble of transmission practices, technology, and tools. These social inventions have developed *within* a particular environmental context. The

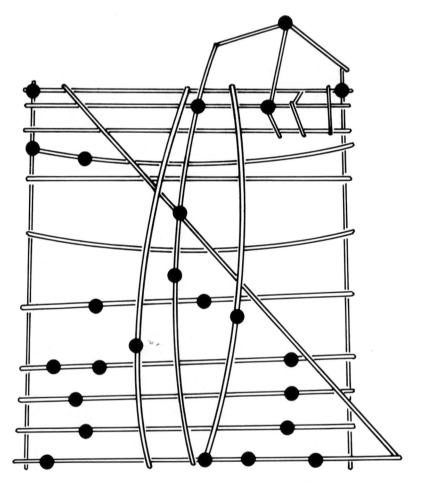

FIG. 6.2   Diagram of stick charts showing islands, currents, and lines of swell used for instruction in the Marshall Islands.

development of these social inventions has generated forms that are distinctive in two senses: first, they are indigenous to the overall sociohistorical context (the South Pacific) and second, they are tailored to particular places within it (the Puluwat Atoll). The extent to which the processes and products of individual and cultural development are repeated and mirrored *across* sociocultural contexts may be illustrated by examining map use for a different purpose in a different place—park exploration in Michigan.

Development in Place: Exploration of Michigan Parks

Western society places strong positive values on the experience of the natural environment. Exposure to, exploration of, comfort in, mastery of, and love of natural settings reflects an idealized sequence of transitions in people–environment relations. Yet, the confrontation of new environments, especially natural environments, may be threatening to children in our society.

One sign of the societal interest in overcoming this fear is revealed by an experimental research approach of Rachel Kaplan (1976). She was concerned with the nature of transitional states as children of various ages were asked to confront two novel environments, an arboretum and a park in Ann Arbor, Michigan. Lack of experience with an unfamiliar type of environmental setting may translate into discomfort and fear. To what extent can the natural environment be *media*-ted to ameliorate or prevent such reactions? Kaplan explored transition experiences that might provide information about an as-yet-unknown environment. To what extent would the encounter with the actual environment be affected by prior experience with an environmental media-tor? Could one modify exploration behavior? Knowledge? Affective responses?

In studies with junior high school and college students, Kaplan presented information in a range of graphic forms and designed a range of activities around these graphic forms.

Four map variants were developed. The first was a picture map; the second, based on topographical data, ". . . converted contour lines to cloud-like patterns resembling lacework" (Kaplan, 1976, p. 48); the third was a traditional, highly abstract contour map with superimposed stream and path information and a grid system; the fourth was an oblique aerial photograph with superimposed paths, streams, and a locator grid.

Activities were comparably wide-ranging and ingenious. At the simplest level, maps were studied prior to visiting the actual environment. Familiarization with the map information was fostered by direct instruction and by Kim-game formats in which periods of map memorization would be followed by orienting questions about the represented environment. Alternatively, board games encouraged active involvement with and communication of the mapped information. For example:

> A "Battleship" game format was used to transmit information about the path structure of the area. For this the students worked in pairs, each having an identical picture map except that the paths shown on the two maps were complementary. Each partner had to guess the location of the paths missing from his map. At the end of about 30 minutes, the partners would compare maps. (Kaplan, 1976, p. 49)

Maps Across Cultures: Contrasts or Similarities?

Kaplan's overall approach will appear familiar to most readers: It fits neatly within the sociocultural tradition of Western empirical research and with our usual expectation about providing "instruction." Although the context and materials may appear very different from those of Gladwin, we would argue that most of those differences are in actuality superficial ones.

Consider, for example, Kaplan's graphic representations in the light of the criteria used to characterize the star map in Gladwin's study. Kaplan's representations draw on readily available materials (paper, ink, etc.); they are flexible (lines can symbolize roads, streams, or terrain elevations); they are adaptable (maps can be processed as Kim-games, Battleship-games, etc.); and they are semi-permanent but ephemeral (except for research data storage, the graphics are not intended for museum preservation).

Similarly, the intent of the sociocultural activity is identical. Both activity systems are concerned with transmitting knowledge about the environment prior to encounters with that environment. Both systems aim for familiarity, comfort, and effective spatial planning. Both systems are designed to enhance individual development and have undergone significant development over historical time spans. For example, the circular form of the star compass has been adapted from an earlier, square form, probably in imitation of the Western compass rose (Gladwin, 1970, p. 130). The photomap is a hybrid graphic form that blends 20th-century aerial photography with age-old cartographic symbolization techniques.

Thus, in considering activities in different sociocultural contexts, we must disentangle the contingent from the universal, the necessary from the sufficient in order to understand individual and cultural ". . . development of skill with societally developed tools for mediating intellectual activity" (Rogoff, 1989, p. 6).

In the next two sections of this chapter, we use the map as a vehicle for exploring the individual and cultural development of a tool system. We begin with a discussion of the functions of maps and the way in which different cultures have responded with different forms to express these functions, and follow this discussion with an analysis of maps in the context of two levels of development: ontogenetic and sociocultural.

In the conclusion, we return to the question underlying this volume: Must one relate development to the environment? We arrive at a similar answer to Rogoff, namely that one must incorporate both Piagetian and Vygotskian approaches. That our answer is reached from a different direction (from tools rather than sociocultural interaction) provides consensual validation of the importance of a contextual approach.

GRAPHIC REPRESENTATIONS OF PLACE

Seeing Through Maps: The World "Revealed" or the World "Realized"?

Tools acquire a taken-for-granted status, more so as they become indispensable in our dealings with the world. Paraphrasing a cliche, familiarity needs no contemplation. Maps — graphic forms that have existed for approximately 5 millennia — exemplify this status.

In the eyes of many people, maps present the world "as it is." Unfolding or unrolling a map is the next best thing to being there because the map is an accurate, true picture of the world as it "really" exists. The map is a miniaturization of the world. Such a view of a map has been called "naive cartographic realism" (see Downs, 1981a, 1981b, 1985). It is captured by Wohlwill's (1973) characterization of maps as ". . . the Gospel according to Rand-McNally" (p. 167). Superimposed on this aura of verisimilitude is the idea that maps are transparent (see Downs & Liben, 1988; Liben & Downs, 1989). One can see through the surface of the map to the world that is immediately available.

Not only is this view wrong but it does a disservice to the map-reader and map-maker alike. It is literally "mindless" because it removes the person from the process of creation and appreciation. In Friedrich Nietzsche's memorable phrase, it is yet another example of the doctrine of immaculate perception.

In its place, we advocate a view of maps as symbolic statements about the world that are as creative in origin as any work of art. As representations, they abstract, generalize, and simplify. They are models. As products of symbol systems, they are not transparent and their meaning is not immediately available. They are opaque. As realizations, they offer one of an infinite variety of views of what the world might be like. They are opinions. As societal tools, they have been shaped by accident and design, by ignorance and knowledge, by convention and invention. They are cultural theories of the social and spatial environment.

We can illustrate this alternative view of maps by considering what for many people is "the" prototypical map of the world (see Fig. 6.3). This is the way that the world *really* is. But on closer inspection, we can "deconstruct" this map to reveal the factors that have shaped its form and to expose how the form has in turn shaped our beliefs about the world it depicts. (For discussions of these concepts, see Committee on Map Projections of the *American Cartographic Association,* 1986, and Monmonier, 1985.)

This rectangular world map is based on a map originally published in 1569 by Gerardus Mercator. Although some details of the mathematical formulae for producing the projection have been modified, in essence, we are presented with a map form developed in the sociohistorical context of 16th-century Western Europe. That map form now appears as the backdrop to 20th-century television newscasts, as the basis for maps in school texts at all levels, and in numerous mass media advertisements.

The Mercator map was a tool designed to meet a specific need: navigation at sea. Given the objective of maintaining a course with a constant geographic direction, a *rhumb,* for convenience, it is easiest if direction appears as a straight line on a map. Thus, the map must have a rectangular graticule of meridians and parallels. A rhumb line intersects the meridians at an angle that is equal to its true bearing on the earth's surface using a

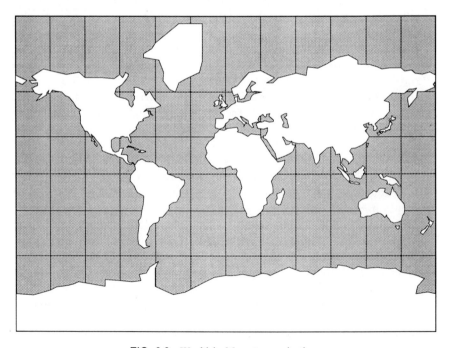

FIG. 6.3   World in Mercator projection.

compass corrected for magnetic declination. Mercator provided the first mathematical solution meeting this intersection requirement and demonstrated the map projection by means of a world map in his atlas. Over the centuries, the basis for constructing a sailing chart has become the basis for seeing the world.

The Mercator map typically appears with the equator in the middle (seen from top to bottom) and the Greenwich meridian in the middle (seen from left to right). Neither choice is necessary. The equatorial aspect comes from the decision to have the map cylinder touch the globe at the equator, prior to "unrolling." The map cylinder could touch along any great circle oriented in any direction on the globe.

There have been numerous prime meridians passing through places as varied as Alexandria (Egypt), the Canary Islands, and St. Paul's Cathedral (London). The consensual choice of Greenwich reflects the political-historical dominance of England in world sea trade and its leadership in navigational astronomy. The decision to assign the "prime" meridian to Greenwich was made in 1884 at a U.S. Government-sponsored conference designed to coordinate international time zones.

"The" map presents a curious view of the world. Meridians (or lines of longitude) are parallel across the entire map, even though this is only true in reality at the equator. Parallels of latitude are of equal length to the equator although this is not true at any point on the earth's two dimensional surface. As a consequence, with increasing distance away from the equator, sizes are greatly exaggerated and shapes distorted. In effect, the North and South poles, dimensionless points, become extended straight lines that are equal in length to the circumference of Earth. The left and right edges of the map depict one line of longitude that has been cartographically "split" into two: the same line appears twice.

The Mercator projection, by dint of repetition, longevity, convenience, neatness, has been transformed from a navigational tool to "the" view of the world. In "seeing" the world through a Mercator-based map, we supposedly "know," of course, that Greenland is not "really" seven times larger than Saudi Arabia. We know that Alaska is "in fact" adjacent to Siberia. We realize that the North Pole is not necessarily at the top of the world and that "down south" is only a colloquial expression. The world does not "really" have four corners and edges.

The potential for discrepancies between what we *see* on the map, what we *believe* about the world, and what we *know* about the world is such that six professional geographic and cartographic organizations passed a resolution in 1989 concluding that: "*Therefore,* we strongly urge book and map publishers, the media, and government agencies to cease using rectangular world maps for general purposes or artistic displays. Such maps promote serious, erroneous conceptions . . ."

As a social invention, the Mercator projection underwent an extended process of cultural reconstruction, during which time it acquired an image of necessity and an aura of realism. Invention became the mother of necessity. All of the contingent decisions that shaped the map's particular form became necessary properties of maps and of the world that they represent. World maps were indispensable and it became taken-for-granted that this is the way that the world really is. Clearly, such is not the case. We can see a similar misunderstanding about the function of a map.

The Functions of Maps

As a model that offers a realization of the world, the map is a powerful, multipurpose tool. Unfortunately, in the same way that we have allowed "the" Mercator map to become the prototypical statement about the world, we have unnecessarily restricted our understanding of what maps are "for." "The" prototypical answer about map purpose is wayfinding. In order to break out of this narrow, although correct conception of a map, we need to contrast the possibilities of direct experience of the environment with those of a media-ted experience of the environment. (For an elaboration of these ideas within context of individual development, see Liben, 1991.)

Maps (and other graphic representations of place) offer two complementary, experiential opportunities. They can substitute for direct experience and they can amplify direct experience with the environment. The idea of substitution depends on the map's ability to stand in place of the environment. Rogoff (this volume) uses a map of an imaginary town as a substitute for spatial planning in a real environment. The map simulates some important, but nevertheless selected dimensions of direct experience in an environment. Unfortunately, the overextension of such a view can lead to the idea of naive cartographic realism wherein the map is falsely equated with the environment.

More interesting is the idea of the *amplification* of experience. Seen in this mode, maps provide information about the environment that would otherwise not be available to the individual. This information serves a variety of purposes that are not necessarily mutually exclusive.

First, maps act as advanced organizers that provide a context for subsequent environmental experience. They shape the influences of later direct experience in the environment. In Kaplan's (1976) study, students who saw a map prior to exploring the park reported more confidence, less fear, and more enjoyment in their encounter with the natural environment than did students not exposed to the map. Maps not only serve an affective function but also obvious cognitive functions. Prior map study can aid in wayfinding and route choice. Although the map versus no-map groups in Kaplan's (1976) study covered similar distances, the map group penetrated a greater range of park areas. Even some 3-year-olds seem to profit from previewing a map prior to entering an environment (Utall & Wellman, 1989).

Second, maps convey information about places that are unavailable. The places may be beyond the immediate spatial range of the individual, as in maps of foreign countries in school textbooks or the islands far removed from Puluwat in the South Pacific; or beyond the possibility of the particular map user's direct experience, as in maps of the surface of the Moon; or be imaginary, as in the town in Rogoff's study or places in children's storybooks.

Third, maps provide a means of realizing otherwise unknowable aspects of the environment. This is perhaps the special genius of the map as a media-tor of the environment. As Treib (1980) argued, "maps are the projections of experience" (p. 22). The map renders the experience of space and place comprehensible (Downs, 1985). The need for comprehensible projections comes from the nature of our fragmentary, time-bound, and sometimes overwhelming experience of space. Maps provide a synthetic overview that allow us to capture a sense of the whole. That synoptic sense is, however, necessarily selective and by taking advantage of this power, we can archive information, see patterns and relations, develop hypotheses, communicate information, and persuade others to see the world as we do.

We can realize an understanding of the otherwise unknowable world in two interrelated ways. On the one hand, we "realize" as in making real through the tangible, physical form of the map. The map invites inspection. On the other hand, therefore, we "realize" as in understanding previously unsuspected ideas. The star chart of the Puluwatans exemplifies both facets of realization. Pebbles arrayed in a circle on a map are a tangible basis on which apprentices can respond to questions of the master navigator about hypothetical courses and directions between islands never previously visited. As substitute or amplifier, the map is an example of Vygotsky's "mediated memory."

The Forms of Maps

At first glance, the range of map forms within and especially between different culture groups is overwhelming. And yet, as the formal and functional parallels between the Puluwatan star chart and the Michigan photomap suggest, there is an underlying unity in diversity in the process of social invention. This unity can be seen at three levels.

At the surficial level of material form, maps have been made from practically every natural and artificial material that can be manipulated. They have been pressed in mud and inscribed in stone in prehistoric periods; they have been sculpted from driftwood by Eskimos and carved on living trees by Delaware Indians; they have been vacuum-pressed on plastic sheets for the visually handicapped and printed on silk in escape kits for aircrews. The list of materials is as long as the capacity of human ingenuity to make use of what is available in the material environment, subject to the dictates of portability and preservability.

At a deeper level of content, maps reflect those social and spatial dimensions of the world that are significant in a particular sociohistorical context. The world maps of 16th-century West Europeans stressed the crucial distinction between land and sea, and on that littoral, depicted the existence of landmarks for navigation, safe harbors, and the political ownership of land. The world was filtered through the values of seafarers who were exploring and carving up space according to the precepts of religion, nationalism, and economic gain. As Wood and Fels (1986) showed, modern "official" state highway maps are not innocent and unbiased depictions of reality. The selection of points of interest, the incorporation of state mottoes, flowers, and birds, the use of colors and line widths to classify road quality, the choice of bold, saturated colors for within-state and pale, anemic colors for out-of-state places; all of these graphic devices promote "the" official self-view of the state government. It is a world of tourism, economic development, and recreation neatly packaged for storage in the glove compartment of the automobile.

At the deepest level of structure, maps display a necessary similarity that is overwritten by the contingencies of the more visible levels of material culture and sociohistorical need. As simplified, abstracted, and generalized models, they are many-to-one mappings. As symbol systems, they are abstract notations. As pseudo-pictures, they bear an iconic relationship to the world. As graphic representations, they present a surface with properties of continuity, proximity, coherence, scale, orientation, and so on.

Stripped of the patina of sociohistorical contingency, the map is a structured realization of the world of experience. If this is the "essence" of the map as a social invention, how can we understand the way in which different societies transmit the skills necessary for using maps? How can we set the essence of the map within the particular context of individual and cultural development?

Learning to See Through Maps

An answer to these questions must again begin with the recognition that maps are symbolic representations and are therefore neither transparent nor immediately accessible to children and adults alike (Downs & Liben, 1988).

We can illustrate this point by reference to examples from our program of work on the development of cartographic literacy in children (Mapping Project at Penn State [MAPPS]). (For detailed presentations, see Liben & Downs, 1986, 1989, 1991; Downs et al., 1988.) Among other tasks, preschool children were presented with various forms of place representations and asked various questions about their content and use. When asked what items a state road map might show, children provided interpretations that suggested they were overinterpreting the iconic characteristics of the graphic symbols. For example, some children thought that the yellow symbol for a built-up area showed "firecrackers" or "eggs." When asked if a line might show a road, some children rejected it as such because it was not "fat enough for two cars to go on." When asked what color a road symbolized in red would be if you stood on it in the real world, the answer for some children was "red." The Rand McNally compass logo was variously identified as a "basketball stadium" and "the place where the lifeguard sits."

These, and numerous other examples of erroneous, but creative interpretations, are not surprising if we remember that maps are complex symbolic statements. Although DeLoache (1989) and Beilin (1991) showed that scale models and photographs, respectively, are understood as standing for the world even by very young children, such an understanding does not imply that the power of graphic representations is fully understood by young children. There is evidence from our work and others that the surface form of the graphic representation intervenes in the process of understanding the information represented. We cannot look through the map immediately to the spatial and social world that is depicted (Downs & Liben, 1988).

As a social invention, the map has evolved into a myriad of different forms. In confronting any particular map, the individual must disentangle a host of shaping factors including: the distinctions between iconic and arbitrary symbols; the role of convention; the use of spatial scale; the intent of the map producer; the date of the map; the roles of abstraction, simplification, and generalization, and so on. Although some of these factors may be explained in the key and/or legend, many are "hidden" from view. These are the unwritten directions for its use, to quote Petroski again. They are part of the tacit understanding that the individual is presumed to have absorbed as part of the socialization process.

And it is precisely this idea of the absorption of tacit understanding that brings us back to the central issues of this volume in general and to Rogoff's chapter in particular. How can we use the idea of maps to explore the interplay between the individual and the environment, between the social and the spatial worlds, and between individual and societal development?

THE PLACE OF GRAPHIC REPRESENTATIONS IN UNDERSTANDING COGNITIVE DEVELOPMENT

Let us begin by restating the steps which have underpinned our argument: that cognitive development occurs in context; that context means environment; that the environment has both social and spatial dimensions; and that these social and spatial dimensions are intertwined in place. The raw material for cognitive development is experience garnered by a self-regulating, constructive individual in interactions with society and space. Experience of and in place can be direct or indirect; indirect experience of place is media-ted; the media include graphic representations of place; the prototypical graphic representation of place is a map.

Does our view of the map as a mediating realization of the world contribute to a theoretical debate central to the field of cognitive development in general, and to Rogoff's (this volume, 1990) discussion in particular, namely, the role of the unique versus the universal in development?

Maps in a Sociohistorical Context

The map is a societal invention. As with the case of most symbol systems, it is impossible to find the precise origins of the map except in the sense of awarding the dubious and temporary accolade, this is the "first" example of a map that we can identify. We cannot state whether the social invention was a singular, spontaneous event that spread or an instance of multiple, even simultaneous discovery. We cannot state why and under what particular and contingent circumstances the invention arose, although we can give a persuasive account of why necessarily it must have arisen. (For a detailed assessment of the history of cartography, see Harley & Woodward, 1987; for a discussion focused on map-makers themselves, see Wilford, 1981.)

We can make four statements, however. First, the map has persisted over at least 5 millennia. Second, the map is pervasive both within and across different cultures. Third, the map has been manifest in a seemingly endless variety of forms. Fourth, the map is used for a wide range of purposes. This picture of longevity, diversity, variety, and utility raises an interesting question: To what extent can we speak about maps as a universal social tool as opposed to a historically contingent social tool? (See Downs, Liben, & Daggs, 1990; Gardner, 1990.) The answer to this question is a necessary precursor for the individual development question: How do individuals develop the skills and acquire the information that are necessary for the use of the map as a tool?

If we return to the examples of Puluwatan star charts and Michigan photomaps, we can draw a contrast between the universal and the unique elements of maps. The charts and photomaps have in common an underlying structure and a set of possible functions. There is a structural and functional universality to maps. The charts and photomaps are differentiated by their specific forms that are tailored to the particular environmental context and sociocultural activity. There is a formal specificity and contingency to the surface appearance of graphic representations of place. The map-reader, child or adult, must understand the structural and functional universality no matter what the sociohistorical context. The map-reader must also understand the formal specificity that derives from the sociohistorical context. The idea of the map is, therefore, universal; the appearance of the map is unique to a particular sociohistorical context.

Maps in a Developmental Context

What does a Puluwatan apprentice navigator need to know about maps? What does a ninth-grade Michigan school student need to know about maps? What does a 9-year-old in Rogoff's study need to know about maps? In each case, where does this knowledge come from?

We need to disentangle the understanding of structural and functional universality from the understanding of formal specificity. Furthermore, we must account for the mechanisms by which these two types of understanding are achieved. Framed in this way, the questions point directly to the complementary contributions of Piagetian and Vygotskian theory in accounting for the processes of cognitive development.

In our work (see Liben & Downs, 1989), we have made use of Piagetian theory in framing the developmental questions surrounding maps. Underpinning the child's ability to use maps is the child's cognitive structure. That cognitive structure will determine the child's ability to understand the particular form of map and the specific activity that the map serves. That cognitive structure is similarly the basis on which the child develops a general understanding of the structural and functional universality of maps.

Our earlier analysis of the presuppositions underlying the use of the imaginary map in Rogoff's study illustrates the hidden depth of knowledge that is required to read a map. Our examples of young children's misunderstandings of a state road map point to the potential early limitations on map-reading ability. We find Piagetian theory to be especially helpful for identifying areas in which children at particular developmental levels may have difficulty in understanding maps. For example, immaturities in spatial concepts are reflected in children's difficulties in understanding relationships among self, map, and space as in locating one's orientation on a map or as in understanding a bird's-eye view of a place (see Downs & Liben, 1990). Immaturities in representational functions are reflected in children's misunderstanding cartographic conventions (e.g., thinking a road shown in red on a map will actually *be* red). Immaturities in logical concepts are reflected in the failure to understand relationships logically implied by maps (e.g., understanding that the hierarchical relationships of towns, counties, states, etc., depend on the logical operations of transitivity, class inclusion, and part–whole relations, see Downs et al., 1988).

In each of these cases, there is an interaction between the child's cognitive structure and the understanding of the form, function, and structure of the map. To the extent that the Piagetian account of cognitive development deals with universals of mental functioning, then that account is particularly appropriate for considering the developing understanding of those functional and structural properties of maps that are universal. Thus, the Piagetian approach would be equally applicable in accounting for the ability of the Puluwatan apprentice navigator, the ninth-grade Michigan student, and the 9-year-old route planner to understand the universal properties of maps. Such an accounting might include the ability to understand: the map as a symbolic representation; the spatial-geometric properties of the map (e.g., its scale and projection); and the map as a possible realization of the social and spatial world.

This Piagetian account of map understanding is, however, incomplete. We must still account for two things: first, the development of the understanding of the formal specificity of maps and second, the mechanisms by which the understanding of map forms, functions, and structure is attained. These two facets are interrelated and suggest the value of extending the contributions of Vygotsky, Rogoff, and others working in a sociocultural perspective.

Unfortunately, there are not yet enough data to explain either the development of the understanding of the formal specificity of maps or the mechanisms by which map understanding is—depending on one's theoretical stance—"constructed," "learned," or "appropriated." To the extent that graphic representations are believed to be transparent and that the information in them is immediately available, there would be little to explain. Nativistic accounts of map understanding (see Landau, 1986), for example, effectively collapse the problem of map understanding into the problem of the genesis of spatial knowledge, itself thought to be present in infancy and subject to little radical development.

We would prefer not to choose between the extremes of seeing the child either as an independent, "lonely" Piagetian operator constructing an understanding of reality or as a passive Vygotskian recipient of sociocultural wisdom transmitted by others. Neither of these caricatures is adequate to account for the Puluwatan student navigator, the ninth-grade Michigan explorer, or the 9-year-old route planner. In each case, Rogoff's notion of guided participation might well explain the "social formation of the mind in society and space." The role of social interaction is central in each case.

In the Puluwatan case of the star chart, there is an adult–child (or expert–novice) dyad engaged in spatial problem solving. For the process to work successfully, the members of the dyad must share an understanding of the formal specifics of the notation system used to symbolize the world. Pebbles represent stars; presumably minor size, shape, and color differences in the pebbles are to be ignored. The stone in the center of the compass (see Fig. 6.1) represents a sailing canoe. The pointer can be used to refer to a specific stone (star or canoe) and to indicate direction (of movement or of angular relationship). Alternatively, the meanings assigned to the pebbles can be "erased" such that they now stand for islands.

In like manner, the children engaged in the "Battleship" game format operate in child–child dyads in a competitive context. Success in this game is predicated on understanding the notation system of the map, being able to use the letter-number system for identifying grid locations on the map, and developing a strategy for asking strings of sequential questions. Differences in access to this understanding and/or skill in implementing it would affect success in the game format.

In neither case, however, is the form of the notation system "obvious" in the sense of being unambiguous and immediate. Although a Piagetian interpretation might focus attention on the idea of symbolization in general, a Vygotskian interpretation might focus attention on the transmission of the specifics of the formal relationships between signifier and signified. To the extent that the signifier–signified relationships are iconic, one might argue that the child could discover (or construct) these relationships. To the extent that the relationships are arbitrary, social transmission might be the more likely mechanism for mastery.

A PICTURE OF THE WHOLE

In closing, we return to the general issue of the relationship between Piagetian and Vygotskian perspectives on cognitive development.

What Rogoff stresses about the particular contribution of Vygotsky (and of others, like herself, who have adapted the Vygotskian approach, e.g., Cole, 1985; Scribner, 1985; Wertsch, 1985) is the central nature of sociocultural context in development. Attention is therefore focused on the ways in which culture—via adult society in particular—shapes the systems of knowing by means of which the child develops an understanding of the social and spatial world. Maps are a pre-eminent system for knowing the social and spatial world. They are a classic example of a powerful social invention that has acquired a taken-for-granted tool status. That the understanding of maps is often taken for granted in no way diminishes the importance of the twin questions: Where, how, and why did the social invention develop? When and how does the individual's understanding of the invention develop?

In addressing such questions, Rogoff paints an interesting contrast between Vygotsky's theory which ". . . was built on the premise that individual mental development must be understood with reference to the sociocultural milieu in which the child is embedded" (Rogoff, this volume,

p. 126). And: ". . . Piaget's speculations on the social world [which] were largely limited to the interpersonal context providing for cognitive conflict, without substantial consideration of the cultural and historical context of the intellectual problems and solutions involved in cognitive development." (Rogoff, this volume, p. 126 order of paragraphs reversed) Leaving aside the putative status of ideas as theory or speculation, we would argue that there is an important sense in which Piaget assigned an equal importance, an assignment that is often overlooked, to the role of the sociocultural milieu.

Piaget had a fundamental concern for the development of knowledge in a discipline or field. Above all, he was interested in explicating the development of human knowledge. One way that knowledge develops is across eras in cultures and in disciplines. Another way that knowledge develops is across the life span of an individual human being. Piaget used the latter to illuminate the former (see Chapman, 1988; Kitchener, 1986). He saw himself first as a genetic epistemologist—not as a psychologist or educator. In undertaking his genetic epistemological project, Piaget was, in fact, very much aware of cultural differences, of culturally defined (or discipline-defined) knowledge, symbol systems, logical procedures, meanings, and so on.

It is equally true that his approach to the project of genetic epistemology was based on an attempt to remove the effect of culture. For example, the opening to the Preface of Piaget and Inhelder's *The Child's Conception of Space* claims that:

> The study of the concept of space, or rather, of the innumerable ideas involved in the concept of space, is for many reasons an indispensable part of child psychology.
>
> • • •
>
> Philosophers and psychologists have argued about the nature of space for centuries. . . . Surely here if anywhere is cause for resorting to experimental psychology, *since only the actual data of mental evolution can reveal the true factors operative in the development of the notion of space.* (Piaget & Inhelder, 1956, vii, italics added)

There is an even more explicit statement of this approach in the Preface to *The Child's Conception of Geometry:*

> Because the present approach is psychological rather than educational, we have deliberately avoided making any use of the knowledge which children acquire in the course of their formal education. To have done otherwise would have meant obscuring important psychological findings. Nevertheless, the fact that the responses given to our questions are spontaneous should prove an

added incentive for working out their implications for education. (Piaget, Inhelder, & Szeminska, 1960, p. iv)

By focusing on individual development, Piaget is endeavoring to strip away the effects of culture and to explore basic concepts in their "uncontaminated" form. In this respect, Piaget did recognize the importance of sociocultural influences: They are more central to this thinking than most people seem to acknowledge.

Having said that, we must also admit that Piaget's decision to ". . . deliberately avoid making any use of the knowledge . . ." from formal education means that he failed to offer us any insights about how these culturally developed and culturally provided systems have an impact on cognitive development. It is unclear how Piaget conceptualized the ways in which the changing knowledge structure at the level of either a society or a discipline has its impact on the knowledge structure of the child. In effect, Piaget chose to avoid precisely the issue of context that is central to the position espoused by Vygotsky and Rogoff: What are the mechanisms by which the societal/disciplinary developments are reflected in the individual's construction of knowledge?

In the case of maps, we need to know the relations among the processes of formal cartographic change (e.g., the invention of map forms such as orthophotoquads or braille maps), the diffusion of these forms from culture to culture (e.g., the adaptation of the circular compass rose form for the Puluwatan star chart), and the adoption of these forms by members of the culture (e.g., the use of modified aerial photographs by ninth-graders in Michigan). The kinds of concepts and empirical paradigms used in Rogoff's program of research could readily be applied to disentangling these relations. As one does so, however, it is important to remember that the processes are occurring at the same time that the individual is coming to grips with a functional and structural understanding of the map concept. We are returned, therefore, to the difference between universal and specific phenomena. We are also forced to address the difference between competence and performance. In simple terms, Piaget's theory is a theory of competence rather than a theory of performance (where the latter is more akin to the Vygotskian position).

The point is much like the one made by Overton (1985) in his discussion of the information-processing approaches to Piagetian theory. These approaches can help to translate a general theory of competence into an explication of performance under particular stimulus and task conditions.

Likewise, the approach by Rogoff and others in the Vygotskian tradition allows us to translate our identification of universal functions and processes into culturally bound, place-determined mechanisms of transmission. The map is but one example of a domain in which we may examine the interplay between individual and society, and thus travel further along on our journey towards an understanding of development in context.

REFERENCES

Beilin, H. (1991). Developmental aesthetics and the psychology of photography. In R. M. Downs, L. S. Liben, & D. S. Palermo (Eds.), *Visions of aesthetics, the environment, and development: The legacy of Joachim Wohlwill* (pp. 45–86). Hillsdale, NJ: Lawrence Erlbaum Associates.

Chapman, M. (1988). *Constructive evolution: Origins and development of Piaget's thought.* Cambridge: Cambridge University Press.

Cole, M. (1985). The zone of proximal development: Where culture and cognition create each other. In J. V. Wertsch (Ed.), *Culture, communication, and cognition: Vygotskian perspectives* (pp. 146–161). Cambridge: Cambridge University Press.

Committee on Map Projections of the *American Cartographic Association.* (1986). *Which map is best? Projections for world maps.* Falls Church, VA: American Congress on Surveying and Mapping.

DeLoache, J. (1989). The development of representation in young children. In H. W. Reese (Ed.), *Advances in child development and behavior* (Vol. 22, pp. 1–39). New York: Academic Press.

Downs, R. M. (1981a). Maps and mappings as metaphors for spatial representation. In L. S. Liben, A. Patterson, & N. Newcombe (Eds.), *Spatial representation and behavior across the life span* (pp. 143–166). New York: Academic Press.

Downs, R. M. (1981b). Maps and metaphors. *The Professional Geographer, 33,* 287–293.

Downs, R. M. (1985). The representation of space: Its development in children and in cartography. In R. Cohen (Ed.), *The development of spatial cognition* (pp. 323–346). Hillsdale, NJ: Lawrence Erlbaum Associates.

Downs, R. M., & Liben, L. S. (1988). Through a map darkly: Understanding maps as representations. *The Genetic Epistemologist, 16,* 11–18.

Downs, R. M., & Liben, L. S. (1990). Getting a bearing on maps: The role of projective spatial concepts. *Children's Environments Quarterly, 7,* 17–27.

Downs, R. M., Liben, L. S., & Daggs, D. G. (1988). On education and geographers: The role of cognitive developmental theory in geographic education. *Annals of the Association of American Geographers, 78,* 680–700.

Downs, R. M., Liben, L. S., & Daggs, D. G. (1990). Surveying the landscape of developmental geography: A dialogue with Howard Gardner. *Annals of the Association of American Geographers, 80,* 124–128.

Gardner, H. (1990). On "On education and geographers: The role of cognitive developmental theory in geographic education" by Roger M. Downs, Lynn S. Liben, and Debra G. Daggs. *Annals of the Association of American Geographers, 80,* 123–124.

Gladwin, T. (1970). *East is a big bird: Navigation and logic on Puluwat Atoll.* Cambridge, MA: Harvard University Press.

Harley, J. B., & Woodward, D. (Eds.). (1987). *The history of cartography, Vol. 1: Cartography in prehistoric, ancient and Medieval Europe and the Mediterranean.* Chicago: University of Chicago Press.

Kaplan, R. (1976). Way-finding in the natural environment. In G. T. Moore & R. G. Golledge (Eds.), *Environmental knowing: Theories, research, and methods* (pp. 46–57). Stroudsburg, PA: Dowden, Hutchinson & Ross.

Kitchener, R. F. (1986). *Piaget's theory of knowledge: Genetic epistemology and scientific reason.* New Haven: Yale University Press.

Landau, B. (1986). Early map use as an unlearned ability. *Cognition, 22,* 201–223.

Lewis, D. (1972). *We, the navigators: The ancient art of landfinding in the Pacific.* Honolulu: The University Press of Hawaii.

Liben, L. S. (1991). Environmental cognition through direct and representational experiences: A life-span perspective. In T. Garling & G. W. Evans (Eds.), *Environment, cognition, and action* (pp. 245–276). New York: Oxford University Press.

Liben, L. S., & Downs, R. M. (1986). *Children's production and comprehension of maps: Increasing graphic literacy* (Final Report to the National Institute of Education, No. G-83-0025).

Liben, L. S., & Downs, R. M. (1989). Understanding maps as symbols: The development of map concepts in children. In H. W. Reese (Ed.), *Advances in child development and behavior* (Vol. 11, pp. 145–201). New York: Academic Press.

Liben, L. S., & Downs, R. M. (1991). The role of graphic representations in understanding the world. In R. M. Downs, L. S. Liben, & D. S. Palermo (Eds.), *Visions of aesthetics, the environment, and development: The legacy of Joachim Wohlwill* (pp. 139–180). Hillsdale, NJ: Lawrence Erlbaum Associates.

Monmonier, M. (1985). *Technological transition in cartography.* Madison, WI: The University of Wisconsin Press.

Overton, W. F. (1985). Scientific methodologies and the competence-moderator-performance issue. In E. D. Neimark, R. De Lisi, & J. L. Newman (Eds.), *Moderators of competence* (pp. 15–41). Hillsdale, NJ: Lawrence Erlbaum Associates.

Petroski, H. (1990). *The pencil: A history of design and circumstance.* New York: Alfred A. Knopf.

Piaget, J., & Inhelder, B. (1956). *The child's conception of space.* New York: Norton.

Piaget, J., Inhelder, B., & Szeminska, A. (1960). *The child's conception of geometry.* London: Routledge and Kegan Paul.

Radziszewska, B., & Rogoff, B. (1988). Influence of adult and peer collaborators on children's planning skills. *Developmental Psychology, 24,* 840–848.

Rogoff, B. (1989). *The social context of cognitive development: Building on Vygotsky and Piaget.* Paper presented at the annual Symposium of the Jean Piaget Society, Philadelphia.

Rogoff, B. (1990). *Apprenticeship in thinking: Cognitive development in sociocultural activity.* New York: Oxford University Press.

Scribner, S. (1985). Vygotsky's use of history. In J. V. Wertsch (Ed.), *Culture, communication, and cognition: Vygotskian perspectives* (pp. 119–145). Cambridge: Cambridge University Press.

Treib, M. (1980). Mapping experience. *Design Quarterly, 115* (Whole Issue).

Utall, D. H., & Wellman, A. M. (1989). Young children's representation of spatial information acquired from maps. *Developmental Psychology, 25,* 128–138.

Wertsch, J. V. (1985). *Vygotsky and the social formation of mind.* Cambridge, MA: Harvard University Press.

Wilford, J. N. (1981). *The mapmakers.* Random House: New York.

Wohlwill, J. F. (1973). The environment is not in the head! In W. F. E. Preiser (Ed.), *Environmental design research, Vol. 2. Symposia and workshops* (pp. 166–181). Stroudsburg, PA: Dowden, Hutchinson & Ross.

Wood, D., & Fels, J. (1986). Design on signs/Myth and meaning in maps. *Cartographica, 23,* 54–103.

Patterns of Interaction in the Co-Construction of Knowledge: Separate Minds, Joint Effort, and Weird Creatures

7

Nira Granott
The Media Laboratory, Massachusetts Institute of Technology

In the last decade, researchers have increasingly acknowledged the importance of social interaction for the development of the individual's cognition. Theorists of different schools, however, suggest different mechanisms for the process, and debate over findings that support one theory or another. In contrast, several researchers view different theories — mainly those of Piaget and Vygotsky — as complementing each other. This chapter follows the latter approach. It attempts to construct a theoretical framework for categorizing and analyzing interactions of different types, while integrating different theories. The study reported here suggests a multifaceted view of interactions and their cognitive effects, and has implications for questions that cognitive researchers commonly ask.

THEORETICAL BACKGROUND

Following the Soviet school, researchers do not see cognitive change as a process that relates to the individual in isolation. Instead, the focus shifts to historical and social origins of thought (Cole, 1985; Laboratory of Comparative Human Cognition, 1983; Luria, 1976; Scribner & Cole, 1981; Vygotsky, 1978); cooperation and interaction (Leont'ev, 1981; Wertsch, 1979, 1984), and the importance of environmental effects on the individual (Bronfenbrenner, 1979; Niesser, 1985; Reed, this volume). Researchers describe the function of shared activities (Newman, Griffin, & Cole, 1989; Resnick, 1987; Rogoff, 1990), and highlight the influence of the context on learning and development (A. L. Brown & Reeve, 1987; J. S. Brown,

Collins, & Duguid, 1989; Fischer, this volume; Lerner & Kaufman, 1985; Rogoff, 1982; Rogoff & Lave, 1984).

Acknowledgment of the social origins of cognitive processes has to be reflected in the unit of analysis of human cognition. Instead of referring to an individual or to isolated psychological processes measured by various tests (LCHC, 1983), units of analysis should reflect the social origins of cognitive processes (Wertsch, 1985). Different levels of activities (Leont'ev, 1981) can serve as units of analysis (Wertsch, Minick, & Arns, 1984). Other units can be socially assembled situations or cultural practices (LCHC, 1983); task-within-practices or job-task (Scribner, 1984, 1986); "whole task" (Newman, Griffin & Cole, 1984), and activity, task, or event (Cole, 1985). By using such units of analysis, the focus of the analysis shifts to the active changes involved in an unfolding event or activity (Rogoff, 1990).

These new units of analysis, however, pose a problem. How can the analysis transcend the specificity of given activities, events, tasks, or situations? What structures can relate to the specifics yet be general enough to unify interactive cognitive experiences across events and contents? This chapter attempts to confront this problem by suggesting factors that affect cognitive change through different types of interactions and across diverse contents.

Different Views of the Cognitive Effect of Interaction

Vygotsky highlights the importance of interaction between children and adults or "more capable" peers (i.e., Vygotsky, 1978; Wertsch, 1979). In this view, cognitive processes, which are initiated by adult–child interaction, are later internalized by the child (Vygotsky, 1978), in the same way that external speech becomes egocentric and then turns to inner speech (Vygotsky, 1962). Studies in the Vygotskian approach analyze adult–child interaction (Rogoff, Malkin, & Gilbride, 1984; Saxe, Guberman, & Gearhart, 1987; Wertsch, 1979; Wertsch et al., 1984), intersubjectivity, and the shared meaning that evolves between the child and a more capable partner. Other studies analyze the cognitive change induced by peer cooperation (Forman, 1987; Forman & Cazden, 1985), showing the function of collaboration, shared meaning, mutual support, and exchange of guidance. Researchers indicate the advantages (Forman & Cazden, 1985) and detriments (Tudge, 1985) of peer interactions, and compare peer versus adult–child interactions (Ellis & Rogoff, 1982; Radziszewska & Rogoff, 1988).

Several researchers compare the Vygotskian and the Piagetian perspective (i.e., Damon, 1984; Forman & Cazden, 1985; Rogoff, 1990; Tudge & Rogoff, 1989). When considering social interaction, the Piagetian school emphasizes cognitive conflict resulting from interaction among peers (i.e.,

Doise & Mugny, 1984; Doise & Palmonari, 1984; Murray, 1972, 1983; Perret-Clermont, 1980; Piaget, 1926). Cognitive conflict generates disequilibrium; by assimilating the other's point of view, equilibrium and cognitive restructuring take place. Piaget's followers show that interaction between unequal peers can also bring cognitive change (Mugny & Doise, 1978; Perret-Clermont, 1980). However, according to Piaget, children's interactions with adults usually generate compliance to adults' authority and prevent cognitive restructuring.

Social learning theory (Bandura, 1977) focuses on human behavior that is learned observationally, through modeling. What children observe in others further guides their own actions. A model reinforces certain behaviors, and the way the individual thinks of him or herself in specific environments affects interaction and cognitive development (Bandura, 1986).

This chapter attempts to show that the patterns of interaction suggested by Vygotsky, Piaget, Bandura, and their followers form only part of the interactive spectrum that affects cognitive change. It follows others who call for considering the Vygotskian and the Piagetian views as complementary (i.e., Damon, 1984; Forman & Cazden, 1985), and who also see social learning theory as complementing those schools of thought (Tudge & Winterhoff, 1991). The chapter suggests a theoretical framework for analyzing interactions. The framework, or interaction model, is based on categories generated from research data, which were further elaborated and structured theoretically. After presenting the model, a few examples from the data illustrate some types of interaction.

THEORETICAL FRAMEWORK FOR ANALYZING INTERACTIONS

The interaction model suggests two major dimensions from which interactions can be analyzed. One is the degree of collaboration. Collaborative patterns can involve high mutuality and evolve through intersubjectivity of shared understanding and common focus of attention (Rogoff, 1990). Yet, other interactions can only involve some exchange of ideas and turn-taking activity. The other dimension refers to the participants' relative knowledge and expertise in the context of the interaction (e.g., a child conserver and a nonconserver, who collaborate on a conservation task).

Figure 7.1 presents these dimensions of analysis. The horizontal dimension, representing degree of collaboration, extends for positive values of collaboration from the intersection of the two axes (indicating no collaboration, or independent activity), through increasing degree of collaboration, to highly collaborative activities. Collaborative interactions are characterized by united effort and continuous sharing. Interactions marked by

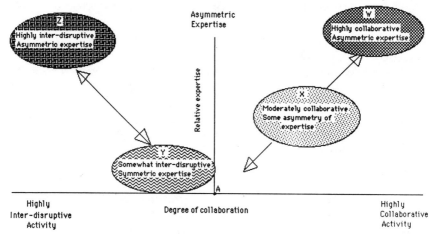

FIG 7.1. A framework for analyzing interactions according to degree of collaboration and relative expertise. Point A, in the intersection of the dimensions, represents symmetric expertise and independent activity.

independent activity, on the other hand, are typical to situations in which participants construct their understanding individually. Disruptive activities are characterized by open conflicts, in which one participant's actions interrupt the other's activity and, to some extent, impede the other's knowledge construction process. For negative values on the collaborative dimension, activities increase in interchange of disruptive interaction toward the far left end of the dimension, culminating in highly interlocked interdisruptive activities.

The vertical dimension characterizes relative knowledge and expertise between the participants. This dimension ranges from symmetric expertise, in which the participants have similar knowledge related to the context of the interaction; it continues through increasing degrees of asymmetry, to a highly asymmetric expertise, in which one participant is more knowledgeable and has greater expertise than the other (in areas relevant to the interaction). Additional factors, other than relative expertise, may affect the types of interaction; these other factors are discussed later.

Many types of interactions map onto the span delineated by these two dimensions. The intersection of the axes is characterized by a situation in which participants with symmetric expertise are each involved in an independent activity. The top-right area (marked W in Fig. 7.1) indicates highly collaborative interactions between participants with asymmetric knowledge and expertise. Adult–child interaction, with evolving shared meaning and highly collaborative support in the Vygotskian-school vein, corresponds to this area. In Area X, interactions are characterized by moderate collaboration between partners of some asymmetric expertise. The Piagetian-school examples of a child conserver and a nonconserver, when each of them tries to explain his or her already formed view to the

186

other, can demonstrate such an interaction. As we see later, other types of positive interactions also map to different areas between these two dimensions.

The area to the left of the intersection of the axes, indicating negative (disruptive) interactions, has a similar structure. For example, interaction between peers (like two classmates) of equal expertise, who are involved in mostly independent activity but disturb each other's actions occasionally, corresponds to the area marked by Y. The top left area (Z), on the other hand, indicates an interaction between partners of asymmetric expertise (expert–novice, or adult–child) that is highly interlocked and disruptive.

Interactions that correspond to different values on the two dimensions have different attributes and different cognitive effects. Collaborative interactions of diverse types can promote the participants' cognitive growth in different ways, as demonstrated by examples below; disruptive interactions can hamper cognitive progress. The following section describes the different types of interactions and indicates some of their cognitive effects.

Collaborative Interactions

Conceptually, the dimensions for analysis (degree of collaboration and relative expertise) are continuous. In order to characterize the attributes of diverse interactions, three ordinal levels — high, medium, and low — are set for each dimension. Figure 7.2 represents collaborative (positive) interactions.

Findings from other studies fit with this analysis (see, e.g., Forman & Cazden, 1985, for levels of procedural interactions; Bandura, 1977, for

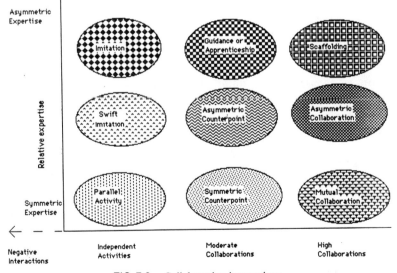

FIG 7.2.   Collaborative interactions.

imitation of a model, and Mugny & Doise, 1978, for cognitive conflict that differs from imitation).

Mutual Collaboration. Mutual collaboration is characterized by a highly collaborative interaction between peers of equal expertise (bottom-right area in Fig. 7.2). This type of interaction is reciprocal and symmetric, and is often accompanied by intensive verbal exchange. The participants are about equally dominant in the activity (when dominance is measured by their utterances or timed actions relative to one another), with quick shifts of dominance from one to the other. They are engaged in a common activity, sharing materials, products, observations, and hypotheses. The participants co-construct their knowledge by continuously sharing their ways of understanding. Their knowledge structures, therefore, evolve simultaneously. The mutual quality of the process is indicated by talking spontaneously, often simultaneously, using abbreviated speech (Vygotsky, 1962), and completing one another's sentences. During mutual collaboration, participants may suggest to one another courses of activities, discuss the suggestions, agree on a common activity, work it out together, share comments on the occurrences, discuss their implications, and co-construct their understanding together (see Table 7.1, for a summary of the attributes of different types of interactions).

Symmetric Counterpoint. Symmetric counterpoint occurs between peers of equal expertise who interact while alternating dominance on an activity. As in musical counterpoint, the participants retain some independent activities, which are woven together into a common moderately collaborative interaction. During symmetric counterpoint dominance shifts from one partner to another for chunks of the activity, but throughout the interaction dominance is about equally distributed. Even when the participants are "passive," they watch their partners attentively.

During symmetric counterpoint the partners share common situations, materials, and feedback on their own and their partners' explorations. However, their understanding of the situation evolves individually, before or during the interaction. Their knowledge, therefore, often develops in unsynchronized spurts. During the interaction, their separate ways of understanding are compared and, if divergent, they may be confronted and changed. After the entire interaction, therefore, the participants' cognitive change may often be similar.

For example, in symmetric counterpoint, during a problem-solving activity, typically one participant at a time tries a solution while the others watch. Another example is a group discussion, in which one participant talks at a time while the others listen.

Parallel Activity.   Parallel activity is an interaction among peers of symmetric expertise, engaged in an activity that is mostly independent. The individuals work in parallel, with some degree of exchange that nourishes and stimulates one another's activity. During the independent segments, the participants are absorbed in their own activity, whereas in the interactive segments they watch the other's activity or talk and exchange information. The interactive parts may be, then, explicit or implicit, verbal or nonverbal (Rogoff, 1990). In contrast to symmetric counterpoint, in which the "passive" participant watches and listens attentively to the other, during parallel activity the independent activities are not shared but rather form separate simultaneous processes. The activities and the feedback to the activities are separate, as are the processes of knowledge construction. The interactive segments generate partial and sometimes unidirectional sharing that confronts and compares some knowledge structures.

A familiar example of parallel activity is young children's parallel play. Although they play separately, there is some interchange that stimulates one another's play. Another example is a research group, in which each member works on his or her research project, but all share a common interest and occasionally exchange information and ideas.

Asymmetric Collaboration.   Asymmetric collaboration represents a collaborative interaction between peers of some asymmetric expertise. The degree to which the participants take part in, or responsibility for, an activity is consistently unbalanced (i.e., one is more dominant, or often directs and guides the other). The participants have common operative goals, share a common activity, and their spontaneous continuous sharing often generates incomplete sentences. While sharing their knowledge and hypotheses, they co-construct their understanding together (see Table 7.1).

Asymmetric Counterpoint.   Asymmetric counterpoint is a moderately collaborative interaction among peers of some asymmetric expertise. As in symmetric counterpoint, the partners share feedback within a common situation but construct their understanding independently. However, the interaction is asymmetric due to the unequal expertise of the participants. There is asymmetric alternations of unequal dominance. The flow of information is often unidirectional (the more capable peer directs the exploration). The processes of knowledge construction are unsynchronized, and the interaction reflects previously or independently constructed knowledge of the more capable partner.

Examples of asymmetric counterpoint occur when heterogeneous groups of students work together on given tasks, or during discussions between experts and novices.

TABLE 7.1
Attributes of Types of Interactions

Imitation	Guidance or Apprenticeship	Scaffolding
Separate activities; a less capable partner imitates a more capable one	Complementing goals; short periods of guidance interspersed throughout independent activities	Common activity with complementing goals
Partial or no sharing	Periods of asymmetric and often unidirectional sharing of knowledge	Sharing the situation, materials, observations; asymmetric sharing of knowledge and hypotheses
Unguided activity and observation	Partially guided activity, observations, and analysis	Guided activity, observations, and analysis
	Alternating shifts of unequal dominance, shifting between independent and guided segments of the activity	Throughout the interaction, a trend of shift of dominance from the scaffolding to the scaffold partner
Asymmetric flow of information, verbal or visual	Asymmetric flow of information	Asymmetric communication
	Guiding and demonstrating (by the expert) vs. task-solving (by the novice) information and action	Guiding (by the scaffolding) vs. task-solving (by the scaffold) information and action
	Mostly complete sentences	Mostly complete sentences, focused on shared understanding
Unsynchronized, separate, and highly unbalanced processes of knowledge construction	Unsynchronized, separate, and highly unbalanced processes of knowledge construction; activity aimed at the novice's construction of knowledge	Unsynchronized, separate, and highly unbalanced processes of knowledge construction; activity aimed at the scaffold's construction of knowledge

Swift Imitation	Asymmetric Counterpoint	Asymmetric Collaboration
Separate activities in which a less capable partner temporarily shifts to imitating a more capable one	Common goal embedded in individually initiated activity, that is unequally alternating among the participants	Common operative goals and activity
Partial or no sharing	Sharing the situation, materials, feedback; possible partial and mostly unidirectional sharing of knowledge structures	Sharing the situation, materials, products, previous knowledge, observations, hypotheses, and understanding
	Partly guided or directed sequence of activity, based on one partner's previous knowledge	Evolving sequence of activity, based on the shared activity of the participants and one partner's previous knowledge
	Alternating shifts of unequal dominance	Unequal dominance
Asymmetric flow of information, verbal or visual	Asymmetric flow of information and action	Asymmetric flow of information and action
		Talking spontaneously; incomplete sentences due to accommodation to the different activity of the other
Unsynchronized, separate, and unbalanced processes of knowledge construction; possible partial comparison or confrontation of knowledge structures	Unsynchronized, separate, and unbalanced processes of knowledge construction; possible partial comparison or confrontation of cognitive structures	Co-construction of knowledge through the interaction, in unbalanced processes

(continued on next page)

TABLE 7.1 *(continued)*

Parallel Activity	Symmetric Counterpoint	Mutual Collaboration
Separate activities with temporary shifts to periods of inter-action	Common goal shared in individually initiated activity that equally alternates between the participants	Common operative goals and activity
Partial or no sharing during the interaction	Sharing the situation, materials, feedback; possible partial sharing of knowledge structures	Sharing the situation, materials, products, observations, hypotheses, and understanding
Separate activities, partial or no continuous common sequence of activity	Evolving sequence of activity, based on previous activity of all partners and on the corresponding feedback	Evolving sequence of activity, based on the shared evolving activity of all participants
	Alternating shifts of equal dominance for chunks of the activity	Equal dominance with very quick shifts from one partner to another
Symmetric or asymmetric flow of information, verbal or visual	Symmetric flow of information and action	Symmetric flow of information and action
	Little information sharing during independent construction of knowledge	Talking spontaneously and simultaneously; abbreviated speech due to shared understanding
Unsynchronized separate processes of knowledge construction; partial comparison or confrontation of cognitive structures	Unsynchronized processes of knowledge construction, but similar during the entire activity; comparison or confrontation of cognitive structures	Co-construction of knowledge through the interaction, in balanced symmetric and shared processes

Swift Imitation.   Swift imitation is an interaction among peers of moderately asymmetric expertise, engaged in an activity that is mostly independent (noncollaborative). The independent activities are interspersed with short periods of imitation of a more capable peer, with or without verbal exchange. The information flow, whether verbal or visual, is mostly unidirectional and asymmetric. The processes of knowledge construction are unsynchronized; the construction of knowledge of the more capable peer may have occurred prior to the interaction (see Table 7.1).

Swift imitation occurs, for example, in the lower grades at school, between children who see each other's drawings, pick up an idea and integrate it in their own drawings. Similar examples occur in older children's writings or in computer graphics they create.

Scaffolding.   Scaffolding (Wood, Bruner, & Ross, 1976) corresponds to a guiding collaborative interaction between partners with asymmetric knowledge and expertise. The guiding partner assists the other's construction of knowledge. In a supportive and approving manner, the guide subtly directs the other's observation and activity step by step, while accommodating to the other's wishes and ability.

Guidance or Apprenticeship.   Guidance or apprenticeship are interactions among participants with asymmetric expertise, characterized by periods of guidance interspersed throughout an activity or discussion. The more experienced partner, parent, expert, or guide gives some directions to the other. These periods of guidance are preceded and followed by unguided activity (which sometimes includes interaction on unrelated issues). The guide may volunteer help, indicate when he or she is available for helping, or be asked for help explicitly. The guidance is unidirectional, from the guide to the guided, and is more informative and directive than the implicit support given during scaffolding.

In familiar examples of guiding, students are engaged in an activity, while the teacher passes from one student (or group) to another, gives feedback or directions, and proceeds to another student (or group). Another example is parent and child, who are each involved in their own activity, when from time to time the child asks the parent for help or information, or the parent approaches the child and offers hints and suggestions. For examples of apprenticeship, see Rogoff (1990).

Imitation.   Imitation corresponds to interaction among partners of asymmetric expertise. It consists mainly of independent (noncollaborative) activities, with limited interaction, in which the less experienced partner imitates the more experienced. In contrast with swift imitation, in which one partner "borrows" a core idea from a peer and then develops it independently, in this type of interaction the imitation may be more substantial to the activity. If the activity is complex or nontrivial for the novice, just borrowing an idea may not suffice. The novice may have to imitate the model of an expert more closely. During Imitation, the more experienced partner may be involved in his or her own activity, and may not explicitly try to guide the novice.

Disruptive Interactions

Disruptive interactions form a mirror image of the collaborative interactions, having a similar structure with negative connotations. Disruptive interactions interfere with a discussion, destroy a product, or stop an exploration; they can impede achievement of a goal, prevent completion of a task, and hinder the related processes of knowledge construction. Disruptive interactions can evolve between partners with different values of relative expertise (e.g., two children with similar ability; different-age siblings, or an adult and a child).

The least interdisruptive interactions, like their low collaborative parallels, consist of mostly independent activities. The participants are each engaged in their own activities, but these are interspersed with short negative interchanges. Highly interdisruptive interactions are characterized by extremely interlocked and interfering activities (e.g., participants who talk simultaneously in a way that neither of them can express his or her views or listen to the other, or children who simultaneously try to use the same materials and dominate an activity). In moderately interlocked activities, there is a counterpoint between the participants' activities, and the activities of at least one participant are disruptive.

Negative interactions occur in research situations as well as in everyday life. For different reasons, negative interactions emerge between parent and child, or among adults (i.e., Glick, 1985; Goodnow, 1990; Hess & Shipman, 1965; Shweder, 1990; Valsiner, 1984). When an expert (or adult) undermines the novice's (or child's) ability, prevents access to materials, stops certain activities, or deprives his or her ability to pursue certain directions of inquiry, the interaction can hinder the novice's (or child's) development in the domain of the interaction.

Other Factors Affecting Interactions

Factors other than asymmetry of knowledge and expertise and degree of collaboration also affect interactions. One factor is knowledge and expertise in irrelevant domains, which may affect participants' expectations of each other's expertise. Another factor is social roles. For example, an authority–submission relationship between two persons at work may affect interaction between them in unrelated contexts. Similarly, a child may comply to adult's authority and defer his or her own point of view (Piaget, 1965). Gender-related patterns may affect boy–girl and man–woman interactions, often giving more dominance on the interaction to the male; race and class differences can have similar effect. Previous patterns of interaction between the same participants, molded through common experiences in the past, can also affect their present interactions. Personality traits (such as leadership, initiative, or passivity) and the individual's self-image will also affect interactions. Finally, participants' interest in the task at hand and the importance they attribute to it may affect the interaction.

In positive interactions, when these factors do not correspond to the participants' relative knowledge and expertise in the context of the interaction, the interaction may be less productive and may have diminished effect on cognitive growth. The interaction model suggested here may help evaluate the effect of these other factors, as discussed later.

The model indicates diverse types of interaction. Before discussing the model and its implications, some of these types of interactions are illustrated by examples from research data.

TYPES OF INTERACTIONS: ILLUSTRATIVE EXAMPLES

The following examples are drawn from a study that investigates the microdevelopment of knowledge structures that develop through adults' collaborative learning (Granott, 1991a, 1991b). Although the subjects in the study were adults, the emerging patterns of interactions are similar to those also observed among children. Clearly, interactions among children differ from adults' interactions in the sophistication of social skills and subject matter knowledge involved. However, especially when adults engage in knowledge construction through spontaneous informal interactions, the underlying structure of their interactive patterns seems to be similar to patterns prevailing across ages.

Method

Thirty-five adults, divided into three groups, explored robots that responded to varied stimuli. During the explorations, the social interactions of the subjects were unstructured — teams formed, changed, and reformed spontaneously. The explorations were unguided and the task ill-defined: The subjects were asked to find out whatever they could about the robots, thus having to define the problem as well as the procedures used. The social context helped to avoid the problem of delayed and distracting verbal reports, caused by the "think-out-loud" technique (Nisbett & Wilson, 1977).

The participants spoke fairly freely with one another, thus exposing their thinking processes (Radziszewska & Rogoff, 1988). The study used an ethnographic method, consisting of observations of the subjects' spontaneous behavior, and generating categories based on the observations.

Procedure

Each group met on 2 consecutive days, for 1½ hours each time. Three participants came for additional sessions or continued their explorations by joining other groups. Videotapes of the explorations served as data for studying the interactive patterns (for further details, see Granott, 1991a, 1991b).

Materials

The study used six robots, built from specialized Lego bricks that incorporated sensors (detecting light, sound, and touch); logic bricks (and, or, inverter, etc.), motor, and battery bricks. Different wiring connections between bricks generated varied and somewhat strange "behaviors," which led to the robots' nickname "Weird Creatures." For example, one robot moved forward and sideways toward shadows, and when bumping into an obstacle it retreated and turned around. Each robot was placed in an environment that generated varied stimuli, some of which were hard to notice, and was activated by only some of the stimuli. The robots' patterns of movement, therefore, were not easy to understand. The subjects could use varied objects that were scattered around to flash lights, cast shadows, make sounds, or create obstacles, in order to test their hypotheses and conjectures as to the causes of the robots' "weird" behaviors.

Examples of Interactions: Co-Constructing Understanding of the Weird Creatures

The socially unconstrained nature of the situation generated rich data. Allowing subjects to interact with one another, without imposing constraints on factors that affect the social interactions, is especially important in studies that investigate interactions, as discussed later. Small segments from episodes, transcribed from the video data, are described and analyzed here. The excerpts are marked by index numbers to which the analyses refer.

Episode 1: Mutual Collaboration. In the following episode, together, three subjects watch little blinking lights that occasionally turn on and off on a robot, and try to understand the related causality.

[1]Yolanda: "The other one is—" [2]Susan: "I think that it's up, once every time it hits-" [3]Yolanda (almost simultaneously): "Any time it hits-" [4](The three together): "Right—aha—ok—" [5]Susan: "And the blue-" [6]Mary (simultaneously, reading aloud): "Blue-" [7]Susan: "-stays on until a-" [8]Yolanda: "Aha." [9]Mary: "So, (reading aloud while writing) the top light on yellow blinks on impact—" [10]Susan: "yeah—[unclear]" [11]Yolanda: "yeah!" [12](The three simultaneously): "Yes! Yeah! Yea! . . . Yep!" [13]Yolanda: "It's also right behind here!" (points). [14]Susan is writing. Mary leans forward to watch). [15]Mary: "Where?" [16]Yolanda (indicates): "Behind this front [deck?]. [17]Now watch—" [18]Mary: "Oh, yeah—" [19](Susan leans forward, watching) [20]Yolanda: "That's the top—" [21](Susan says something unclear, simultaneously). [22]Mary (simultaneously): "It only blinks when—" [23]Yolanda (simultaneously): "I don't know of the—" [24]Mary (continues) "[it goes?] forward. ."

In the episode, Mary, Susan, and Yolanda work in close collaboration. Dominance of the exploration and the discourse is distributed among them with quick shifts from one to the other. Mary shares her notes with the others by reading them aloud (9). In an evolving intersubjectivity, the three talk in abbreviated speech, agreeing with one another to half formulated sentences (3-4; 7-8). Only when one does not understand, is there a need to be more explicit or even to point. This happens when Yolanda notices another light (13), which Mary does not see (15). Yolanda describes explicitly where the light is (16) while indicating it, further directing her partner's attention: "Now watch" (17). The three often talk simultaneously (4, 6-7, 12, 21-24), but at the same time they listen and respond to what the other says (4, 8). They share observations (1, 7, 13-17) and co-construct their knowledge by together formulating rules for the phenomena they observe (2-3, 5-9, 20-24).

Episode 2: Symmetric Counterpoint.   In this episode, Sam and Dorothy explore a robot that has a light sensor. The robot moves backward in the shade and forward in the light, but only when the light falls directly on the sensor.

[1]The robot moves forward, reaches the wall and gets stuck there. [2]Sam approaches it, extends his hand and reaches for the robot. [3]The robot makes a sudden back-and-forth jerk. [4]Sam stops, [5]puts his hand on top of the robot, and slowly moves his hand back and forth above it. [6]The robot doesn't respond. [7]Sam takes a flashlight and illuminates the robot. [8]Still no response. [9]Sam takes the robot carefully, holding it from behind. [10]He turns the robot around, watches it, then illuminates it with the flashlight. [11]Still no response. [12]Sam puts the robot, facing a different direction, on the floor. [13]The robot starts moving, bumps into a box and gets stuck there. [14]Dorothy approaches the robot and carefully puts her hand on top of it, close to the robot. [15]The robot reacts—it starts moving backward instead of forward.

After previous shifts of dominance, in this segment Sam is dominant (2–13) while Dorothy watches him. After the surprising reaction of the robot (2–3), Sam attempts to find what causes it (5; 7; 10), while Dorothy watches without interrupting. When Sam stops exploring (12–13), Dorothy takes over (14). However, this time (unlike her previous explorations) she can control the robot in her first attempt (15), which indicates that she was attentively watching Sam, learning from the robot's responses to his interventions, and forming her own understanding through his explorations. Between the two, there is no collaborative planning, nor shared analysis. Their knowledge, then, develops for the most part independently, in unsynchronized spurts. Yet, at the end of the interaction, their knowledge is similar — Dorothy understands the robot while watching Sam, and Sam, later, while watching her.

Episode 3: Asymmetric Collaboration.   In the following episode, Mary and Abigail are building a new robot together. They connect a special brick to the new robot and try to find out the function of that brick.

[1]Mary is holding the new robot. [2]Abigail says: "This is a . . ." [3]Mary: "Timer . . . [4]and I don't know what this is." [5]Abigail takes the new robot and checks it. [6]Mary is watching her and the robot. [7]She adds: "Sometimes it would [unclear] (. . .) [8]Mary indicates a certain brick on the robot that Abigail is holding, turns the brick and continues: [9]"It looks like they told him what to do. (. . .) [10]Abigail returns the robot to Mary and says: [11]"We need to [connect a sensor?]" [12]Mary: "But where? I don't see any [unclear] where it's supposed to go on this, that's one thing. Maybe just . . ." [13]Abigail turns around, takes the ready-made robot, and checks it. [14]Mary watches her and continues: [15]"It's like this, they're connecting — [16](while looking at the robot that Abigail examines) Oh, here?" [17]Mary indicates something on the ready-made robot that Abigail is holding, and continues: [18]"This one?" [19]Mary takes apart a similar brick on their own robot and shows to Abigail: [20]"Look, this one doesn't work any more. It appears to have . . ." [21]Mary checks it and Abigail watches the brick Mary is showing her. (. . .) [22]Mary: "Let's just try it. Let's try it here." (. . .) [23]Abigail: "All right." (. . .) [24]Mary: "Oh, oh, look, maybe we have to figure out where to put some wires in?" (. . .) [25]Abigail turns around, checks the ready-made robot. [26]Then she turns back to Mary, takes their own robot, indicates an extension on the sound sensor and says: [27]"That's where it is." [28]Abigail takes a wire, connects it to the sound sensor at the place she indicated before, and connects the other side of the wire to another brick. [29]Mary: "Ahaaa! !"

In the episode, Mary and Abigail set for themselves common operative goals (11; 22–23; 24). They share a common activity and are continuously interacting. When Abigail is checking the robot, Mary is not just watching her, waiting for her turn, but rather continues to share her way of understanding the robot (7; 9; 18; 20), indicating to Abigail what she's referring to (8; 17; 19). Abigail's exploration (13) triggers Mary to generate more hypotheses, which she immediately shares (17–18). In turn, when Abigail finds out where to connect the wire, she doesn't simply do so, but rather shows Mary first where the wire should be connected (27), and only then connects it (28).

Mary and Abigail share their understanding and hypotheses (2–4, 7, 9, 11–12, 18, 20, 24; 27). In contrast to abbreviated speech in mutual collaboration, what causes incomplete sentences in this case is not that "the subject is the same in the two minds" (Vygotsky, 1962, p. 239), but rather accommodating to the different activities of the other (15–16; 20–21; 25–29). The collaboration is asymmetric: Mary shares more information with Abigail than vice versa: since the beginning of the episode the asymmetric structure of the interaction is set when Mary completes Abigail's sentence (2–3). Mary continues to tell Abigail what she knows and does not know about the robot and specific bricks (4, 7, 9, 12, 20). Mary is more dominant in the interaction—she talks more and is more elaborate in her suggestions and hypotheses. Yet, Abigail contributes to their common understanding too—and she, in fact, finds the solution to their problem (27–28).

Episode 4: Swift Imitation. In the following episode, Tim, Lucy, Jill, and Sherry are about to start their exploration for the first time, when one of them sees Lynn's exploration. Lynn already participated in two sessions with another group and joined this group to continue her explorations.

[1]Tim, Lucy, Jill, and Sherry observe a robot move, and [2]consult with one another how to explore it. [3]Tim says: "—Since there are apparently different things here . . ." [4]Others say: [5]—"We must have [unclear] here something we can try . . ." [6]—"Maybe looking at the forwards and backwards movement?" [7]—"Let's make it—" [8]At that moment, light flashes on them. [9]Lynn is passing by, following her robot. [10]She holds a flashlight, projects light on the robot, and explores its reaction. [11]Sherry says: "Oh, look at that! [12]. . . Let's see, the forward behavior is with the light, right?" [13]While talking she approaches a nearby box, picks up a flashlight, and uses it to project light on their robot. [14]The others join her.

The episode shows a short and partial interaction, based mainly on imitation of a peer, Lynn, who has greater expertise. Tim, Lucy, Jill, and Sherry, are engaged in their own activity, before (1–7) and after (13–14) their encounter with Lynn. While the four are discussing how to start their exploration (2–7), Lynn's light flashes on them (8) and calls Sherry's attention. When seeing Lynn flashing light on her robot (9–10), Sherry suggests that they do the same thing (12). In this case, the interaction is partial and nonverbal. The four participants pick up an idea, and then integrate it in their own exploration (13–14).

The data included examples of other types of interactions, through not all those delineated by the interaction model. Due to space limitations, these cannot be described in this chapter.

CONCLUDING DISCUSSION

This chapter indicates two problems. One refers to the unit of analysis used by research that explores cognitive change in relation to social interaction. Units of analysis such as activities, events, tasks, and the like are prone to specificity. The way cognitive processes evolve depends on their context (e.g., Granott, 1991a). However, the progress of research depends on the possibility to compare and integrate results of different studies.

The second problem relates to the various theories concerned with the effect of interaction on cognitive development. Existing theories, developed by Vygotsky, Piaget, Bandura, and their followers, each suggest different mechanisms for the way interaction affects cognitive change. Studies within the conceptual approach of each theory have assessed the theory's claims, often challenging other theories. However, there is no common ground on which the theories can meet and become integrated.

The model suggested in this chapter attempts to tackle these problems. Without undermining the context of the interactive events under scrutiny, the model indicates dimensions for analysis that could be compared across studies. These two dimensions — degree of collaboration and relative expertise — are suggested as major factors affecting the attributes of interactions and the cognitive change they generate, and (as discussed later) can serve as a baseline for evaluating the effect of other factors.

The two dimensions open a span within which different types of interactions can be compared and analyzed. The model indicates how the theories suggested by Vygotsky, Piaget, and Bandura map onto this span. It shows the variables along which situations addressed by one theory can be transformed into situations addressed by another, and suggests how other types of interactions, not discussed by these theories, could be integrated too.

The following section compares the attributes of different types of interactions, and maps the theories of Vygotsky, Piaget, and Bandura onto the proposed model.

Framework for Comparing Different Types of Interactions

Different types of interaction, portrayed by the interaction model, have different dynamics and attributes, and differing implications for cognitive processes of knowledge construction. Yet, there are overlaps and similarities between types of interactions. Interactions that map to different values on one dimension (e.g., have different levels of relative expertise) but have a similar value on the other dimension (e.g., highly collaborative interactions) overlap in their attributes that characterize the latter (characteristics of high collaborations).

Collaborative Interactions. On the most collaborative end, mutual collaboration, asymmetric collaboration, and scaffolding have some similar attributes (see Table 7.1): The partners share the activity, situation, materials, observations, and hypotheses. Within that shared context, interactions are characterized by shared meaning and evolving intersubjectivity, as maintained by the Vygotskian approach. Although Vygotsky focused on adult–child interaction, such intersubjectivity exists also in interactions between peers of equal and unequal expertise. Within intersubjectivity, knowledge is co-constructed.

Some of these attributes, however, change along the relative–expertise dimension. Sharing the observations and hypotheses becomes increasingly asymmetric toward the asymmetric–expertise end. Spontaneous talk and abbreviated speech, generated by intersubjectivity, gradually lose their abbreviated quality as the expertise becomes more asymmetric (when the expert needs to make sure his or her less experienced partner understands, he or she tends to use clear and well-defined communication). Similarly, the processes of knowledge co-construction of the participants become less similar and less synchronized as the interactions shift toward the asymmetric–expertise end, and culminate in scaffolding, in which the goal of the expert partner is not his or her own construction of knowledge, but that of the novice.

Moderately Collaborative Interactions. The moderately collaborative interactions (symmetric counterpoint, asymmetric counterpoint, and guidance or apprenticeship) are all characterized by decreased degree of shared meaning and evolving intersubjectivity. The participants' individual voices, therefore, are distinctly detected in a counterpoint of activities that do not mesh into one another. Hence, the shift of alternating dominance: A segment of the activity dominated by one participant is qualitatively distinct from a segment dominated by another. The processes of knowledge construction evolve separately, through partial sharing. The resulting intersubjectivity resembles the Piagetian model of intraindividual processes, in which one is working on the other's ideas (Rogoff, 1990; Tudge & Rogoff, 1989). Because the participants' knowledge structures develop separately, they are often unsynchronized. Their comparison and confrontation through partial sharing may create cognitive conflict, according to the Piagetian theory. Although the Piagetian school focused on interaction among peers of some asymmetric expertise, similar processes may occur between peers of equal expertise or highly asymmetric expertise.

Some of the attributes of these interactions change along the relative-expertise dimension: Sharing the situation, materials, and feedback becomes more unidirectional and partial toward the asymmetric-expertise end. Similarly, the knowledge construction processes become more separate and asymmetric for interactions that are closer to the asymmetric-expertise end.

Less Collaborative Interactions.   In the less collaborative interactions (parallel activity, swift imitation, and imitation), a considerable part of the activity is independent. The social context supplies ideas, examples, and models for the individual, in line with social learning theory. Imitation can be continuous or can happen at a glance. Furthermore, parallel activity (i.e., young children's parallel play) is also a version of interactive influence, which is mainly based on independent activities. The independent activities are interspersed with segments of interaction, which may be verbal and explicit or visual and implicit (Rogoff, 1990). The processes of knowledge construction of the participants evolve separately, in part during independent activities, and in part during interactive segments. Along the relative expertise dimension, the activities in the less collaborative interactions become increasingly dependent on the model of a more experienced partner.

Disruptive Interactions.   Disruptive interactions form a mirror image of the collaborative interactions. Disruptive interactions range from highly interdisruptive interactions (with extremely interlocked, interfering activities), through moderately interlocked, disruptive activities, to least interdisruptive interactions (represented close to the intersection of the dimensions) that are mostly independent.

This analysis portrays prototypes of interactions. In reality, interactive patterns are often more complex: For a given team, different patterns may evolve. For example, in Episode 4, between the group of four and Lynn, the interaction is characterized by swift imitation. At the same time, the interaction among the four evolves along different patterns. A person can have one type of interaction with one partner while maintaining a totally different type with another. By the same token, for a given team, patterns of interaction may change throughout an activity. Furthermore, interactions do not always fit neatly within the aforementioned prototypes. The dimensions (degree of collaboration and relative expertise) are continuous. Therefore, sometimes a finer grain subdivision to interactive types, covering only a limited segment of the span of interactions, may be needed for the data available.

Other Factors Affecting Interactions

Other factors also affect interactions and the resulting cognitive change (e.g., expertise in irrelevant domains, social roles, gender, race, previous interactions, personality traits, etc.; see pp. 194–195), although these could not be elaborated in this chapter. In many circumstances, these factors overpower the evolving interaction. In the context of these factors, certain types of interactions may be more prevalent than others; persons who "deserve" to be more dominant in an interaction, considering their expertise, become dominated. The poignant effect of these factors, it seems, stems from the discrepancy between the resulting interaction in such cases and the interaction that could have been expected otherwise (according to distribution of types of interaction in other populations, or to objectively assessed relative expertise). The framework of analysis suggested here may, then, provide a baseline against which the effect of these other factors can be assessed.

Implications

Multi-Interaction Approach. The suggested model and the examples from the study indicate that there is no one "right" type of interaction that promotes cognitive change in one way, but rather many types that affect cognitive change in various positive and negative ways. This multi-interaction view has several implications for research. First, it is important to find out what kinds of interactions evolve in given cultures, contexts, and conditions. There may be cultural variations in patterns of interaction. In addition, in a given culture, the same individuals may develop different types of interactions in different situations and contexts and with different people. Second, in this multi-interaction view, an interesting question is not only which type of interaction best induces cognitive change, but also how prevalent is that type of interaction in a person's life. For example, scaffolding may prove very powerful in promoting cognitive change, but may be rare for children from certain socioeconomic backgrounds and family structures. Third, the interrelations among the different types of interactions and their cognitive implications is crucial. Cognitive change at a specific time is an end result of complementing or compensating effects of diverse interactions. (A similar phenomenon relates to developmental problems: These result from combination of various factors; see Kopp,

1983.) A child conserver, for example, may temporarily regress to nonconservation after interacting with a nonconserver adult (i.e., Kuhn, 1972). The temporary nature of this regression may reflect the child's other experiences and the continuous interactions the child has with other people. A multi-interaction approach, therefore, may better suit the complex issue of interactions and their cognitive effects.

Spontaneous Versus Constrained Interactions.   Many studies that explore interactions and the related cognitive change use a context that constrains the interactions. The experimenter often teams peers together for the experiment's sake (e.g., conserver and nonconserver), sets specific goals for the activity, or enforces collaboration by putting constraints (such as turn taking or imposed coordinated actions). When activities serve as units of analysis and interactions are the subject and the goal of the study, it seems improper to constrain these aspects of an experiment. The ensuing activity will necessarily be influenced by these constraints. Therefore, the results will reflect and often confirm what the researcher is looking for. However, when the participants choose their own goals, team up and interact spontaneously, the emerging types of interactions and their cognitive change may be richer, more diverse, and more complex.

This chapter suggests a model for analyzing interactions and their cognitive effects, while integrating various theories and without sacrificing the contingency of interactions on specifics of context, situation, culture, and so on. The model suggested in this chapter may contribute to compare results of different studies. The issue of interactions and their cognitive effects is intricate and complex, and includes several puzzling phenomena. Many questions still remain open: When does interaction among peers of some asymmetric expertise generate regression, resulting in adoption of less advanced knowledge structures (Forman, Cordle, Carr, & Gregorius, 1991; Tudge, 1985)? What is the effect of cultural practices on interactive patterns? What are the specifics of the mechanism of cognitive change through interaction? These questions, as many others, are subject to further research.

ACKNOWLEDGMENTS

I was most fortunate to get illuminating comments, advice, encouragement, and support from mentors, colleagues, and friends whom I admire and with whom I have pleasure to work. I want to give special thanks to Kurt Fischer, Howard Gardner, Edith Ackermann, Seymour Papert, Aaron Falbel, and Mindy Korenhaber. Many thanks also to Ellice Forman, Addison Stone, Joe Becker, and Robert Wozniak for their comments that stimulated further thinking. To my family and friends, and above all to Daniel, for their encouragement and comments, I am most grateful. The research reported here was supported by the The National Science Foundation (Grant # 8850449-TPE) and the LEGO Systems A/S. Earlier versions of the model were presented at the 21st Symposium of the Jean Piaget Society, 1991, and at the annual meeting of the American Educational Research Association, 1991.

REFERENCES

Bandura, A. (1977). *Social learning theory*. Englewood Cliff, NJ: Prentice-Hall.

Bandura, A. (1986). *Social foundations of thought and action: A social cognitive theory*. Englewood Cliffs, NJ: Prentice-Hall.

Bronfenbrenner, U. (1979). *The ecology of human development: experiments by nature and design*. Cambridge, MA: Harvard University Press.

Brown, A. L., & Reeve, R. A. (1987). Bandwidths of competence: The role of supportive contexts in learning and development. In L. S. Liben (Ed.), *Development and learning: Conflict or congruence?* (pp. 173–223). Hillsdale, NJ: Lawrence Erlbaum Associates.

Brown, J. S., Collins, A., & Duguid, P. (1989). Situated cognition and the culture of learning. *Educational Researcher, 18*(1), 32–42.

Cole, M. (1985). The zone of proximal development: where culture and cognition create each other. In J. V. Wertsch (Ed.), *Culture, communication and cognition: Vygotskian perspectives* (pp. 146–161). Cambridge: Cambridge University Press.

Damon, W. (1984). Peer education: The untapped potential. *Journal of Applied Developmental Psychology, 5*, 331–343.

Doise, W., & Mugny, G. (1984). *The social development of the intellect*. Oxford: Pergamon Press.

Doise, W., & Palmonari, A. (Eds.). (1984). *Social interaction in individual development*. Cambridge: Cambridge University Press.

Ellis, S., & Rogoff, B. (1982). The strategies and efficacy of child versus adult teachers. *Child Development, 53*, 730–735.

Forman, E. A. (1987). Learning through peer instruction: A Vygotskian perspective. *The Genetic Epistemologist, XV*(2), 6–15.

Forman, E. A., & Cazden, C. B. (1985). Exploring Vygotskian perspectives in education: The cognitive value of peer interaction. In J. V. Wertsch (Ed.), *Culture, communication and cognition: Vygotskian perspective* (pp. 323–347). Cambridge: Cambridge University Press.

Forman, E. A., Cordle, J., Carr, N., & Gregorius, T. (1991). *Expertise and the co-construction of meaning in collaborative problem solving*. Paper presented at the 21st annual symposium of the Jean Piaget Society, Philadelphia.

Glick, J. (1985). Culture and cognition revisited. In E. D. Neimark, R. De Lisi, & J. L. Newman (Eds.), *Moderators of competence* (pp. 99–115). Hillsdale, NJ: Lawrence Erlbaum Associates.

Goodnow, J. J. (1990). The socialization of cognition: What's involved? In J. W. Stigler, R. A. Shweder, & G. Herdt (Eds.), *Cultural psychology: Essays on comparative human development* (pp. 259–286). Cambridge: Cambridge University Press.

Granott, N. (1991a). *From macro to micro and back: On the analysis of microdevelopment*. Paper presented at the 21st annual symposium of the Jean Piaget Society, Philadelphia.

Granott, N. (1991b). Puzzled minds and weird creatures: Phases in the spontaneous process of knowledge construction. In I. Harel & S. Papert (Eds.), *Constructionism*. Norwood, NJ: Ablex.

Hess, R. D., & Shipman, V. C. (1965). Early experience and the socialization of cognitive modes in children. *Child Development, 36*, 869–886.

Kopp, C. B. (1983). Risk factors in development. In P. H. Mussen (Ed.), *Infancy and developmental psychobiology, Vol. 2: Handbook of child development* (pp. 1081–1188). New York: Wiley.

Kuhn, D. (1972). Mechanism of change in the development of cognitive structures. *Child Development, 43,* 833–844.

Laboratory of Comparative Human Cognition (1983). Culture and cognitive development. In P. H. Mussen (Series Ed.) & W. Kessen (Vol. Ed.), *Handbook of child psychology: Vol. 1. History, theory, and methods* (pp. 295–356). New York: Wiley.

Leont'ev, A. N. (1981). The problem of activity in psychology. In J. V. Wertsch (Ed.), *The concept of activity in Soviet psychology* (pp. 37–71). Armonk, NY: Sharpe.

Lerner, R. M., & Kaufman, M. B. (1985). The context of development in contextualism. *Developmental Review, 5,* 309–333.

Luria, A. R. (1976). *Cognitive development: Its cultural and social foundations.* Cambridge, MA: Harvard University Press.

Mugny, G., & Doise, W. (1978). Socio-cognitive conflict and structure of individual and collective performances. *European Journal of Social Psychology, 8*(8), 181–192.

Murray, F. B. (1972). Acquisition of conservation through social interaction. *Developmental Psychology, 6*(1), 1–6.

Murray, F. B. (1983). Learning and development through social interaction and conflict: A challenge to social learning theory. In L. S. Liben (Ed.), *Piaget and the foundations of knowledge* (pp. 231–247). Hillsdale, NJ: Lawrence Erlbaum Associates.

Newman, D., Griffin, P., & Cole, M. (1984). Social constraints in laboratory and classroom tasks. In B. Rogoff & J. Lave (Eds.), *Everyday cognition: Its development in social context* (pp. 172–193). Cambridge, MA: Harvard University Press.

Newman, D., Griffin, P., & Cole, M. (1989). *The construction zone: Working for cognitive change in school.* Cambridge: Cambridge University Press.

Niesser, U. (1985). Toward an ecologically oriented cognitive science. In T. M. Shlechter & M. P. Toglia (Eds.), *New directions in cognitive science* (pp. 17–32). Norwood, NJ: Ablex.

Nisbett, R. E., & Wilson, T. D. (1977). Telling more than we can know: Verbal reports on mental processes. *Psychological Review, 84*(3), 231–258.

Perret-Clermont, A.-N. (1980). *Social interaction and cognitive development in children.* London: Academic Press.

Piaget, J. (1926). *The language and thought of the child.* New York: Harcourt, Brace.

Piaget, J. (1965). *The moral judgment of the child.* New York: The Free Press.

Radziszewska, B., & Rogoff, B. (1988). Influence of adult and peer collaborators on children's planning skills. *Developmental Psychology, 24*(6), 840–848.

Resnick, L. B. (1987). Learning in school and out. *Educational Researcher, 16*(9), 13–20.

Rogoff, B. (1982). Integrating context and cognitive development. In M. E. Lamb & A. L. Brown (Eds.), *Advances in developmental psychology* (Vol. 2, pp. 125–170). Hillsdale, NJ: Lawrence Erlbaum Associates.

Rogoff, B. (1990). *Apprenticeship in thinking: Cognitive development in social context.* New York: Oxford University Press.

Rogoff, B., & Lave, J. (Eds.). (1984). *Everyday cognition: Its development in social context.* Cambridge, MA: Harvard University Press.

Rogoff, B., Malkin, C., & Gilbride, K. (1984). Interaction with babies as guidance in development. In B. Rogoff & J. V. Wertsch (Eds.), *Children's learning in the "zone of proximal development." New directions for child development* (No. 23, pp. 31–44). San Francisco: Jossey-Bass.

Saxe, G. B., Guberman, S. R., & Gearhart, M. (1987). Social Processes in early number development. *Monographs of the Society for Research in Child Development, 52* (2, Serial No. 216).

Scribner, S. (1984). Studying working intelligence. In B. Rogoff & J. Lave (Eds.), *Everyday cognition: Its development in social context* (pp. 9–40). Cambridge, MA: Harvard University Press.

Scribner, S. (1986). Thinking in action: Some characteristics of practical thought. In R. J. Sternberg & R. K. Wagner (Eds.), *Practical intelligence: Nature and origins of competence in the everyday world* (pp. 13–30). Cambridge: Cambridge University Press.

Scribner, S., & Cole, M. (1981). *The psychology of literacy.* Cambridge: Harvard University Press.

Shweder, R. A. (1990). Culture psychology—What is it? In J. W. Stigler, R. A. Shweder, & G. Herdt (Eds.), *Cultural psychology: Essays on comparative human development* (pp. 1–43). Cambridge: Cambridge University Press.

Tudge, J. (1985). The effect of social interaction on cognitive development: How creative is conflict? *The Quarterly Newsletter of The Laboratory of Comparative Human Cognition, 7*(2), 33–40.

Tudge, J., & Rogoff, B. (1989). Peer influences on cognitive development: Piagetian and Vygotskian perspectives. In M. H. Bornstein & J. S. Bruner (Eds.), *Interaction in human development* (pp. 17–40). Hillsdale, NJ: Lawrence Erlbaum Associates.

Tudge, J., & Winterhoff, P. (1991). *Vygotsky, Piaget, and Bandura: Perspectives on the relationship between social interaction and cognitive development, with special reference to peers.* Paper presented at the annual meeting of the American Educational Research Association, Chicago.

Valsiner, J. (1984). Construction of the zone of proximal development in adult–child joint action: The socialization of meals. In B. Rogoff & J. V. Wertsch (Eds.), *Children's learning in the "zone of proximal development." New directions for child development* (No. 23, pp. 65–76). San Francisco: Jossey-Bass.

Vygotsky, L. S. (1962). *Thought and language.* Cambridge, MA: MIT Press.

Vygotsky, L. S. (1978). *Mind in society: The development of higher psychological processes.* Cambridge, MA: Harvard University Press.

Wertsch, J. V. (1979). From social interaction to higher psychological processes: A clarification and application of Vygotsky's theory. *Human Development, 22,* 1–22.

Wertsch, J. V. (1984). The zone of proximal development: Some conceptual issues. In B. Rogoff & J. V. Wertsch (Eds.), *Children's learning in the zone of proximal development. New Directions for child development* (No. 23, pp. 7–18). San Francisco: Jossey-Bass.

Wertsch, J. V. (1985). *Vygotsky and the social formation of mind.* Cambridge, MA: Harvard University Press.

Wertsch, J. V., Minick, N., & Arns, F. J. (1984). The creation of context in joint problem solving. In B. Rogoff & J. Lave (Eds.), *Everyday cognition: Its development in social context* (pp. 151–171). Cambridge, MA: Harvard University Press.

Wood, D., Bruner, J., & Ross, G. (1976). The role of tutoring in problem solving. *Journal of Child Psychology and Psychiatry, 17,* 89–100.

III SOCIAL SYSTEMS AS SPECIFIC CONTEXTS FOR DEVELOPMENT

8 Socialization of Cognition: The Distancing Model

Irving E. Sigel
Elizabeth T. Stinson
Myung-In Kim
Educational Testing Service

This chapter presents a portion of a larger research program designed to investigate the influential role parents play in the development of representational competence in their children. After describing our working model and defining the concepts guiding our research effort, we present some of the findings and then discuss their implications in terms of developmental theory and further research.

Our approach is based on the proposition that representational competence in particular, and cognition, in general, are products of social experiences that generate within the family. Parents as primary socialization agents serve as educators for their children, employing socialization techniques that provide children with introductory experiences into the social, cultural, and physical world. In this manner, children come to know the cognitive, linguistic, and social requirements for functioning in a particular milieu. Moreover, parental actions are embedded in a familial context that includes siblings and extended family members. From this perspective, the family serves as a microcosm of the larger social world in which individuals of different ages and genders interact. However, for our purpose here, we address the family unit of mother, father, and target child, only.

Parents are sources of primary knowledge about how to behave in this complex environment. The early learning engendered in the ecosystem of the family may well define how the child will eventually proceed to engage socially with other adults and children in extrafamilial environments. Much of the learning acquired by children is indirect and covert. However, the class of socialization behaviors that communicates parental wishes, desires, goals, and notions of right and wrong to the child is characterized by actions we can readily observe and identify as *teaching* strategies. It is the effect of this class of interactive behaviors that is the focus of this chapter.

Defining the role of parents as teachers is consistent with the view that parents socialize their children's orientation to the culture and to the various social categories embedded in that social system. The socialization function thus incorporates the acquisition and use of knowledge, ways of representing that knowledge and ways of thinking and reasoning with that knowledge (Luria, 1976). This concept of the socialization of cognition as a developmental process originating within the familial context is foundational to our research program.

To be sure, some attention over the years has been given to parental influence on children's intellectual and academic achievement. Yet, much of this research has tended to focus on the various roles of parenting styles (Baumrind, 1971), beliefs (McGillicuddy-DeLisi, 1982a, 1982b, 1985), and academic expectations or attributions (Dix & Grusec, 1985; Holloway & Hess, 1985) in relation to the child's cognitive–social functioning. The missing link in most socialization studies is the quantity and quality of the discourse between parents and children as critical sources of influence.

Studies examining the role of language in the home have been concerned primarily with the effects of the child's linguistic experiences relative to language development rather than thinking and reasoning. Our model, on the other hand, is based on the premise that what the parent does, or says, and how and when the parent acts, are the events that merit attention. We presume that parental behaviors are expressions of underlying attitudes, values, and beliefs. However, it is the parents' actions that are directly communicated and evident to the child. This is not to say that parents' attitudes, values, and beliefs about children are irrelevant. Rather, we view these covert cognitive dimensions as indirect sources of influence on the child (see Sigel, 1985).

Emphasis on the function of the parent as teacher is relatively new among developmentalists, so many gaps in our knowledge still exist. The research reported here demonstrates that parental socialization strategies do, in fact, have a significant influence on children's intellectual functioning as defined by representational competence.

REPRESENTATIONAL COMPETENCE

Representation is a cognitive function. *Cognition* is a broad domain encompassing many processes such as memory, reasoning, judgment, or thinking. The set of cognitive functions central to the model being developed here is referred to as *representational competence,* herein defined as the ability to understand the meanings of signs and symbols and transform experiential events into mental events. Representational competence is essentially determined by the individuals' understanding of the *representational rule* (i.e., that any event, object, or person can be represented in some sign or symbolic form and still retain its original meaning). A three-dimensional object (e.g., a car) retains its identity whether represented by a word or a picture. Although the picture and the three-dimensional object clearly differ, they share a common meaning. Understanding that this is the case reflects a knowledge of the representational rule that forms the basis for representational competence.

The question is: What is the developmental course of representational competence? Or, to put it another way: How does understanding of the representational rule come about? Arguing that such competence evolves in the course of socialization, it follows that the search for understanding begins with the family. We maintain that representational competence develops, in part, as a consequence of the kinds of discourse parents have with their children in everyday interactions.

Parents engage their children through discourse (i.e., by talking to them). Parent–child discourse provides a source of intellectual stimulation as it places demands on the child to think, reason, and understand. The use of language includes referents to different temporal relations, to objects seen and unseen, and to symbols representing different objects and events. How the parent constructs a linguistic environment and creates discourse opportunities for engaging the child plays a pivotal role in the child's acquisition of the representational rule. Discerning the process of parent–child engagement is central to our conceptual model because acquisition of the competence under study can only emerge in a social context.

The four basic developmental concepts that form the cornerstones of this relational model are: *distancing, discrepancy, dialectics,* and *representation.* We view these interdependent components as contributory factors in the evolution of representational competence. The nature of their interaction is described in the following sequence: A distancing behavior instigates a discrepancy which, in turn, triggers the dialectical interaction presumed to contribute to cognitive restructuring and developmental change.

Let us turn now to a detailed description of these components and how they function as aspects of an overall cognitive system.

DEFINITION OF BASIC CONCEPTS

Distancing Strategies.   Distancing behaviors are conceptualized as a class of exogenous events personal and nonpersonal that function as communication strategies when employed by individuals in an interactive situation. In our case, parents' use of distancing strategies constitutes cognitive demands that encourage the child's own thought processes. Moreover, the cognitive demands set the stage for a potential dialogue between parents and children in which discrepancies may be generated.

Distancing strategies function to create temporal and/or spatial, and/or psychological distance between self and object. Thus, the distancing construct may be viewed as a spatial metaphor representing the mental separation of the self from the ongoing present.

As illustrated in Table 8.1, distancing strategies vary in level, from those making minimal demands for the child to separate self from the ongoing present and involving minimal representation, to high-level demands to mentally extend beyond the information given, to make inferences, and use propositional and hypothetical thinking. Because distancing strategies are essentially verbal, they contain characteristics common to all such communication (e.g., form, content [meaning], and syntactical structure). In our categorization system, distancing strategies are delineated in terms of their mental operational demands (i.e., what does the message in the utterance ask of the subject?). For example, a strategy might ask the child to make inferences, or describe an object, or recount an experience. Incorporated within the distancing strategy is the message to engage and the level at which engagement is expected to occur.

The argument is that the cognitive demands made by these distancing strategies provide the child with the experience of engaging in particular mental processes such as drawing inferences, describing, and reconstructing events. These encounters provide the child with the opportunity to employ

TABLE 8.1
Types of Distancing Strategies Categorized by Levels

High-Level Distancing	Medium-Level Distancing	Low-Level Distancing
Evaluate consequence	Sequence	Label
Evaluate competence	Reproduce	Produce information
Evaluate affect	Describe similarities	Describe, define
Evaluate effort and/or performance	Describe differences	Describe – interpretation
Evaluate necessary and/or sufficient	Infer similarities	Demonstrate
Infer cause–effect	Infer differences	Observe
Infer affect	Symmetrical classifying	
Generalize	Asymmetrical classifying	
Transform	Enumerating	
Plan	Synthesizing within classifying	
Confirmation of a plan		
Conclude		
Propose alternatives		
Resolve conflict		

these mental processes in a meaningful and relevant context, thereby enabling the child to construct and use representations. Experiencing opportunities to generate representations combined with parental acceptance of the child's efforts are presumed to pave the way for the development of representational competence. However, one critical factor influencing the developmental course of representational competence is the level of distancing strategies that parents employ and the way parents follow through on the child's responses to distancing strategies.

A second important feature of the dialogue relates to the form (e.g., statement, question, or imperative) of the distancing strategy that may well be a key element of influence. For instance, distancing strategies in the form of a question, such as, *"What other way might you do this?"* place a demand on the child to separate self from the ongoing present and to seek options. Thus, the child engaging in option-seeking is activating representational mentation. In contrast, a statement such as, *"You may solve the problem in one of two ways"* does not provide the same demand quality or impetus for the child to generate her or his own options.

Discrepancy.   The second critical construct in our model is discrepancy. A discrepancy is created by distancing strategies, particularly in the form of open-ended inquiries. Discrepancy arises when there is a mismatch or a conflict between internal and external states occurring at one of three levels: "(1) *a mismatch between an internal event and an external event, . . . (2) a mismatch between two internal events . . . and (3) a mismatch between two external events . . ."* (Sigel & Cocking, 1977, p. 216). These mismatches reflect situations in which the person comes into conflict with the ongoing state of events and resolution requires modifying one's behavior. Discrepancies propel the individual to change because of an inherent discomfort with discrepancies. Distancing strategies serve to induce discrepancies because they "function as *instigators, activators,* and *organizers* of mental operations" (Sigel & Cocking, 1977, p. 213). The only way a child can respond to the mental demands is to be actively engaged, complying with the demands of the message in the strategy.

Dialectic.   As can be surmised from the description of parent–child interactions discussed in the context of distancing and discrepancy, there is the implication of a dialectic. Dialectical laws cover most of the conditions relevant to thinking and reasoning and are pertinent to our discussion here. First, there is the law of unity and opposites that holds that concurrent, mutually exclusive categories presuppose one another (i.e., there cannot be dark without light; Sigel & Cocking, 1977). The second law of dialectics relates to transition stages of cognitive growth during which quantitative changes of sufficient magnitude bring about sudden changes in quality (i.e., objects take on new identities with new characteristics). Finally, there is the law of the negation of the negation (Wozniak, 1975), wherein the old is continually replaced by the new. "All forms have within themselves the seeds of their own destruction; they will be assimilated in the new, and the new will be the old" (Sigel & Cocking, 1977, p. 219).

A parent–child dialogue, activated by distancing strategies, provides the conditions for emergence of discrepancies that may be perceived as contradictions by the child and generates opportunities for resolving them. As we see here, the use of a dialectical approach in a teaching situation can be a key impetus to cognitive reorganization and growth.

Cognitive Growth, Distancing Strategies, and Representational Competence

In summary, cognitive growth as conceptualized here refers to the organization and reorganization of mental structures as a response to distancing strategies. Strategies contribute differentially, however, to the process of mental reorganization. For example, if parents tend to ask open-ended questions, then follow through on the response by establishing a dialogue and furthering the discussion, the child will have more opportunities to be actively engaged and more experiences with generating answers. Contrast this with a child who experiences closed-ended question with little opportunity to "think" or dialogue. That child would have less chance to reorganize his or her mental processing. To some researchers and educators, this process has been relegated to the category of skill development, but in our minds this reorganization is a functional set of changes that precede skill development.

Cognition describes a process of knowing and that which is known is a representation of experience. The experience takes many forms and involves many activities. These experiences are assimilated and constructed as schemes that are mentally represented figuratively and conceptually.[1] According to our model, activation of representational mentation is an outcome of distancing dialogues occurring in this context between parents and children.

As important as distancing, discrepancy, dialectic, and dialogue functions are individually, their significance lies in their unity. In fact, these are not functionally independent dimensions. Rather, they tend to occur simultaneously. For example, a distancing strategy that generates a discrepancy that, in turn, leads to a dialectical dialogue, creates an opportunity for cognitive growth. Although all three components are necessary, the power

---

[1]The various ways knowledge is represented are not elaborated in this discussion. The interested reader may find discussions of these questions in Piaget (1962).

of the components to influence cognitive reorganization will depend on (a) the level of cognitive demand made initially by the distancing strategy, (b) the intensity of the conflict generated by the discrepancy, and ultimately (c) the nature of the dialogue.

The distancing model provides a conceptualization of social interaction that we claim reflects the socialization of cognition. However, although the emphasis in this presentation is on the social aspects of cognitive organization, to flesh out the model, we include the biological and affective features implicated in the socialization process.

Biological and Affective Aspects of the Model. Let us be clear that this perspective accepts biological givens that define the cognitive capabilities of the human infant. The central nervous system as well as musculatures involved in learning and remembering are the givens with which every human infant is endowed. The quality of these biosystems will vary, as we know, as a function of genetic and nutritional factors, which, in their own right, may serve as inhibitors or facilitators of subsequent development. The various ways these systems serve the individual are not in the purview of the psychologist and therefore we must acknowledge that our research accounts for a limited source of the variance. It is incumbent at this time, however, to keep in mind that data from disciplines other than our own will have to be entered into the system at some point. Keep the room unrented for the entry of the biosystem, among others.

The biological factors involved in our socialization model are those that enable the child to process the engagement experience (i.e., to use and to understand the language employed, to retain the experience, and to be aware). These are the substrates that allow the child to comprehend what is going on. The child also reacts to these social engagements with feelings and emotions of varying intensity. It is assumed that all responses have some affective aspects that in their totality lead to attitudes and feelings toward self. Engaging in dialogue may well contribute to the child's sense of confidence because the responses are attended to by the adult and hence present an egalitarian-type interaction. Moreover, the parent who enters into a reasoned exchange of thoughts and ideas with the child reflects acceptance of the child's point of view and conveys the message that the child has something worthwhile to say. The distancing model that ostensibly focuses on the child's cognitive functioning, in reality, involves the total individual's cognitive, social, and affective experience.

MAJOR HYPOTHESES OF THE DISTANCING MODEL

The hypotheses guiding our efforts, then, are as follows: The more experience children have with high-level distancing strategies, the more likely they are to develop representational systems that promote competence in planning, anticipating, and recalling of experience. A corollary of this premise argues that exposure to distancing will facilitate the child's development beyond these early representational systems toward transformation of competencies to academic tasks such as mathematics and reading that require representational skills in notational contexts.

On the other hand, low-level distancing strategies that place minimal demands for the child to restructure his or her thinking and that implicitly indicate the authoritative perspective of the adult, do not encourage the child to become actively engaged in the interaction. Hence, we hypothesize that parents' use of low-level distancing strategies and parental structuring of the child's experience should relate negatively to representational competence.

PREVIOUS RESEARCH WITH THE MODEL

The results that are discussed in this chapter come from a comprehensive program of research investigating the distancing hypotheses just mentioned. Primarily, we present relevant findings from our recent 5-year follow-up study of a subsample of two-parent families who returned to Educational Testing Service to participate in our ongoing investigation begun in 1980. At that time, the children ranged in age from 3½ to 7½ years, while at follow-up, we were dealing with preadolescents averaging 11 years of age. However, before going into the recent study it would be useful to briefly describe our earlier work with the distancing model to help put the entire research program into focus. Over more than a 15-year period, three major projects were undertaken to test our distancing hypotheses using observations of parent–child teaching situations.

In our initial study, distancing theory was examined within the context of birth order and spacing among working-class and middle-class families (Sigel, McGillicuddy-DeLisi, & Johnson, 1980). Subsequent studies enrolled parents with children who were communication handicapped in order to focus on effects of atypical children on family communication patterns. Yet, each study employed a similar research strategy with similar outcome measures to evaluate children's representational competence whether we were looking at the influence of the parent on the child or the child on the parent (Sigel, McGillicuddy-DeLisi, Flaugher, & Rock, 1983).

To test for the long-term effects of parental distancing behaviors, we followed up a subset of the typical middle-class families we had seen 5 years previously. Participants included 40 families with a child who had been diagnosed as communication handicapped (CH) at the time of the earlier study and 40 families with a nonhandicapped child (NCH) of the same age, selected as matched controls.[2] For our purposes here, however, we primarily report the results for the nonhandicapped children in order to test the theory more precisely and to permit generalizations to normative populations.

In the early studies, parents' distancing strategies were assessed by observing them while they taught their children two tasks, a paper-folding Origami task (structured) and a story-reading task (unstructured). To permit comparisons across time, our later study was designed to use similar, but more age-appropriate tasks. A knot-tying task replaced paper folding and a verbal problem-solving task replaced the story. In all cases, each parent was instructed to help the child learn how to do the task. All parent–child interactions were approximately 10 minutes long; they were videotaped and subsequently coded for parents' distancing behaviors.

Although the codes were more elaborated than those mentioned in Table 8.1, the basic codes used in the current study were fundamentally the same as those used earlier in terms of their basic definitions. Differences in frequencies of coded parent behaviors observed at the two time points were attributed to expected developmental changes in family functioning as the maturing child assumed a more prominent role as an active, verbal participant in task resolution.

Child measures at the two time points were selected on the basis of their relation to representational competence. When children were between the ages of 3½ and 7½, their representational ability was assessed by tests of general mental ability and by a series of Piagetian tasks tapping memory, planning, and anticipatory imagery. At follow-up, 5 years later, academic indices of intellectual performance such as math and reading achievement were used as proxies for the representational competence measures employed in the earlier studies.

In summary, we found that the results of our continuing investigations of the distancing model in relation to representational competence tended to form a congruent pattern from study to study. The following statements briefly illustrate some of the relevant findings:

1. Parents' teaching behaviors were significantly associated with children's representational competence. The strongest set of relationships was the negative correlation between low-level distancing and structuring and virtually all of the cognitive outcomes. As predicted, low-level distancing strategies do seem to function as depressors of representational competence, at least as measured by anticipatory imagery, memory, seriation, and general mental ability.

---

[2]Families were matched on parents' education, income, gender of target child, and when possible, birth order of target child.

2. Parental teaching strategies of the didactic-controlling type were associated with low performance by all children on the cognitive assessment tasks, as predicted by the model. Authoritative teaching approaches are intrinsically definitive by nature, thereby permitting little opportunity for disagreement or dialogue between parent and child.

3. Parental teaching strategies varied as a function of the intellectual level and a pathogenic status of the child (i.e., parents' of a child with a communication handicap altered their strategies to match their child's intellectual level, indicating the influential role of the child's characteristics on parent–child interactions). Path analyses confirmed that the higher the child's IQ, the more likely the parent was to use high-level strategies; the reverse was true for lower IQ children (within normal range) in that the parents were more likely to use low-level didactic strategies.

4. Parents' distancing strategies tended to vary as a function of task. Moreover, fathers tended to differ from mothers in the types of strategies they used with these tasks. What this suggests is that generalizations about parent behavior must be constrained by the nature of the context in which parent–child interactions occur.

Influence of Family Structure on Representational Competence

In our initial study we looked at two-child and three-child families, equally divided by socioeconomic status (SES; e.g., working class and middle class). We examined the representational competence of children from each of these groups using discriminate function analyses and found that SES and the configuration of the family did make a significant difference in children's cognitive functioning. Additionally, parents' distancing strategies were differentially related to child outcomes for each group. Working-class children that were closely spaced performed better on cognitive tasks than children who were far-spaced, but middle-class children who were far-spaced performed better on cognitive tasks than near-spaced children from the same class group.

It appears that parental teaching strategies might make a greater difference to children's cognitive functioning in the middle-class group due to the fact that parents in this group may have more time to spend interacting with each child. Whereas, among working-class families, siblings who were close in age appeared to provide intellectual stimulation for each other (McGillicuddy & Sigel, 1991)

Long-Term Consequences of Distancing Behaviors

Even as these results inform us of the impact of parent behaviors on young children's representational competence at one point in time, new questions begin to emerge, such as: What, if any, are the long-term consequences of these early distancing interactions? When parents use distancing strategies with the older child, are the outcome effects similar or different from those observed earlier?

Our follow-up study with a subset of the original 1980 sample of families was designed to answer these questions. Of the 80 two-parent families who agreed to participate, 78 (40 NCH and 38 CH) returned to ETS to complete the second phase of the study.[3] Although the methodological format of this investigation was designed to be as similar as possible to our earlier effort, it was not a true replication because we had to alter the teaching tasks to make them age-appropriate. However, the task demands of each interaction (e.g., one structured and the other verbal) were comparable to those used earlier. For our dependent measures, we assessed children's achievement in mathematics and reading using standardized scores as proxies for representational competence. These academic areas embody the logical manifestation of representational skills acquired earlier because each of these knowledge domains requires comprehension and the use of representational systems (e.g., mathematic notations and words).

Looking at the NCH sample ($N = 40$) only, significant albeit modest relationships between mother's use of high-level distancing on the structured task (knot-tying) and children's achievement were obtained for mathematics ($r = .35$ p > .02)[4] but not for reading. Use of low-level distancing strategies by either parent generally tended to yield negative but nonsignificant achievement outcomes. Structuring of the task for the child by mothers also yielded negative correlations with achievement that just missed significance.

On the other hand, fathers' influence on child main achievement was apparent with the verbal problem-solving task as well as the structured task. (Knot-tying). Fathers' tendency to offer relatively low levels of information to the child during problem resolution was associated with significant decrements in the childs, over and above child IQ ($r = .29$ p > .04). A negative trend was also found between fathers' use of structuring on the knot-tying task and their children's mathematics achievement.

What was not anticipated, but intuitively reasonable, was the role of parental approval across time. For both fathers and mothers, parental approval of the young child's efforts on both learning tasks yielded strong positive relationships with academic outcomes as measured currently. In fact, these robust findings would seem to reflect the long-term effect of

---

[3]Due to the severity of two of the children's handicap condition, complete data could not be obtained on academic measures and the families were subsequently dropped from the study. For the CH group: $N = 38$ for all data analyses.

[4]Correlations reported were for one-tail tests of significance.

parents' positive support for children's task performance (Sigel, Stinson, & Flaugher, 1991).

Basically, the general hypotheses were supported. Parents' use of distancing strategies did have an effect on children's representational competence as demonstrated by the young child's proficiency with Piagetian tasks and the school-aged child's achievement in mathematics. However, contrary to our predictions, reading achievement was less associated with the use of distancing strategies and more highly related to parents' earlier expressions of approval while reading stories to their young children. What we are documenting here may be related to Vygotsky's developmental notion of internalization processes (Wertsch, 1985). Parental teaching strategies, such as joint book-reading, provide children with opportunities for adult–child dialogues that promote the child's own self-regulatory mechanisms (Pellegrini, Brody, & Sigel, 1985). Children learn to plan and guide their own behavior in the context of the dialectical interaction as they internalize the learning strategies and problem-solving approaches employed by parents. In terms of our own findings, it would seem that parents' expressions of approval (e.g., positive verbal feedback), while sharing a book-reading experience with their young children, may have facilitated the internalization processes underlying early linguistic competence and subsequent levels of reading achievement observed in these children 5 years later.

There also may be a "ceiling effect" operating with regard to parental influence on the child's acquisition of language skills that may explain our differential findings for math and reading achievement. Our results would indicate that parental use of distancing strategies with the older, school-aged child becomes particularly salient to enhanced math achievement, but bears little relationship to reading achievement. This may be due to the fact that the novel and complex representational demands inherent in mathematical competence require the ongoing intellectual activation that distancing strategies provide. The mechanisms underlying reading achievement, on the other hand, are presumably activated earlier in the course of the child's development when parental approval nurtures the young child's acquisition of linguistic competence.

CONCLUSIONS

The results reported here demonstrate that there is a relationship between parental distancing strategies and children's representational competence both in the short run and in the long run. However, the roles of fathers and mothers differ in terms of the direction and the strength of their influence on the growing child's representational competence. Differences in findings relative to parent–child interactions are also attributable to the nature of the learning task employed. These qualifications may either be considered as noise in the system or as evidence of constraints upon our knowledge regarding the role of the family in the development of the child.

These results, microgenic as they are, open the window to examination of the importance of discourse between parents and their children. Although many studies have focused on parent–child discourse, they have tended to assess outcomes within the context of language development, not in terms of children's intellectual achievement. Yet by inference, it is often said that the way in which parents actually engage their children in dialoguing influences their intellectual development. Our current results provide some of the details that may furnish an explanation for individual differences in children's representational competence.

This is not to say there are not a number of conceptual and methodological issues remaining that merit investigation. For example, attention needs to be paid to the affective environment in which the particular strategies are employed. Also, the sequence of the interaction or the mechanisms by which parents and children maintain dialogues requires closer examination. These are but some of the issues remaining that we hope to address in future publications. Our results to date, however, encourage us to continue our investigation of the role of parental teaching strategies as influential factors in the development of children's representational competence.

> We proceed and cautiously define areas that appear to have conceptual quasi-independence which can be treated as a subsystem of the whole. Ultimately the hope is that — as the research continues — the subsystem can be embedded into a larger system. It is with this perspective that we conceptualized the family as a *learning environment,* where the roles of the parent are those of teacher and provider of human (e.g., affection) and material resources. (Sigel, 1982, p. 48)

ACKNOWLEDGMENT

Part of the research reported in this chapter was supported by the National Institute of Child Health and Human Development Grant No. R01-HD10686 to Educational Testing Service, National Institute of Mental Health Grant No. R01-MH32301 to Educational Testing Service, and Bureau of Education of the Handicapped Grant No. G007902000 to Educational Testing Service.

REFERENCES

Baumrind, D. (1971). Current patterns of parental authority. *Developmental Psychology Monographs, 4,* 1–103.

Dix, T. H., & Grusec, J. E. (1985). Parent attribution processes in the socialization of children. In I. E. Sigel (Ed.), *Parental belief systems: The psychological consequences for children* (pp. 201–233). Hillsdale, NJ: Lawrence Erlbaum Associates.

Holloway, S. D., & Hess, R. D. (1985). Mothers' and teachers' attributions about children's mathematics performance. In I. E. Sigel (Ed.), *Parental belief systems: The psychological consequences for children* (pp. 177–199). Hillsdale, NJ: Lawrence Erlbaum Associates.

Luria, A. R. (1976). *Cognitive development: Its cultural and social foundations.* Cambridge, MA: Harvard University Press.

McGillicuddy-DeLisi, A. V. (1982a). Parental beliefs about developmental processes. *Human Development, 25,* 192–200.

McGillicuddy-DeLisi, A. V. (1982b). The relationship between parents' beliefs about development and family constellation, socioeconomic status, and parents' teaching strategies. In L. M. Laosa & I. E. Sigel (Eds.), *Families as learning environments for children* (pp. 261–299). New York: Plenum.

McGillicuddy-DeLisi (1985). The relationship between parental beliefs and children's cognitive level. In I. E. Sigel (Ed.), *Parental belief systems: The psychological consequences for children* (pp. 7–24). Hillsdale, NJ: Lawrence Erlbaum Associates.

McGillicuddy-DeLisi, A. V., & Sigel, I. E. (1991). Family environments and children's representational thinking. In S. Silvern (Ed.), *Advances in reading/language research: Vol. 5. Literacy through family, community and school interaction* (pp. 63–90). Greenwich, CT: JAI Press.

Pellegrini, A. D., Brody, G. H., & Sigel, I. E. (1985). Parents' book-reading habits with their children. *Journal of Educational Psychology, 7*(3), 332–340.

Piaget, J. (1962). *Play, dreams and imitation in childhood.* New York: Norton.

Sigel, I. E. (1982). The relationship between parents' distancing strategies and the child's cognitive behavior. In L. M. Laosa & I. E. Sigel (Eds.), *Families as learning environments for children* (pp. 47–86). New York: Plenum.

Sigel, I. E. (1985). A conceptual analysis of beliefs. In I. E. Sigel (Ed.), *Parental belief systems: The psychological consequences for children* (pp. 345–371). Hillsdale, NJ: Lawrence Erlbaum Associates.

Sigel, I. E., & Cocking, R. R. (1977). Cognition and communication: A dialectic paradigm for development. In M. Lewis & L. A. Rosenblum (Eds.), *The origins of behavior: Vol. 5. Interaction, conversation, and the development of language* (pp. 207–226). New York: Wiley.

Sigel, I. E., McGillicuddy-DeLisi, A. V., Flaugher, J., & Rock, D. A. (1983). *Parents as teachers of their own learning disabled children* (ETS RR 83–21). Princeton, NJ: Educational Testing Service.

Sigel, I. E., McGillicuddy-DeLisi, A. V., & Johnson, J. E. (1980). *Parental distancing, beliefs and children's representational competence within the family context* (ETS RR 80–21). Princeton, NJ: Educational Testing Service.

Sigel, I. E., Stinson, E. T., & Flaugher, J. (1991). Socialization of representational competence in the family: The distancing paradigm. In L. Okagaki & R. J. Sternberg (Eds.), *Directors of development: Influences on the development of children's thinking* (pp. 121–144). Hillsdale, NJ: Lawrence Erlbaum Associates.

Wertsch, J. V. (1985). *Vygotsky and the social formation of mind.* Cambridge, MA: Harvard University Press.

Wozniak, R. H. (1975). Dialecticism and structuralism in Soviet philosophy and psychology. In K. F. Riegel & G. C. Rosewald (Eds.), *Structure and transformation: Developmental and historical aspects.* New York: Wiley.

9

Cultural Organisms in the Development of Great Potential: Referees, Termites, and the Aspen Music Festival

David Henry Feldman
Tufts University

This chapter presents some relatively recent efforts to reflect on my own and others' efforts to conceptualize environments as they affect and are affected by the development of extreme talent in individuals. In doing so I have had something of a *crystallizing experience,* to use a term I dreamed up almost 20 years ago (although it has also become associated with my colleague Howard Gardner in the interim; cf. Walters & Gardner, 1986). I have found that the need to say something about how specific environments or environmental processes affect development of exceptional potential has provided a set of conditions for me to refine a view of environments that has been more or less there for the better part of two decades, but that has become somewhat more explicit as a consequence of the current exercise.

My burden in this chapter is to say as clearly as I can what I have learned from studying extreme cases of talent development (particularly prodigies) that might shed light on how environmental influences release, shape and refine great potential.

I begin with an idiosyncratic review of what some others have said about how to conceptualize environments, move to my own previous (if unsystematic) efforts to do so, and then try to describe certain phenomena that might be of use in extending our understanding of how environment and individual interact over extended periods of time toward the realization of great potential (cf. Gruber, 1982; Wallace & Gruber, 1989).

ENVIRONMENTS CONCEPTUALIZED

As early as 1970 or so I was aware of attempts to make sense of environments in more interesting ways than as sources of reinforcement

225

histories or contingency relationships. In particular, I knew about Urie Bronfenbrenner's (1974) efforts to conceive of ecological issues in child development, to argue for the value of analyzing environments in terms of system, pattern, and organization. Although these efforts made sense to me, they unfortunately did not make much impact, as I was still very much tied up with the individual notion of development a la Piaget.

I knew a bit about work on classroom environments being done at Stanford by Rudolf Moos and others, and appreciated the value of this approach in the work of my Yale colleague, Ed Trickett. But this work was about community psychology and making a difference in the lives of students being pulverized by schooling, a much more practical goal than anything I was working on at the time. Trickett's mentor, Moos, had done some nice conceptual work in describing dimensions of environments (Moos, 1973) and I could see how this kind of analysis could be of real value, but again, no sale.

What was preoccupying me in those days (and still) were issues of qualitative shifts in reasoning, in particular questions of how one moves through the levels of developmental domains, particularly domains of the sort I have come to call *nonuniversal* (Feldman, 1980, in press). Probably the most potent influence on my thinking at the time were several developmentalists whose ideas continue to hold important places in my mental landscape. First were Jerome Bruner and David Olson (Bruner & Olson, 1974), whose work on cultural "prosthetics" stunned me into realizing that everything does not necessarily spring from the inside, spontaneously and purely, as a diehard Piagetian would tend to believe. Their 1966 book (Bruner, Olver, & Greenfield, 1966), which reported work done in other cultures, was especially moving. Bruner laid out the theoretical and conceptual basis for arguing that pedagogy, prosthetics, and culturally evolved forms of assisting the young to learn were powerful ingredients of development, a lesson I eventually learned.

Somewhere along the way, Vygotsky's (1962) *Thought and Language* was put under my nose, I expect by Joe Glick, who taught me a great deal of what I know while we walked together through Minnesota winters on the way to work in 1969 and 1970. Although I apparently repressed the powerful influence Vygotsky had on me for several years, as readers of *Beyond Universals in Cognitive Development* (Feldman, 1980) know all too well, the striking resonance between my own formulations and those of Vygotsky are ever more apparent to me. Knowing now that Bruner was himself greatly influenced by Vygotsky makes it only more apparent that I was on a collision course with environment long before I was aware of it.

The distinction between "spontaneous" and "scientific" concepts in chapter 6 of *Thought and Language* (Vygotsky, 1962) bears (unfortunately mute) testimony to its place in my own central theoretical distinction between "universal" and "nonuniversal" developmental domains. It is one of my deepest regrets and embarrassments that Vygotsky's insights did not receive proper credit in the more widely read version of universal to unique (Feldman, 1980; although see Feldman, in press). In the achievement of all nonuniversal, nonspontaneous advances in understanding, active, systematic, and sustained intentional efforts on the part of those who would teach the child are absolutely necessary. Although I tried to be more detailed than Vygotsky had been in my presentation of environment in the earliest published version of "universal to unique," (Feldman, 1974), my notion of crystallizing conditions in that work was, to put it mildly, sketchy.

I suppose I should also point out that by this time (the early 1970s) I was becoming increasingly uneasy with the relatively minor role environment plays in Piaget's theory. Having read Beilin's critique of Piaget (Beilin, 1971), which claimed Piaget was more of a maturationist than he admitted, and having read Kessen's (1962), Bruner's (Bruner & Olson, 1974), and Flavell's (1971) general critiques of stage theories, I was impressed with the need to articulate a position that included systematic roles for agents of the culture in cognitive development. Writing in 1971, Flavell put it in this way:

> Beilin argues that Piaget's view of cognitive development is actually more maturationistic and preformationistic than Piaget himself admits it to be. I believe that Beilin is correct in so arguing. . . . It is obvious, however, that consideration of environmental effects must continue to figure very prominently in any such genetically determined, maturationistic, conception of how development proceeds, if that view is to be taken seriously, and I would submit that there is at present no good theory about these environmental effects. (Flavell, in Mischel, 1971, pp. 121–122)

Recognizing how difficult a task it would be to specify how environment works in development, Flavell continued:

> I personally take as a major objective for our field the search for possible *universal* outcomes of human cognitive development . . . The point I am making is that the role of environment within a more maturationistically oriented view of development is subtle and hard to conceptualize, but its conceptualization is a necessary task. (p. 122)

This charge from such a powerful source had to be taken seriously.

The other work that most influenced my thinking during that period was the book by Cole, Gay, Glick, and Sharp (1971) *The Cultural Context of Learning and Thinking*. The importance of sensitivity to cultural context in assessing cognitive capabilities was driven home with full force in this elegant and compelling work in which The Kpelle of Liberia were found to be subtle and high-level thinkers, given an appropriate context for revealing their capabilities. Again, however, the message was that all individuals in all cultures can be expected to reach high levels of reasoning ability (i.e., the emphasis was on universals).

NONUNIVERSAL DEVELOPMENT: CRYSTALLIZING CONDITIONS

Given the consensus that a theory of cognitive development must include systematic accounts of how environment contributes to advances in reasoning and, given the preoccupation with universals in thought structures as the target of theory and research, I did the only honorable thing. I sidestepped the issue and turned my attention to other matters, and until very recently most of the rest of the field has sidestepped it as well.

John Flavell, William Kessen, Jerome Bruner, and Michael Cole, the people who might reasonably be expected to chart the way, headed for the high ground of the experimental laboratory, the computer network, the policy arena, or other safer places. There have of course been exceptions, including an ambitious recent effort by Frances Horowitz (1987) to integrate environment and maturation, behavioral and cognitive developmental frameworks, and universal and nonuniversal developmental changes. But remarkably little progress in conceptualizing context in cognitive development has been made since the early to mid-1970s. Some promising recent work has now become available (cf. Rogoff, 1990, for a summary).

For my part, as the 1970s opened, there was a practical problem to be confronted. *Child Development* rejected the article I wrote based on my dissertation on map understanding, and I needed to find a way to get the work into print. So I somehow came up with the idea of a set of hypothetical conditions I called "crystallizers of cognitive structures" as an ex post facto rationale for the research I had done on stage and skill sequences in map drawing. The ruse worked, and the study was published (Feldman, 1971). But there was now this idea that I found myself intrigued by, the idea of "crystallizers of cognitive structures." What was a crystallizer and how did it work?

A crystallizer was originally conceptualized as an already existing part of the environment that played a critical catalytic role in the formation of new cognitive structures. It was a set of conditions that had been crafted to provide just the right kind of stimulation at the proper moment to precipitate a transition in cognitive development. In its earliest form, there was no distinction made between a crystallizer of universal structures and any other kind of crystallizer. Here is how I introduced the idea:

The rationale for the present study follows from the premise that there may be tasks which function as "crystallizers" in the development of cognitive structures; that is, tasks which are significantly related to cognitive development but which are also influenced in important ways by patterns and sequences of planned experience provided by the environment. It would follow that if such tasks exist, they would merit the attention of the educational researcher because of their possible long-range importance for later learning. (Feldman, 1971, p. 486)

When the map-drawing work was published in 1971, it had not occurred to me (yet) that map drawing might be seen as a *cultural* activity as much as a manifestation of the development of universal spatial reasoning capabilities in children, which was how Piaget and Inhelder (1956) viewed the task. It was in working with my student at Yale, Sam Snyder, that the importance of cultural knowledge became clear, or at least clearer.

I had seen maps as perhaps having qualities that gave them special status when universal spatial reasoning structures were ready to become transformed to more advanced developmental levels. If it could be demonstrated that such activities were at least in part teachable, it would indeed follow that they would merit the attention of educational researchers. Crystallizer tasks, as the argument went, would have the potential to significantly transfer to broader areas of capability than most other parts of the curriculum. A crystallizer would provide more "bang for the buck."

Although I never did follow this line of research very far, I did go so far as to think about two further sets of issues. I tried to imagine what other kinds of things might be nominated as crystallizing activities, and came up with a few possibilities like writing paragraphs and stories, playing and composing songs, or starting and running a small business (Feldman, 1981). I also extended the general formulation of crystallizers into realms of development beyond those of the typical universal sort; I did this in an essay on creativity published in 1974 in which I introduced the idea of "nonuniversal" developmental change (Feldman, 1974).

In that essay I proposed four sets of crystallizing conditions: universal, cultural, idiosyncratic, and creative. I tried to outline what kinds of environmental entities and experiences might fall under each of these broad rubrics. Re-reading the proposed crystallizers with hindsight is a humbling experience. Yet, what is clear from these early efforts is that I was trying to conceptualize environment in a systematic way that would relate to the conditions under which progressive changes in various knowledge domains might take place. More important was the tendency to divide environment into broad conceptual categories ranging from universal to unique, a tendency that persists into, and very likely beyond, the present effort.

I had in mind that stored in a culture's bag of tricks were a few preorganized and relatively readily available knowledge domains, ready to engage the energies of individuals prepared to acquire them. Rather than informally passed from elders to youngsters in culturewide activities, these more specialized opportunities are always present but not actively imparted, at least not actively imparted to all youngsters. Some domains, if introduced properly, even permit young children to comprehend the nature of their abilities and find life direction through them (the crystallizing experience of Walters & Gardner, 1986).

All cultures maintain domains of expertise in which early prodigious achievement occurs, although the domains vary from culture to culture. I thought that the study of such situations might reveal how talent is crystallized. The more extreme the talent under investigation, I reasoned, the clearer would be the processes through which that talent revealed itself and was developed (Feldman, 1979).

Sensing that the most promising place to learn about the interplay of specific environmental conditions and individual development might be with child prodigies, I embarked on a study of six prodigies that was to span more than a decade (Feldman, 1976, 1979, 1982, 1986/1991). I saw the main purpose of that work to tease apart the environmental influences, especially family and teachers, that went into the developing of the prodigy's natural talents.

I also believed that a vital set of crystallizing conditions resided in the body of knowledge that the prodigy was mastering, and that it was therefore necessary to understand something of the specific structure of the knowledge domain in which the child was active. Broader contextual matters such as the place of the domain in the value system of a society, current economic and institutional conditions, and so on, were also raised. Some of these conditions are now referred to as having to do with the "field" rather than the domain itself, following the important conceptual distinction made by my colleague Mihalyi Csikszentmihalyi (cf. Csikszentmihalyi, 1990; Csikszentmihalyi & Robinson, 1986).

CULTURAL ORGANISMS

It was not until I began work on this chapter that I started to conceptualize entities that organize domain and field into purposeful entities for the development of great potential. I focus on three sorts of environmental entities that were particularly crucial in the development of my own six subjects, especially the three who turned toward music. These are of course the "cultural organisms" referred to in my title. Before turning to the specific features of the cultural organisms that gave form to the talents of the prodigies, however, I acknowledge the conceptual debt I owe to Lewis Thomas (1974), the author of *The Lives of a Cell,* who has elegantly described qualities of the natural world that provide models for most of what I present; indeed, the label *cultural organism* is based on the title of one of his essays: "On Societies as Organisms." Much of what I describe here does indeed exist in one form or another in other parts of nature, among other organisms — much, but crucially, not all.

Perhaps because he is such a keen student of nature, Thomas in fact missed seeing the cultural organism that is most vital to my story, perhaps because what I observed were in some respects uniquely *human* forms of organization. As Vygotsky did before me, I see an adequate explanation of development, of both the humble and the more exalted sort, as requiring an appreciation of the distinct qualities that set human experience apart from the rest of the organic world (Vygotsky, 1934/1962, 1978).

Still, one cannot help but be impressed, even humbled, by the realization that creatures we typically think of as beneath us have evolved social organizations that rival our own. Consider what Thomas said about termite society:

> Two or three termites in a chamber will begin to pick up pellets and move them from place to place, but nothing comes of it; nothing is built. As more join in, they seem to reach a critical mass, a quorum, and the thinking begins. They place pellets atop pellets, then throw up columns and beautiful curving symmetrical arches, and the crystalline architecture of vaulted chambers is created. It is not known how they communicate with each other, how the chains of termites building one column know when to turn toward the crew on the adjacent column, or how, when the time comes, they manage the flawless joining of the arches. The stimuli that set them off at the outset, building collectively instead of shifting things about, may be pheremones released when they reach committee size. They react as if alarmed. They become agitated, excited, and then they begin working like artists. (Thomas, 1974, pp. 13–14)

Because the interpretation of what I observed in the development of prodigies is ex post facto, and because the data were not gathered with the current conceptualization in mind, what is reported are largely impressionistic, descriptive, and unsystematic observations, which are also of course based on only a small number of cases. These observations are buttressed to some degree by complimentary findings of other investigators of extreme cases, particularly those of Bloom (1985) and his associates. This said, I still find the descriptions in Thomas' work strikingly appropriate.

In an example that I discuss in more detail later, Thomas likened the system through which scientific knowledge is organized and cumulated into an overall body of knowledge to the social activity of termites, not the building of termite hills as in the previous quote, but in the accumulation of information. Thomas opined that one of the most significant social structures created by humans is an *information structure,* and we are as unconscious of these as the termites seem to be of their architecture.

The initial, more solitary aspects of scientific work Thomas likened to the aimless activity of the termite alone or in small groups. It is when there is effort to let others know what is going on that a larger and vastly more important part of the enterprise is engaged. For better or worse (Thomas seems only to think for better), referred journals are a vital part of this process. Thomas put it this way:

> Perhaps, however, we are linked in circuits for the storage, processing, and retrieval of information, since this appears to be the most basic and universal of all human enterprises. It may be our biological function to build a certain kind of Hill. We have access to all the information of the biosphere, arriving as elementary units in the stream of solar photons. When we have learned how these are rearranged against randomness, to make, say, springtails, quantum mechanics, and the late quartets, we may have a clearer notion of how to proceed. (Thomas, 1974, p. 15)

My own preoccupation for many years has been with what is suggested in the last part of this quote, the part about how things are rearranged into patterns of exquisite form from time to time. Although prodigies generally are not the ones who themselves rearrange things, they may reveal some of the processes that make such rearrangements possible.

Our concern is thus with the social conditions that make it *possible* for major new works to be done, the broader structures within which potential is harnessed and organized and directed toward greater mastery and expression. These are not the conditions that directly lead to the creation of a grand new citadel from which new vistas are glimpsed for the first time. They are rather the more humble entities that, in turn, make possible those rare ascents toward the heavens that mark human life as unique in the universe, a sort of base camp for scaling a mountain of our own creation.

As I think of them, cultural organisms are specialized social structures designed to carry out human intentions; in the current context their special purpose is to nurture and direct the expression of extreme talent. They evolve and change according to their utility (as contrasted with those of termites that are essentially stable). Such structures are designed to be stable enough to develop exceptional talent, a process that takes a decade at the very least, yet supple enough to allow for changes that seem better suited to the task (Bruner & Haste, 1987; Vygotsky, 1978).

A *cultural organism* is therefore defined in the present context as "a cooperative structure that is formed and reformed in order to enhance the possibilities for discovery, development, and optimal expression of human talents in various domains." They also serve as repositories of knowledge and wisdom about how to select, preserve, and enhance the qualities of the domain itself.

Cultural organisms are constructed with humanly crafted tools, techniques, technologies, symbol systems, traditions, rules, customs, and beliefs organized around a particular human purpose. That purpose may be more or less explicit, more or less conscious, more or less shared, more or less sanctioned by larger cultural organisms, more or less common, or more or less rare.

A nuclear family may be thought of as a relatively small cultural organism when it focuses its resources on the development of one or more of its members (Deakin, 1972). An extended family or a family with several generations of sustained activity focused on a specific domain might provide a somewhat larger vehicle for preserving, transmitting, and protecting a tradition of expertise in a particular field. The Zildjian family, for example, has been making the world's best percussion cymbals for several centuries. This use of family resources is a phenomenon we have called *transgenerational influences* and have explored them in the case of violinist Yehudi Menuhin and his family (Feldman & Goldsmith, 1986).

The question may be asked whether it adds anything to the discussion to propose yet another term for entities that are for the most part already known and appreciated for their functions and purposes. If there is value in doing so, it lies in directing attention to certain features of these entities that may not have been highlighted before. It also may serve the purpose of revealing commonalities and distinctions among human environments.

As Vygotsky emphasized in his cultural psychology, the central purpose of introducing the notion of cultural organisms is to try to highlight some of the uniquely human qualities that are reflected in them. This does not mean that the uncanniness of Thomas' descriptions of termite hills, ant nests, and beehives should not give us pause and remind us of our kinship with other living creatures. At the same time, however, no other living thing *sets out* to build a particular sort of social structure, then tinkers with that structure constantly, devises variations, and creates significant changes in the environments of others (including sometimes the termites) by virtue of this process.

As Karl Marx (cited in Vygotsky, 1978) wrote in *Capital:*

> The spider carries out operations reminiscent of a weaver and the boxes which bees build in the sky could disgrace the work of many architects. But even the worst architect differs from the most able bee from the very outset in that before he builds a box out of boards he has already constructed it in his head. At the end of the work process he obtains a result which already existed in his

mind before he began to build. The architect not only changes the form given
to him by nature, within the constraints imposed by nature, he also carries out
a purpose of his own which defines the means and the character of the activity
to which he must subordinate his will. (p. XIV)

And Friedrich Engels (cited in Vygotsky, 1978), in *Dialectics of Nature,*
wrote this about human activity: "It is precisely *the alteration of nature by
men,* not nature as such, which is the most essential and immediate basis of
human thought" (p. XIV).

It seems clear that Thomas, the inveterate biologist, ran wide of the mark
in drawing such a close parallel between human and nonhuman social
structures. Not seeing the distinct kinds of social structures that human
beings construct as essential either to survival or (and more to the point), to
the nature of human cultural life, he suggested that the cathedral at
Chartres, computers and lasers, synthetic proteins, and the like, do not hold
the keys to human survival and well being.

In Thomas' view, it is *language,* only language, that ties human beings
together, because language is inherited into the genes of all of us in a
biologically programmed language acquisition device (Thomas, 1974, pp.
104–106). In those examples where Marx and Engels and Vygotsky (and
humanistic psychology too) have endeavored to make their case, Thomas
found ephemeral, fleeting, by-products of human wanderlust and tinkering,
however beautiful the result. The argument is not that the great cathedral
does not possess surpassing beauty (as does the termite hill); it is that its
importance in the sense of biological survival is minimal.

And yet, a few pages later in *The Lives of a Cell,* Thomas (1974)
recognized that there is something quite unique about human language, and
this is its ability to entertain *ambiguity* and deviate from the precise point.
"The great thing about human language," he wrote, "is that it prevents us
from sticking to the matter at hand" (pp. 111–112). Without this quality, he
said, it is "unlikely that we would have been able to evolve from words to
Bach." And it is precisely the possibility of evolving from "words to Bach"
that is at issue. Thomas seemed to sense this, but not to know what to do
with it. He nonetheless wrote with real feeling about the majesty of human
creativity, such as in the following passage:

> The real surprises, which set us back on our heels when they occur, will always
> be the mutants . . . They have slightly different receptors for the information
> cascading from other minds, and slightly different machinery for processing
> it, so that what comes out to rejoin the flow is novel, and filled with new sorts
> of meaning . . . In this sense, the Art of the Fugue and the St. Matthew
> Passion were, for the evolving organism of human thought, feathered wings,
> apposing thumbs, new layers of frontal cortex. (1974, pp. 168–169)

Somehow, appreciating the significance of great works of creativity as major shifts in the evolution of thought is not enough to get Thomas to connect his earlier ideas about social insect behavior with his later thoughts about language and invention.

This is the connection that underlies my interest in cultural organisms, because what is at issue is precisely the relationship of social behavior of the sort that I am at pains to describe with the prodigies and creativity of the sort that Thomas saw as marking major turning points in the evolution of thought. I believe that cultural entities such as particular kinds of family structures, structures for preparing and nurturing neophytes in various fields, technologies for storing and transmitting information, and larger entities are (perhaps unconsciously) designed to set conditions that will increase the likelihood that "mutations" of the Bach and Einstein sort will occur.

Thomas seems to think that we should not try to analyze such things, but rather to trust that the good stuff will simply emerge from the random and undirected flow of information around the species. Or perhaps because we know so little about how to form productive structures to carry out the essential mission of organizing and directing information, it is better to leave well enough alone. By describing what I have noticed in studying extreme cases of talent development, the productive link between culturally formed social structures and powerful mental mutations, it is hoped, will be more apparent. It is clear that, language notwithstanding, there is more to the process than ambiguity, random reorganization, and slight variations in information receptors.

Humans, uniquely among living things, create environmental structures specifically designed for the purpose of talent development. The most powerful feature of these environments is that they can be modified and refined, fine-tuned as it were, to accomplish their purposes. My own interest in these uniquely human tendencies is somewhat different from that of Marx and Engels; for me the most interesting quality about such human constructions is that they serve collective as well as individual interests. With prodigies, what is striking is how a collective enterprise serves the purpose of providing the precise conditions under which the individual prodigy's talents will be enabled to develop.

In fact, I have come to see the prodigy as dramatic testimony to a kind of reciprocity between nature and culture. What little evidence there is on the subject suggests that the natural talents of prodigies have been available for milennia (Gould, 1981). What has changed with time are the critical cultural conditions for detecting, developing, and refining such talents, the cultural organisms of the current discussion.

I have often thought about what it would be like for a musical talent of the quality of Mozart or a chess talent of the quality of Bobby Fischer to have appeared in a time and place that provided little specific opportunity for the expression of those talents, both of which quite likely have occurred. The Indian boy of poverty Ramanujan is perhaps the best example in recent decades of a mismatch of time and circumstances (Gardner, 1981; Sykes, 1988). Consensus within the mathematics community seems to be that Ramanujan was as naturally gifted a mathematician as any during this century, perhaps ever. But opportunities for learning mathematics as well as for finding appropriate mentors, books, and colleagues were very limited in the slums of Ramanujan's native Madras.

When Ramanujan wrote to Professor Hardy of Cambridge University in England asking for advice on his work, Hardy knew at once that he was dealing with a mathematical mind of the first rank. By the time he found his way to Cambridge at 26, Ramanujan had reinvented much of Western mathematics and mastered many of its most challenging problems, although in highly idiosyncratic ways. And yet Hardy was to learn after several years as Ramanujan's mentor that culture and time were too much out of synch to fully develop his great potential.

Ramanujan's methods were highly intuitive, unconventional, and defied rational analysis. Indeed, the profoundly religious Ramanujan attributed the source of his mathematical insights to the goddess Namagiri. His methods of proof were completely unconventional, and all but defied rational analysis even by mathematicians trained in the specific field in which his work was done (Sykes, 1988). Ramanujan's creativity and flashing insights and intuitions may have been crystallized by the very same environmental conditions that also limited his ability to achieve conventional technical skill.

Sensing that the full development of his gifts required a different environment from what was available in India, Ramanujan decided to place himself within the world of mathematics as best he could, knowing that it might require the sacrifice of his own well being. In fact, the shock of moving to a completely different culture eventually proved too much for Ramanujan, and after many illnesses he died at the age of 32; not however before he and Hardy created a formula for calculating the number of primes of any number, a stunning solution that stands as one of mathematics' greatest achievements of the 20th century.

Hardy knew, however, that by the time he reached Cambridge, Ramanujan's gifts were too crystallized to be much affected by instruction. Hardy, the Cambridge don, perhaps the most highly respected mathematician of his day, wrote that the opportunity to know Ramanujan was the highlight of his life as well as its greatest frustration.

Therefore, when we see a prodigy, a child who has mastered the fundamentals of a highly challenging field in a fraction of the time it takes even a talented adult to do so, we are witnessing a triumph of humanity's patient construction of a receptacle and nurturer for some of nature's most powerful gifts. When opportunity, timing, and treatment are optimal, a prodigy is able to find full expression of his or her natural talents and gifts through the guided mastery of a culturally preserved nonuniversal developmental domain. Were Ramanujan to have been born in England and not India, were his gifts recognized earlier so that he could be better withstood the shock of relocation, the world might have had much greater benefit from his enormous talent.

On the other hand, the possibility must be recognized as well that the striking originality and unwillingness to accept constraints that characterized Ramanujan's approach to mathematical problems may have developed *because* his early experience was so unusual (Gardner, 1988). A distinction must therefore be made between mastery of a domain as it exists, which is the province of the prodigy, and transforming it, which is the mark of creative accomplishment (Feldman, 1988, 1989).

Glimpses of Three Cultural Organisms Stimulated by the Study of Prodigies

What began in 1975 as an informal study of two 8-year-old chess players and a 9-year-old composer (see Feldman, 1979, 1980) evolved into a 10-year longitudinal study of six prodigies and their families (reported in detail in Feldman, 1986/1991). One of the conclusions reached in the study of prodigies was that the appearance and development of a prodigy depends as much on the state of a body of knowledge at a particular period in its own development as it does on a child with extreme talent. When both child and domain seem opportune for prodigy development to occur, whether or not it happens depends on the availability of culturally preserved and protected intermediaries, which become the crystallizers and developers of the prodigy's talents.

Once initial engagement has occurred, a prodigy becomes a prodigy through sustained, systematic, specific, and appropriate experiences under the guidance of attentive and devoted mentors, who use techniques and technologies passed down from generation to generation, and who operate through structures such as guilds, unions, schools, and the like. If it happens that talent is developed fully, it happens because of the existence and support of the cultural organisms of the title, accessed and used in appropriate ways by families, teachers, mentors, and others associated with a field of expertise.

Of the many social structures that struck me during the prodigy research, three stand out (Feldman, 1986/1991). These are what I have labeled *cocoons, gatekeepers and barriers,* and the *grand edifice.* Although there was evidence of such entities in all of the areas where I found prodigies (writing, chess, science, and music), their presence seemed more coherent and better organized in music. With one exception drawn more from my own experience in an academic field, I focus on cultural organisms that function to develop talent in music.

Cocoons.   I have noticed two cocoonlike cultural organisms that play important roles in the preparation of prodigies in music, particularly instrumental music. The first of these is simply a more extreme version of the nuclear family that is a waning ideal in this society. I recall being struck with how "quaint" and perhaps old fashioned the families in the study seemed to be: very traditional, deeply held values on the primacy of family and the importance of committed parenting, particularly mothering.

All of the mothers in my study gave the major portions of their time to caretaking; in the one partial exception to this, mother and father constructed an elaborate scheme for pursuing their jobs with minimum intrusion into their primary mission, which was to provide continuous, complete, and unlimited attention to the needs of their offspring. Such dedication to childrearing may not be uncommon for 6 months or a year or so, but to sustain it for well over a decade, as was the case in these families, is striking.

The cocoon type of family arrangement works best when there are only three members: parents and one child. Where there were other children, the effect was diluted, with some reduction in the sense of protective isolation that was created. To carry off the isolation and keep the sense of distance from the outside world with more than one child is much more difficult. The only documented case I know of was not in my study, but was the family of four children reported in the fascinating work by Deakin (1972), *The Children on the Hill.*

The three children (out of six) in my study who pursued music were all reared in cocoonlike families. Two were only children; the third contained two boys 5 years apart. In the latter case, my subjects' parents acknowledged that they put vastly more energy into the preparation of their first-born for a career in music than was expended on their second, perhaps equally musically talented, son. Later on, when I read about the family of violinist Yehudi Menuhin, whose family has produced prodigies for centuries, I could not help but be struck by similarities between what I had been observing and descriptions of the Menuhins in biographical and autobiographical material. The families in our studies, extreme though they were, were less extreme than the Menuhins (Feldman & Goldsmith, 1986; Menuhin, 1977; Rolfe, 1978).

It is not clear the degree to which cocoonlike families might be important in other cultures, but in this culture at this moment, the need to form thick boundaries between what exists within the family unit and what exists outside seems clear, at least when it comes to the development of exceptional talent. Japanese and Chinese families are often described in terms like the ones we have used to describe our prodigy families (Gardner, 1989). Perhaps in another cultural setting the need to form cocoonlike structures would not be as necessary.

Were the families in my study to have been themselves highly musical (which they were not), or to have been located within more musically oriented communities (which they were not), the situation might also have been different. At least when it comes to the development of exceptional talent, the importance of music and the necessary devotion to pursuing it has to be actively supported. If a passion for music is not supported by an entity like the community or the state, a cocoonlike family can serve such a purpose in the earliest and perhaps most crucial phases.

The second sort of cocoonlike social organism I observed was within the field of music itself. It is described in some detail in *Nature's Gambit* (Feldman, 1986/1991), so I only briefly touch on it here. It was most evident in the "middle period" of preparation of the prodigy, coming after the inwardly protective family, after the warm, accepting initial teacher, but before the masters who bring the student to final readiness for entry into the professional field, usually by the late teens in the case of a prodigy (Bloom, 1985).

How common such entities are is difficult to say, but the one we saw was so interesting and peculiar that its existence must be noted. Furthermore, it was of real importance in providing one of my subjects with certain fundamentals of musical knowledge and skill, fundamentals that served him in good stead as he moved to the next level of preparation (which in his case was the collegiate division of the Juilliard School).

What was striking about this structure for musical preparation was its claim for total control over the process, including dicta about personal habits such as nutrition, exercise, and sexual activity. It could be described as a school except that it had no formal status. It was a collection of individuals under the direction of a charismatic older leader, located in various spots around Boston, but with each node in close coordination with the center. My subject's musical education with this group during the time I observed him included piano, composition, and violin lessons, as well as solfège at a local university where the group had contacts.

The hallmarks of this peculiar cultural organism were its isolation from other groups and its self-consciously "superior" understanding of how to achieve the best preparation for a career in music. The group was so intense partly in reaction to its peripheral place among the more established musical community. Indeed, as my subject became involved in more established schools and programs elsewhere, the response of his mentors within the "Jovanovich Group" (as it was called in *Nature's Gambit*) was to become disturbed, suspicious, and ultimately self-destructive, at least in the sense of losing a prized, perhaps uniquely talented student.

One of the problems with this particular cultural organism is that it did not seem to perceive its limitations, had not accepted its place in the larger context. From the perspective of our longitudinal work, as well as from Bloom's (1985) retrospective work on world class performers, a transition to another level of preparation may have been inevitable in the case of my subject Nils Kirkendahl (a pseudonym). But the Jovanovich group did not recognize itself as a "middle level" preparation experience, and did not gracefully accept the loss of its most prized student.

Two other features of the musical preparation cocoon I observed were that it was held together by a set of beliefs about reincarnation and spirituality that all members were expected to embrace completely, including sexual abstinence. And that the leader of the group not only had remarkable musical capabilities but charismatic and intuitive powers as well. She was also exempt from the strictures on other members' behavior.

The group had an unmistakable cultlike quality about it, although for the most part was harmless enough. This does raise the question of the possible significance of cults or cultlike entities for the development of extreme talent. Perhaps extreme cultural organisms exist at least in part to bring out extreme potential. For something remarkable to occur, in some instances it may be necessary to construct a social entity that stands outside established boundaries, isolated and inwardly directed, self consciously superior in its beliefs about the domain in question.

At the age of 12, my subject chose to leave the Jovanovich group and to pursue a more conventional course of preparation, a decision he does not regret. Yet he acknowledges that the Jovanovich group gave him a great deal and may have been crucial to his successful entry into the ranks of concert violinists.

Within the context of middle level entities, it may be that the cocoon is but one of several social constructions, and the key to successful preparation lies in the *match* (cf. Hunt, 1961) of a specific form of cultural organism to specific possibilities of the aspiring musician, a process I have in a broader context called co-incidence (Feldman, 1979, 1980, 1986, 1986/1991; Feldman & Goldsmith, 1986).

Cocoons of two types, then, small nuclear families and highly centralized musical collectives, were found when extreme potential in music was developed in my subjects. The former were apparent in all cases studied, whereas the latter was evident in only one case. The database is meager in any event, and we will not know if the observations reported here will prove durable until more studies have been done.

Gatekeepers and Barriers. Moving to the second type of cultural organism, the example discussed here has nothing directly to do with music.

I was rereading Thomas' (1974) *The Lives of a Cell* and was struck with his description of scientific journals and the crucial role they have played in the creation of modern science. The analogue in music would probably be the various juries, contests, panels, and prizes that stand between the promising young composer or performer and the recognition and rewards that come from winning contests and so forth.

I am in no position to discuss how music organizes these purposes, having never experienced them directly nor observed them systematically (although I have certainly witnessed them as part of the prodigies research). I confine my discussion to a kind of quality control and standards setting that is closer to my own experience, the academic journal. In particular, I am interested in the specific human social constructions that serve the purposes of organizing into larger units contributions to knowledge by individuals. The main point I wish to make is that human constructions have a different epistemological status from natural ones, making them subject to conscious transformation.

As for the creation of journals and systems for judging quality and scientific merit, Thomas quoted Ziman, who in the (scientific journal) *Nature* wrote: "the invention of a mechanism for the systematic publication of *fragments* of scientific work may have been the key event in the history of modern science" (pp. 16–17). Thomas continued with a longer quotation, of which the following is an excerpt:

> *This technique, of soliciting many modest contributions to the story of human knowledge, has been the secret of Western science since the seventeenth century, for it achieves a corporate, collective power that is far greater than one individual can exert* (pp. 16–17)

As suggested earlier, the enterprise is likened to the building of a termite nest, a brilliant if somewhat misleading observation.

It is true enough that there is often an unreflective and unselfconscious tendency among humans to construct entities, including conceptual and social entities, without a clear guiding plan or purpose. Some seem pure whimsy, others appear to grow like topsy. Thomas' emphasis on the similarity between people and termites is in this sense well taken.

Even with an entity as seemingly purposeful as an academic journal, few who are involved in the business of starting and maintaining journals, let alone those who have to deal with them as potential contributors, think a lot about why they exist or what their larger purposes might be. And yet a reflective scholar (like Ziman) was able to perceive some of the more profound purposes of such an enterprise, making it possible to understand this particular human creation more fully. By virtue of these reflections, the likelihood of conscious change also increases, so that the entity may carry out its now more clearly understood purposes more effectively. Termites don't do this.

It is the ability to reflect, to take an intentional stance to use Dennett's (1978) term, that distinguishes human behavior from all other. It is what makes real thought possible. Language is the vehicle of human thought par excellence (Piaget's work showing thought before language notwithstanding) because language more than any other medium permits humans to reflect on their own behavior, the behavior of others, and the effects of intentional changes on cultural entities, a conclusion that gives Piaget his due but not more (Feldman, 1988, 1989).

Language, however, is not the only human creation that encourages reflection and awareness of purposeful change; all human symbol systems have this feature (Gardner, 1983). Thomas, therefore, puts too great an emphasis on language as the only real difference between humans and other animals, and by virtue of this overlooks the unique ontological status of crafted objects, systems, technologies, and yes, scientific societies and journals, that are put into the world by people with a purpose, however aware of it or not they may be at the time (Feldman, 1988, 1989).

For Vygotsky (1978), the greatest moment in a human being's life, according to a passage in *Mind in Society,* is that moment when speech and tool use begin to engage and influence each other. Vygotsky (and Marx and Engels before him) recognized that human culture is itself an everchanging, evolving set of shapers and formers of thought, although they tended to overemphasize the power of these things. What exist in the world as crafted objects, symbols, systems, and myths, made by human beings, are epistemologically different from what exists as a consequence of nonhuman natural forces, *and humans uniquely recognize this difference.* The Marxists, including even Vygotsky probably, overestimated the power of human history and culture to determine the form and content of thought, but their great virtue was to make explicit how and why such forces are as influential as they are. It is because, to a degree, they offer the possibility of control and direction of the course of cultural evolution.

The impression one gets from Thomas, on the other hand, is unmistakably of a collection of organisms basically bewildered about what they do and why they do it, as are the termites. But the extent of human unselfconsciousness must not be exaggerated. Often the purposes of human activity are anything but dim, as Gruber's brilliant work on Darwin's quite conscious desire to construct a theory of evolution makes clear (Gruber, 1981). Indeed, the most likely reason for Darwin's decades long delay in publishing his theory of evolution through natural selection is that he understood all too well just what he was doing, why he was doing it, and what its likely ramifications and implications would be. Not all instances of intentional behavior have such explicitly comprehended purposes, of course, but they all share the essential quality that they are done by people with a purpose. No termite has ever done that either, so far as we know.

Now what does all of this have to do with the realization of great potential? Are there cultural organisms that contribute to the process of placing novel variations into the world, variations that come about through the intentional efforts of reflective human enterprise? This, as Bruner (1986) pointed out in a valuable essay on Vygotsky, was the most problematic aspect of marxist thought, and even Vygotsky didn't get all that far with it. As Bruner wrote:

> Marxism has always had difficulty with its Principle of Spontaneity, a principle to account for generativeness and creativity in human affairs beyond historical determinism. Vygotsky strived mightily . . . to provide a means of bridging the gap between historical determinism and the play of consciousness. (p. 78)

Perhaps, if we think about scientific journals as cultural organisms, a glimmer of an explanation moves into view concerning a relationship between "historical determinism" and "the play of consciousness" thought of not so much as a gap to be bridged as a boundary to be transcended (cf. Perkins, 1988).

I am reminded again of my experience almost two decades ago when I was confronted with having my work rejected by a well-established scientific journal. Although I did not see it this way at the time, I found the challenge of having to find a way of getting my work out to the scientific community, or at least into print, to be a crucial stimulus in forcing me to come up with the idea of crystallizing experiences, catalysts of cognitive structures, and a middle level theory to link learning and development (Feldman, 1971, 1980, 1987; Strauss, 1987). Had the rejection not occurred, it is possible I would not have thought of these things at all. Without evaluating the significance of my own "innovations," the point is that their very existence may have crucially depended on being confronted with a stubborn gatekeeper.

Therefore, it seems plausible that human constructions such as scientific societies, journals and the like serve a vital, if in a sense negative function. They make it difficult for something brought into the world by a single person or small group to be shared with and connected with that of others, at least shared under conditions of implicit approval of their scientific status and thereby sanctioned in their right to be taken seriously. In my own case, these challenges may have catalyzed some new ideas that were spurred by my intention to succeed in getting the work published. The sheer bulk of established knowledge, received wisdom, and ingrained prejudice comprise the weight against which the lone innovator's lever must be applied.

Were such cultural organisms not to exist, or be impossible to intentionally change, then the possibility of novelty, creativity, transformation, revolution, in short, of significant change understood as significant change, would hardly exist at all. However, the evidence of significant changes brought about through intentional human effort, recognized as such by others, is overwhelming, in fact is virtually beyond argument (Feldman, 1989).

It can be said, then, that cultural organisms that organize, distill, select, and communicate knowledge are constructed to guard against frivolous innovation, to resist insignificant transformation, and ultimately to mark as clearly as possible the landmarks and boundaries that must be transcended when something new is to become part of culture (Perkins, 1988).

Whether these thoughts give comfort to the many who have suffered the humiliation of rejection from a valued journal, it is vital to acknowledge the tension between this kind of cultural organism and the achievement of human potential. This tension is a plausible source of a relationship between "determinism" and "spontaneity." One can only hope that a deeper awareness of the function of journals as providing necessary resistance, and thereby serving as catalysts for innovation, might lead their editors to be somewhat more receptive to new ideas—but of course not *too* receptive or their vital purpose would be compromised.

As for the individual aspiring to establish a place, the existence of the sort of cultural organism we have been discussing can be a source of great challenge or of equally great discouragement. The extent to which a given person's capabilities are well understood and appreciated by current gate-keepers will predict a great deal about the fate of that person's chances for the development of his or her potential within the field, and more importantly, for the chance to have one's works placed permanently among the selected works that make up the knowledge structures of a domain.

The Grand Edifice.   I now turn to the third form of cultural organism I have observed in my work on the development of great potential, that of the grand edifice. It was in the summer of 1988 at the Aspen Music Festival (the title of this chapter should be more comprehensible now) that the idea occurred to me of a much larger entity than anything I had considered before. I was invited to give a talk on musical prodigies to a meeting of physicians who specialized in medical problems of performers, and was sent a flier (a beautifully done flier at that) about the festival. What struck me first was that the list of guest musical faculty ran well over 150 people; the sheer number impressed me.

Then I glanced at the schedule of events and was likewise moved by the variety and number of these. The magnitude, the grandeur of the festival overwhelmed me. I reflected on the numbers of people, working in concert, who had to have collaborated to make the festival run, from the teenagers who picked up trash around the major event tent to the guest conductor who arrived by chartered flight for a last minute substitute performance for a fallen colleague. The level and degree of organization and cooperation required to pull the festival off was remarkable.

This is of course not a novel thought. Many have been impressed with the coordination, organization, management, and interpersonal skills required to make a major festival like the Aspen function well. What my experience with extreme cases may have added to the usual reaction was the realization that the primary purpose of such a cultural enterprise may be to provide precisely the conditions under which great potential in music could be extruded from the collective talents of all the participants, including (and perhaps most specifically) from those whose talents transcend the technical, musical, and aesthetic boundaries lovingly (and sometimes not so lovingly) provided by the musical community. When a truly wonderful performance occurs, as sometimes happens at Aspen, there is a collective affirmation of the rightness, the worthiness, the importance of the whole enterprise.

I then found myself thinking somewhat differently about the nice lady in the neighborhood who gives piano lessons. People like her have provided many children their initial exposure to the wider world of music. I also saw nobility in the little music store on Massachusetts Avenue in nearby Cambridge that provides an anchoring point and support network for aspiring performers and composers. It exists as a vital part of the large base on which the structures of music are meticulously built, level by level.

After leaving the festival, I began talking with musician friends about a large-scale, loosely organized cultural structure that is constructed to serve the purpose of bringing forth the best music that all the participants, individually and collectively, are able to produce. The idea seemed to make sense to people who participate in music, and even provide some comfort to those who toil in obscurity many levels down from the rarified heights of musical expression in evidence at such festivals as the Aspen.

To recall an earlier quote from Thomas, humans seem to have access to, as he said, all the bits of information in the biosphere, but do not know yet what to do with them. "When we have learned how these are rearranged against randomness, to make, say, springtails, quantum mechanics, and the late quartets, we may have a clearer notion of how to proceed" (p. 15).

I began to see the social structures of music as perhaps the most advanced prototype of a system for knowing what to do to rearrange nonsense into wonder, to take the bits and make them into functional cultural entities. To see the musical community in this way makes it important for what it directly contributes to culture through music itself, but of perhaps of greater importance as a source of understanding how human cultural organisms are formed, sustained, transformed, and refined to fulfill their purposes. In this case, the purpose seems to be to give large numbers of people a worthy, overarching goal to pursue, with each having an important place and important part to play.

Without necessarily being aware of it (Thomas' point of course), people willingly devote their lives (or a portion of them) to making the Aspen Music Festival, the Philadelphia Music Festival, the Asbury Park Music Festival, and so on, the very best they can be. And when a prodigy appears, is prepared well, and in time plays superbly, the entire cultural organism rejoices.

The grandest edifice among the cultural organisms, then, is also the most humble. It seems to allow virtually everyone who wishes to participate an important role at some level, and it organizes and channels talent from the most modest to the most exalted. It is not the Aspen Music Festival alone that must be understood, because that event is for a selected few, but the much larger organism of which Aspen is a part. The Aspen festival exists as one of the most demanding and most extreme tests of talent, where the gatekeepers and hurdles to overcome are raised almost impossibly high, so that the fruits of the other levels of the musical hill (or hive) can be gathered, for all to rejoice.

CONCLUSION

I have tried to do three things in this chapter. The first has been to recapitulate some of my own previous efforts to conceptualize specific environmental influences on the development of human potential. From this perhaps self-indulgent effort I realized that I have been working on various ways of reckoning humanly crafted environments for quite awhile, from crystallizing conditions to nonuniversal developmental domains. The opportunity to reflect on these matters has made me realize that even as I doggedly held to my individualist training and bias, I was in fact reaching for some way of bringing systematic, specific environmental constructs into the way I look at development.

The second theme of this presentation has been to describe certain forms of what I have called *cultural organisms,* or humanly constructed systems for detecting, developing, protecting, promoting, and rejoicing in great potential within certain selected domains. For the most part, the cultural organisms that struck me as the most effective and most refined have been in music, although a comparative study of such entities in other domains recommends itself forcefully. Cocoonlike families and teaching groups, organizers and boundary setters described as institutionalized gatekeepers, and a grand edifice with many layers of contributing units, including high level, major events like the Aspen Music Festival, were presented as vital parts of the process of the development of talent, particularly great talent.

To mount an ascent of one of the great mountains of civilization (which, paradoxically, may show peaks that were previously unknown) requires monumental efforts, superb organization, sustained application, and great resources. No less than the coordinated efforts of the entire domain-related community will make that ascent possible. This means that when a truly great performance occurs, it reflects the combined efforts of countless individuals working in voluntary harness over long periods of time. By virtue of their natural gifts, prodigies are especially well equipped with the talent and energy to carry forward the aspirations of the community that gives them nurture and support. When all goes well, prodigies fully justify the enormous resources that are invested in their preparation.

I have also hinted at the limits of the pure prodigy, since for the most part she or he produces epiphany through a perfect match with an already existing domain. The boundaries and landmarks and hurdles all appear to be set just right for the prodigy; indeed, prodigies are perhaps most useful for showing how far along in the process are various domains toward coherence and organization of purpose (Gardner, 1988).

Citing the example of my own experience with rejection of a manuscript as the catalyst for generating some new ideas, I tried to suggest that cultural organisms of this type serve a purpose beyond organizing fragments of knowledge. They help establish the gap that has to be transcended in order for a new idea to be integrated into that evolving body of knowledge we call a developmental domain. I was motivated through rejection of a manuscript to come up with the idea of crystallizing conditions, an idea that has had a profound role to play in the work I have done in the past 20 years.

The purposes of orderly transformation are thus served by the marking of boundaries and by transcending them. An interesting line of research would be to try to measure how well marked and how permeable the boundaries of various fields are at a given moment, and how large a gap can be bridged while still maintaining the orderly movement of the knowledge base of the domain. Genius, in this context, would represent a resetting of boundaries based on altered principles of organization governing the accumulation of knowledge in that domain (Feldman, 1982).

It seems to me that a most worthy goal of developmental science should be to try to understand better how these truly grand cultural organisms are formed, how they function, and how they organize themselves around certain shared purposes or goals. The observations reported here are of course anecdotal and unsystematic, lacking in the virtues of good empirical work. As self-appointed explorer and scout, I have merely pointed out what a small number of cultural organisms look like, or more accurately, have recast things that we perfectly well know exist into a framework where they are intended to take on new meaning.

In particular, the role of cultural organisms, as I have called them, in the discovery, development, refinement, and expression of extreme potential is a necessary compliment to an understanding of the nature of potential itself. To comprehend one requires the comprehension of the other. I have simply extended the target of inquiry and tried to give it form.

Indeed, a fruitful way to think about human potential may be as a set of possibilities ranging from universal to unique that may or may not occur through the ministrations of the available set of cultural organisms. To know the specific conditions under which human potential, humble or great, is realized and the much more common conditions under which it is not, may be as good a way as any to describe the goal of the cultural organism we call the field of cognitive development.

SUMMARY OF COMMENTARY BY PROFESSOR ROBBIE CASE[1]

Immediately following the presentation of the preceding thoughts (which have been edited some in the interim), Professor Robbie Case presented a most stimulating commentary. That commentary was divided into two parts: the first was based on the imposition of a life-cycle context on the notion of cultural organisms; the second attempted to place cultural organisms in the context of my own life cycle, suggesting that they represent both a distillation of the past 20 years of work, as well as foreshadowing work likely to come in the next 20. Finally, some "modest" proposals for extending the idea of cultural organisms were laid before the audience for discussion.

Using the universal-to-unique continuum as a guide, Professor Case reviewed my efforts in research and theory going back to the crystallizing conditions of the early 1970s. In doing so, he found that there has been steady movement from universal to unique in my research interests. My earliest work dealt with Piagetian themes and universal stage sequences. It moved from there to a cultural task (map drawing), even though I was not altogether aware of the fact that I had made such a shift. From there I became preoccupied with transition mechanisms within specific developmental domains, and next moved toward extreme cases of early prodigious

---

[1] I am grateful to Professor Case for sending me copies of his notes. He also sent photocopies of the overhead slides used in his discussion. As anyone who has heard Robbie Case knows, he is a master of the use of overheads. Therefore, much of the richness and flavor of his presentation is lost in the translation from lively discussion to sober summary.

achievement, creative transformations, and individuality. These efforts he characterized as my "early" and "middle" periods. Having moved from universal to unique in this fashion, I was prepared to take the step that is represented in the idea of cultural organisms (i.e., to give context to the entire universal to unique continuum of developmental sequences).

In turning to the cultural organisms work, Case saw the beginnings of another chapter in my work, one that can be perhaps characterized as contextual. The cultural organisms I identified all attempt to deal with contextual entities that give direction, shape, and form to the potentials an individual might develop. They range from relatively small (families as cocoonlike cultural organisms) to very large (the grand edifice of music preparation), with the gatekeeper structure of the professional journal of intermediate size.

Although on the whole sympathetic to the idea of cultural organisms, Case saw a number of problems and limitations with the current conception. Perhaps most problematic is the fact that much of what I reported came from my work with prodigies, whose developmental trajectory is anything but typical. Therefore, Case argued, the cultural organisms I discovered may be limited in their application to extreme cases. Other possible cultural organisms might be more critical to examine, particularly when less extreme situations are the focus of inquiry.

A number of extensions and alternatives were also presented in Case's discussion. By using Daniel Levinson's (1978) concepts of "adult life structures" as a framework, Case tried to show how unusual the prodigy is, how much the exception rather than the rule for the development of great potential. Nevertheless, he concluded that the study of prodigies has led to a way of looking at the development of great potential that has real promise. By examining such sharply etched and rarified instances of development, we are, he concluded, in a better position to identify the forces and contexts that must be taken into account in all instances of talent development. The interplay among these forces, including whatever cultural organisms are found to be involved, holds the key to understanding the development of great potential.

ACKNOWLEDGMENT

A similar version of this chapter appears in Feldman (1993) under the title "Cultural Organisms." I wish to thank the society for permission to use material from this chapter for that purpose. The work reported here was supported by grants from The Grant Foundation, The Mellon Foundation, The Rockefeller Brothers Fund, and The Spencer Foundation. Members of the Developmental Science Group at Tufts University made valuable suggestions and comments on earlier drafts.

REFERENCES

Beilin, H. (1971). Developmental stages and developmental processes. In D. Green, M. Ford, & G. Flamer (Eds.), *Measurement and Piaget* (pp. 172–189). New York: McGraw-Hill.

Bloom, B. (Ed.). (1985). *Developing talent in young people.* New York: Ballantine Books.

Bronfenbrenner, U. (1974). Developmental research, public policy, and the ecology of childhood. *Child Development, 45,* 1–5.

Bruner, J. S. (1986). *Actual minds, possible worlds.* Cambridge, MA: Harvard University Press.

Bruner, J. S., & Haste, H. (Eds.). (1987). *Making sense: The child's construction of the world.* New York: Methuen.

Bruner, J. S., Olver, R., & Greenfield, P. (1966). *Studies in cognitive growth.* New York: Wiley.

Bruner, J. S., & Olson, D. R. (1974). Learning through experience and learning through media. In D. R. Olson (Ed.), *Media and symbols* (pp. 125–150). Chicago: University of Chicago Press.

Cole, M., Gay, J., Glick, J., & Sharp, D. (1971). *The cultural context of learning and thinking.* New York: Basic Books.

Csikszentmihalyi, M. (1990). The domain of creativity. In M. Runco & R. Albert (Eds.), *Theories of creativity* (pp. 190–212). Newbury Park, CA: Sage.

Csikszentmihalyi, M., & Robinson, R. E. (1986). Culture, time and the development of talent. In R. J. Sternberg & J. E. Davidson (Eds.), *Conceptions of giftedness* (pp. 264–284). New York: Cambridge University Press.

Deakin, M. (1972). *The children on the hill: One family's bold experiment with a new way of learning and growing.* New York: Bobbs-Merrill.

Dennett, D. C. (1978). *Brainstorms: Philosophical essays on mind and psychology.* Montgomery, VT: Bradford Books.

Feldman, D. H. (1971). Map understanding as a possible crystallizer of cognitive structures. *American Educational Research Journal, 8,* 485–501.

Feldman, D. H. (1974). Universal to unique: A developmental view of creativity and education. In S. Rosner & L. Abt (Eds.), *Essays in creativity* (pp. 47–85). Croton-on-Hudson: North River Press.

Feldman, D. H. (1976). The child as craftsman. *Phi Delta Kappan, 58,* 143–149.

Feldman, D. H. (1979). The mysterious case of extreme giftedness. In H. Passow (Ed.), *The gifted and the talented* (NSSE Yearbook #78, pp. 335–351). Chicago, IL: University of Chicago Press.

Feldman, D. H. (1980). *Beyond universals in cognitive development.* Norwood, NJ: Ablex.

Feldman, D. H. (1981). Beyond universals: Toward a developmental psychology of education. *Educational Researcher, 11,* 21–31.

Feldman, D. H. (1982). A developmental framework for research with gifted children. In D. H. Feldman (Ed.), *Developmental approaches to giftedness and creativity* (pp. 31–45). San Francisco: Jossey-Bass.

Feldman, D. H. (1986). How development works. In I. Levin (Ed.), *Stage and structure: Reopening the debate* (pp. 284–306). Norwood, NJ: Ablex.

Feldman, D. H. (1987). Going for the middle ground: A promising place for educational psychology. In L. Liben (Ed.), *Development and learning: Conflict or congruence?* (pp. 159–172). Hillsdale, NJ: Lawrence Erlbaum Associates.

Feldman, D. H. (1988). Creativity: Dreams, insights, and transformations. In R. Sternberg (Ed.), *The nature of creativity.* New York: Cambridge University Press.

Feldman, D. H. (1989). Creativity: Proof that development occurs. In W. Damon (Ed.), *Child development today and tomorrow* (pp. 240–260). San Francisco: Jossey-Bass.

Feldman, D. H. (1991). *Nature's gambit.* New York: Teachers College Press (Original work published 1986).

Feldman, D. H. (1993). *Beyond universals in cognitive development* (2nd ed.). Norwood, NJ: Ablex.

Feldman, D. H., & Goldsmith, L. T. (1986). Transgenerational influences on the development of early prodigious behavior: A case study approach. In W. Fowler (Ed.), *Early experience and the development of competence.* San Francisco: Jossey-Bass.

Feldman, D. H., & Goldsmith, L. T. (1989). Child prodigies: Straddling two worlds. In E. Bernstein (Ed.), *Medical and health annual* (pp. 32–51). Chicago: Encyclopedia Britannica.

Flavell, J. H. (1971). Stage-related properties of cognitive development. *Cognitive Psychology, 2,* 421–453.

Gardner, H. (1981, May). Prodigies progress. *Psychology Today,* pp. 75–79.

Gardner, H. (1983). *Frames of mind: The theory of multiple intelligences.* New York: Basic Books.

Gardner, H. (1988). Creative lives and creative works: A synthetic scientific approach. In R. Sternberg (Ed.), *The nature of creativity* (pp. 298–321). New York: Cambridge University Press.

Gardner, H. (1989). *To open minds: Chinese clues to the dilemma of contemporary education.* New York: Basic Books.

Gould, S. J. (1981). *The mismeasure of man.* New York: Norton.

Gruber, H. (1981). *Darwin on man: A psychological study of scientific creativity* (2nd ed.). Chicago: University of Chicago Press.

Gruber, H. (1982). On the hypothesized relation between giftedness and creativity. In D. H. Feldman (Ed.), *Developmental approaches to giftedness and creativity* (pp. 7–29). San Francisco: Jossey-Bass.

Horowitz, F. D. (1987). *Exploring developmental theories: Toward a structural/behavioral model of development.* Hillsdale, NJ: Lawrence Erlbaum Associates.

Hunt, J. McV. (1961). *Intelligence and experience.* New York: Ronald Press.

Kessen, W. (1962). "Stage" and "structure" in the study of children. In W. Kessen & C. Kuhlman (Eds.), *Monographs of the Society for Research in Child Development, 27,* 53–70.

Levinson, D. (1978). *The seasons of a man's life.* New York: Knopf.

Menuhin, Y. (1977). *Unfinished journey.* New York: Knopf.

Mischel, T. (Ed.). (1971). *Cognitive development and epistemology.* New York: Academic Press.

Moos, R. H. (1973). Conceptualizations of human environments. *American Psychologist, 28,* 652–665.

Perkins, D. N. (1988). The possibility of invention. In R. J. Sternberg (Ed.), *The nature of creativity* (pp. 362–385). New York: Cambridge University Press.

Piaget, J., & Inhelder, B. (1956). *The child's conception of space.* New York: Norton.

Rogoff, B. (1990). *Apprenticeship in thinking.* New York: Oxford University Press.

Rolfe, L. (1978). *The Menuhins: A family odyssey.* San Francisco: Panjandrum/Aris Books.

Strauss, S. (1987). Educational-developmental psychology and school learning. In L. Liben (Ed.), *Development and learning: Conflict or congruence?* (pp. 133–158). Hillsdale, NJ: Lawrence Erlbaum Associates.

Sykes, C. (Producer & Director). (March, 1988). *Ramanujan.* Boston: WGBH TV (NOVA).

Thomas, L. (1974). *The lives of a cell: Notes of a biology watcher.* New York: Bantam Books.

Vygotsky, L. (1962). *Thought and language.* Cambridge, MA: MIT Press. (Original work published 1934).

Vygotsky, L. S. (1978). *Mind in society: The development of higher psychological processes.* Cambridge, MA: Harvard University Press.

Wallace, D. B., & Gruber, H. E. (Eds.). (1989). *Creative people at work.* Oxford: Oxford University Press.

Walters, J., & Gardner, H. (1986). The crystallizing experience: Discovering an intellectual gift. In R. J. Sternberg & J. E. Davidson (Eds.), *Conceptions of giftedness* (pp. 306–331). New York: Cambridge University Press.

IV COMMENTARIES

10

Where Is the Social Environment? A Commentary on Reed

John A. Meacham
State University of New York at Buffalo

I take as my task the weaving of a suitable commentary out of the variegated strands that are available to me: Reed's (this volume) tightly argued and provocative chapter on actions and intentions, a chapter that has renewed my interest in Gibson's (1979; Reed, 1988a) ecological approach to perception; the theme of this volume, the impact of specific environments on cognitive development; my own view that the impact of societal, cultural, and historical conditions upon development has been neglected (Meacham, 1984a, 1989); my view that the basis for psychological development is not individual cognition but interpersonal relations, communication, and cooperation (Meacham, 1984b, 1991; Meacham & Emont, 1989); the fact that simultaneous with our annual meeting a short distance from Independence Hall in Philadelphia, a symbol of freedom, thousands of people were gathered together in Tiananmen Square; and, of course, Piaget's structural-developmental theory. Each of these strands might serve as the warp or as the woof — each might provide a context for interpretation of the others, each might be interpreted in terms of the others — and so which one of the many strands I select to begin the weaving becomes, for better or worse, a critical choice that will give shape and texture to the whole cloth.

ACADEMIC FREEDOM

My thoughts continue to return to chapter 6 of Reed's (1988a) account of Gibson's life and his research on perception. The chapter was titled "The Unmaking of a Social Psychologist, 1941–1955," and so it is with this strand that I will begin. Reed (this volume) argues that a standard criticism of Gibson's concept of affordances, namely, that although the concept might have utility with respect to the physical environment it is of little use in understanding the social world, is not valid. Instead, Gibson viewed his work as providing a way of overcoming the false dichotomies between the biological and the cultural and between the physical and the social worlds (Reed, 1988a, p. 309). Indeed, Gibson had a long-standing interest in such mainstream social psychological issues as group cooperation, stereotypes, education and propaganda, socialization of behavior, and so forth, and during the 1940s was active within the Society for the Psychological Study of Social Issues (SPSSI).

In 1948, Ralph Gundlach, a social psychologist at the University of Washington, a member of SPSSI, and a long-time acquaintance of Gibson, refused to answer questions about political beliefs and associates before an investigative committee chaired by Albert Canwell, a Washington State legislator. Previously, an experienced witness, most of whose testimony was later proved false, had testified that members of the Communist party held many positions at the University of Washington. Gundlach had not been a member of the Communist party and was not officially accused of being a member. Even if he had been, the American Association of University Professors and a University of Washington faculty committee had made clear that political associations were not relevant to the question of suitability for teaching. Nevertheless, Gundlach was fired by the president of the University of Washington for refusing to cooperate with the investigative committee and was unable to obtain another academic position (Reed, 1988a, pp. 107–109).

Gibson was one of a group of SPSSI members who viewed what had happened to Gundlach as an attack upon academic freedom and upon the possibility for social psychologists to pursue research of social relevance. He became involved in the defense of Gundlach as well as other psychologists (e.g., Edward Tolman, Herbert Kelman) who were being attacked, circulating petitions and organizing fund raisers. The Federal Bureau of Investigation (FBI) began interviewing Gibson's neighbors and colleagues, who criticized Gibson for, among other activities, his opposition to increased armaments, his concern for the plight of Negroes, and his leadership of the local teachers union. Subsequently, Gibson's security clearance was cancelled and he became unable to obtain research contracts with the U. S. Air Force. Reed (1988a, chapter 6) suggested that the unfavorable climate for social psychological research as well as the questioning and harassment from the FBI are among the reasons why Gibson turned his attention away from research related to social issues and toward the further refinement of his work on visual perception.

Is it possible to interpret this series of events in Gibson's professional development in terms of the constructs provided in Reed's chapter (this volume)? Gibson argued that socially constructed entities, such as post-boxes and baseball bats, are real and exist in the environment alongside natural objects, such as trees. These entities are psychologically salient aspects of our environment, or affordances, because they are perceived as objects within the framework of social systems. Is it stretching the concept of affordances too far to consider academic freedom and the possibility of research on social issues as affordances? These might be considered as instances of a comprehensive and uniquely human affordance, the potential for entering into discourse with one another. (I use the term *discourse* to mean, following Habermas, 1984, the deciding of issues through the force of the better argument within a community of persons in dialogue; McCarthy, 1978, pp. 310–333.) If this usage of the construct of affordance is permissable, then the social entity of academic freedom was an aspect of Gibson's Field of Promoted Action and his Field of Free Action; furthermore, Gibson might be said to have been intentional with respect to this particular affordance.

Reed (this volume) provides a framework within which a number of questions that could be raised at this point, for example, regarding the establishment and maintenance of this particular intention with respect to academic freedom, might be addressed. Yet this series of events from Gibson's professional development contrasts with what I take to be the general perspective of Reed's chapter. Although the primary concern in development is with expansion of the Field of Free Action so as to take advantage of the affordances within the Field of Promoted Action, in these events from Gibson's life we witness a contraction of the Field of Free Action, as Gibson (along with SPSSI) suffered defeats in the attempt to defend academic freedom and as he was forced through harassment to turn away from his research program in social psychology. The processes of interest are no longer scaffolding and the establishment of intentions, but processes of defense against potential loss, such as Gibson's circulation of petitions and organization of fund raisers, and processes of adjustment to the actual loss of an affordance that had been provided within the social environment. It appears that Gibson adjusted reasonably well to the loss. What can we say about the adjustment of Gundlach and the many other academics who lost their jobs during the McCarthy era, the people in Tiananmen Square whose expectations of freedom were crushed, and the impact of increasing disadvantage on the development of children in the United States? The common strand among these is the loss of affordances, the loss of psychologically salient aspects of the social environment.

THE REPRODUCTION OF SOCIETY

I would like at this point to pick up a new strand and introduce it into the commentary that I am weaving. The theme of this volume concerns the impact of specific environments on cognitive development. Family, school, peer, work, and other environments are all deserving of our attention. Nevertheless, the impact of these environments on development must be understood within a more general context, namely, a specific societal or cultural environment. When we ask questions about cognitive development, that is, about what it is that individuals know and how they come to know it, both the questions and the answers must be meaningful within the context of what we believe about how societies maintain themselves, reproduce themselves from one generation to the next, and transform themselves.

Let me begin with some very simple questions about the relationship between individual cognitive development and societal development. What is the role of individuals qua individuals in the maintenance, reproduction, and transformation of human society? Why is psychological individualism so peculiar to human society yet apparently not at all essential to other societies? Compare, for example, ant and bee societies, in which ants and bees of course exist as individual entities yet do not exist as psychological entities, that is, with a sense of agency, intentionality, personhood, awareness, responsibility, freedom, and so forth. (I do not wish to pursue the question of what importance society has for individuals, that is, what benefits might accrue to individuals by their coming together and forming interpersonal and societal relations. The assumption underlying this question, namely, that psychological individuals preexist society, is faulty. This traditional approach to conceptualizing the relationship between the individual and society was also rejected by Gibson; Reed, 1988a, p. 59.)

I argue that psychological individuals are essential in the maintenance, reproduction, and transformation of human society and, furthermore, it is psychological individualism that makes possible that unique quality of human society, its ability to adapt rapidly to changing environmental conditions. In the case of ants and bees, society is maintained primarily through the genetic structure. Societal change takes place slowly, through changes in the genetic structure, but not through changes in the knowledge of particular ants about the interpersonal and societal relations in which they are immersed.

Human societies are able to adapt rapidly to changing environmental conditions because the primary mechanism is no longer the genetic structure but instead the structure of our individual knowing and understanding. It would be impossible for transformations of roles within the hives of ants and bees to take place within a few years or even a few generations; yet in the case of human society, changes in the roles of women, of slaves, of workers, and so forth have been dramatic within only a few decades or a few generations. What holds human society together, as well as providing the possibility for rapid transformation in the nature of society, is not merely the genetic structure, but the psychological knowing structures.

But although the human species is thus provided with a mechanism for rapid societal change, there are costs or dangers associated with this mechanism. One danger is that the structure that maintains society is very fragile. The guarantee of friendship, cooperation, community, and societal harmony is not locked into our genetic structure, but is carried within the psychological structures of knowing. Unfortunately, knowledge can be distorted or forgotten. And societal change might readily be taken in a direction that is not adaptive for society, for example, through the arguments of a persuasive leader such as Senator Joseph McCarthy. Furthermore, individuals might decide not to cooperate in what is best for society as a whole. Why should individuals cooperate when to cooperate means to subordinate ones own goals or purposes to those of the group? Human society would not have these problems if the guarantee of our cooperation were entirely genetic, but if so then our society would be much more rigid and less adaptable.

So there is a paradox, namely, that although the psychological structures of knowing are sufficiently flexible to permit rapid transformation and adaptation by human societies, they are at the same time, at least as traditionally conceived, too flimsy to ensure the stability and coherence required for effective functioning of human societies. As traditionally conceived, what the individual learns about society is information that is transmitted to the individual through the process of socialization. In short, society reproduces itself by each generation transmitting the knowledge about society to the next generation (roughly analogous to the process of genetic transmission). The paradox can be resolved by making the structures of knowing stronger, that is, strong enough to provide an adequate guarantee for the long-term maintenance of society as the genetic structure does for ants and bees, yet not so strong that they impede societal transformation and adaptation when this is appropriate.

The solution, of course, is entirely consistent with Piaget's structural–developmental theory, namely, the strength of what the individual knows about society comes from the fact of children having constructed society for themselves, so that the child believes firmly in, desires, and even loves his or her society (Furth, 1990). In short, society reproduces itself not by transmission from one generation to the next, but instead by each new generation constructing a new society for itself. Because the child and subsequently the adult firmly believes in his or her own construction, the danger inherent in knowing structures as the fragile basis of society can be substantially contained, for the individual will act, as Gibson did in circulating petitions and organizing fund raisers, to maintain and defend his or her own construction.

The process of societal adaptation and transformation necessarily involves a knower who can reflect — to a modest extent — on society's basis in structures of knowing and on the fragility of society and who, in the face of this partial knowledge, strives to construct a new and better framework for interpersonal and societal relations, one that not only more securely defends against the problem of fragility but also permits the individual greater freedom qua individual within the constraints of society. To cooperate and participate in society means to subordinate ones goals to those of the group. But the boundary between friendship, cooperation, and community, on the one hand, and structures of hierarchical control, domination, and power (e.g., structures of racism, sexism, and social class), on the other, is not always clearly perceptible. In ant and bee societies, there is no individual protest against hierarchy, domination, and power; in contrast, the emancipatory interest has been a constant in human history.

The problem of the fragility of societal relations is never fully solved: too much fragility leads to the collapse of society, too little yields a rigid society, one that is unable to adapt and so will ultimately collapse. Similarly, the problems of hierarchy, domination, and power are never resolved. Too little reflection by individuals on these issues, too little emancipatory protest, leaves a society that is sterile, unchanging, and stagnant; too much attention to these issues yields merely a collection of conscious, rational individuals, each acting in his or her own apparent interest, but likely not in the interest of maintaining and reproducing society itself. As psychological individuals, we can acknowledge but I suspect we can never fully accept either the relativism of our own constructions of society or the necessary subordination of our interests to those of society. And there is no reason that we should, for the maintenance and the adaptive transformation of society depend upon the continued illusions both that the society that we have constructed is valid and real and that our motives and goals as individuals really do matter.

It is time to cut this strand and tie it with a knot: Traditional approaches to understanding the relationship between the individual and society have taken for granted the existence of autonomous individuals and have asked what benefits accrue to the individual in belonging to a society. I have raised a question from the perspective of a society that has an interest in maintaining, reproducing, and transforming itself, namely, of what use are psychological individuals to human society? Of course, neither the individual nor the society preexists the other; the nature of each depends on the simultaneous existence of the other.

WHERE IS SOCIETY LOCATED?

The theme of this volume, the impact of specific environments on cognitive development, constitutes another strand in my commentary. The child is immersed in specific family, peer, school, and community environments, as well as in specific cultural and historical conditions, and all of these presumably have explanatory roles in the child's development. Any number of developmental textbooks, book chapters, and overhead slides show the developing child at the center of a set of concentric circles representing specific environments embedded within more encompassing environments. It is true that a child walking in a straight line would first leave his or her home and then the school district, the community, the state, the nation and culture, and so forth. Yet there is no reason to suppose that this linear progression corresponds to the psychological significance of each of these environments for the child. Indeed, I take one of Gibson's and Reed's major points to be that we must get beyond thinking of environments merely in such physical terms as time and space and instead in terms of the possibilities that environments afford for action.

For Gibson in the early 1950s, the Field of Promoted Action included among its affordances academic freedom and the possibility of research on social issues. When there was a threat to the Field of Free Action (the attacks on Gundlach and other academics and the harassment by the FBI), Gibson responded by defending the Field of Free Action through circulating petitions and organizing fund raisers. Later, following defeat and contraction of the Field of Free Action, he sought to expand the Field of Free Action through strengthening his ties with European psychologists and increasing his research productivity in the area of perception (Reed, 1988a, p. 113).

Gibson's actions were far more profound than merely knowing about the societal environment through acting within it. Rather, either Gibson was acting in order to restore the affordances that he understood to be intrinsic to the societal environment, or he was acting to transform the societal environment to include those affordances that he believed would provide both greater stability to society and greater opportunity for individual freedom. In either case, Gibson's actions appear to be instigated not by the societal environment as given, but rather by the societal environment as he had constructed it, that he firmly believed in, and that he desired and even loved. Academic freedom and the possibility of research on social issues were significant for Gibson and worth defending not because these aspects of the societal environment had been transmitted to him by a preceding generation, but rather because he had constructed for himself an understanding of society in which academic freedom and research on social issues were among the affordances.

Reed (1988a) noted that one of Gibson's research interests had been the problem of social change in general, and that Gibson recognized as the key problem for any theory of social change explaining "how an individual raised in one society with one set of proprieties comes to be able to perceive the limits of that tradition. How can awareness break through the encrusted ideology of the dominant group" (p. 65)? In other words, the key problem addressed by Gibson's theory of social change, as for Piaget's structural--developmental theory, is the problem of novelty.

Where was this specific societal environment that Gibson as an individual had constructed, the societal environment that afforded academic freedom and research on social issues? Traditionally, in our textbooks, chapters, and overhead slides, cultural modes of discourse and values such as academic freedom are located among the outermost of the concentric circles, yet as psychologically constructed and salient aspects of Gibson's environment it would seem far more appropriate to locate them at the center, within the mind of Gibson himself. In short, the societal and cultural environment is not "out there" along with the physical environment but is instead "inside."

I find myself persuaded by much of what I read both in Reed's chapter (this volume) and about Gibson's ecological approach to perception (Reed, 1988a; see also Reed, 1988b). Yet it would appear at first glance that by locating the societal environment within the mind of the individual rather than "out there" along with the physical environment I might be giving rise to a fundamental disagreement between us. After all, in his chapter Reed (this volume) makes clear, for example, that social norms are not private, subjective states, but instead are public and exist in the environment; that socially constructed entities, such as mailboxes and baseball bats, exist in the environment alongside natural objects such as trees; and that all meaningful aspects of the environment, including social events, can be perceived directly (as opposed to processes of information detection, symbolic interpretation, or the formation of mental representations).

One way to reconcile the apparent difference between us would be to grant Reed's and Gibson's position for all social events that are, as Reed says, sufficiently embodied so that some aspect is perceptible, but to reserve for a societal environment constructed within the mind of the individual those cultural modes and values that are not sufficiently embodied. This is an awkward reconciliation, at best, as there would seem to be a continuum of embodiment rather than a clear separation between that which might be embodied and that which typically cannot be sufficiently embodied so as to be perceptible.

A far better reconciliation, however, is to grant that Reed and Gibson are correct regarding the direct perception of what is in the social environment, because this follows directly from the notion I have advanced here that the social environment is not "out there" but is in fact constructed in the mind of the individual. Obviously, the individual has no difficulty perceiving directly that which he or she has previously constructed.

One of the important changes that has taken place in recent years in how we understand psychological development has been what I call the *externalizing* of cognition into the environment. That is, cognition is no longer understood as an attribute located within the mind of individual persons, but rather as developing within the framework of interpersonal relations within which the child is immersed. Several theorists have found it useful to abandon individual cognition and consciousness as the starting point for individual and societal development in favor of interpersonal relations, communication, and cooperation as the starting point (Habermas, 1984; Harre, 1984; Meacham, 1984b; Vygotsky, 1978). For example, Habermas rejected intrasubjectivity as a starting point for understanding the individual and society, arguing instead for basing these in intersubjectivity, in the community of persons in dialogue. A similar perspective is advanced by Harre, who argued that the primary reality is the array of persons in conversation, with the psychological realities of human minds brought into being only as secondary entities.

Reed's and Gibson's emphasis on the role of joint intentions in the process of cognitive development, on perceiving what the environment affords for others as well as oneself, and on the treatment of cognition ecologically not as merely mental but also as public is certainly consistent with this trend toward the externalizing of cognition. What should be the complementary—but not antagonistic—trend is that which I have woven into this commentary: the *internalizing* of the environment into the mind, that is, the *constructing* of the environment by the child. Piaget, of course, would point out that it is not merely the societal or cultural environment that is constructed by the child but also the interpersonal and physical environments.

And so it is appropriate to cut this strand as well and tie it with a knot. In answering the question implicit in the theme of this volume, regarding the impact of specific environments upon cognitive development, we must first transcend the false separation of environment from mind. Mind has its origins within the environment of interpersonal and societal relations; the environment of interpersonal and societal relations is produced and reproduced through mind. My argument is not that mind contains a constructed representation of interpersonal and societal relations; rather, the knowledge that is mind is co-extensive with the relationships that constitute our interpersonal and societal environments. Locating society within the mind, as I have suggested, makes sense only if it is understood that mind must be located within society. The question posed by the theme of this volume regarding the effects of specific environments on cognitive development thus appears inappropriate with respect to the societal and cultural environment, for the form of the question appears to assume an environment that is separable from the processes of cognition when in fact there is an *interpenetration* of both cognitive development and how the societal environment is conceived. All this would be familiar to Piaget (1971, p. 361; see also Chapman, 1986), for whom the operations of intelligence and the operations of social interaction are the same, for whom the most general forms of thought are either forms of cognitive exchange or of interindividual regulation.

WILL OUR SOCIETY BE REPRODUCED?

There remain more than a few loose strands to be pulled together: What are the implications for cognitive development of a contraction or a stunting of the Field of Free Action? More important, to be consistent with the perspective I have adopted within this commentary, what are the implications for the maintenance and reproduction of society? How can we assess the loss of expertise, creativity, and spirit in American society as a result of the persecution and the forced conformity of the McCarthy era? And how can we assess the loss to Chinese society as a result of the massacre that followed the demonstrations for freedom in Tiananmen Square? And now for the critical question: Can we as adults be confident that the next generation of American children will construct its society so as to reproduce what we regard as our best traditions, values, commitments, and hopes?

Let's consider some basic facts about the specific environments in which American children are now developing. Almost one of every four children under age 6 in the United States is developing in a family environment that is below the standard of living established by the poverty line. The "poverty line" is the minimum standard of living based on pretax income and adjusted for family size and changes in the cost of living, as defined by the United States Government. In 1989, the poverty line was $9,890 for a family of three and $12,675 for a family of four. In 1987, according to a study by the National Center for Children in Poverty at Columbia University ("Report raises alarm," 1990), 32.5 million Americans lived below the poverty line. Of these, 13 million were less than 18 years old and 5 million were age 6 or younger.

More than 40% of all U.S. children living in poverty are White, although the rate of poverty is substantially higher among Blacks and Hispanics. More than half of poor children under age 6 live outside urban areas. More than half have at least one working parent, but minimum wage jobs in 1987 paid only $6,968. Since 1980, federal programs initiated in the 1960s to assist low-income families, such as the Head Start preschool education program, the food stamp program, the school-lunch program, the Upward Bound precollege preparation program, and funds for housing, have all had their funding severely reduced. The funding for Head Start, for example, is not adequate to provide education for even one fifth of the low-income children who are eligible.

In major U.S. cities, children are developing in neighborhoods in which an average of one person every 3 days is beaten, robbed, or shot (Kotlowitz, 1987). The sound of gunshots is common. Children are taught to walk rather than run when they hear gunshots. Otherwise, in panic and not knowing where the gunshots are coming from, they run directly through the gunfire. Children grow up with the experience of seeing other children shot, either inadvertently or as victims of rival gangs. Children worry about being asked to join gangs; parents purchase burial insurance on their children. The children suffer nightmares, depression, and personality disorders, and become withdrawn or aggressive.

In the midwestern United States, the emotional stresses associated with the financial collapse of large numbers of independent family farms has been described as more brutal than during the Depression (Wall, 1985). Farm children, who often work closely with their parents in farm chores, are now growing up in an environment of worry, hopelessness, alienation, and fear. The frustrations and loss of confidence in losing farms that have been within the same family for generations are vented in increased rates of family abuse, alcoholism, violence, and suicide. Children are scared when they see that their parents are scared.

"Not since slavery has so much calamity and ongoing catastrophe been visited on black males," said Health and Human Services Secretary Louis Sullivan; "We are watching our own demise," said Ed Pitt, former director of health and environmental services for the National Urban League (McAllister, 1990). Urban Black men face a 1 in 10 chance of being killed during their lifetimes, compared to a 1 in 80 chance for White men. For young Black males, homicide is the leading cause of death. Among the other problems Black males experience are persistently high unemployment, continued high poverty rates, a decline in real income, a drop in college enrollments, and decreased life expectancy due to higher death rates than Whites in virtually every disease category, including heart disease, stroke, and cancer.

Certainly many additional dreadful statistics and poignant accounts could be appended to these few paragraphs. The point, as this strand is woven into my commentary, is that great numbers of children in the United States are no doubt constructing for themselves a bleak version of society, one that they firmly believe in and are committed to as real, but one in which they foresee only limited roles for themselves and limited prospects for significant improvement in the conditions for development (the Field of Promoted Action). Societies are not transmitted from one generation to the next, but are reconstructed anew by each successive generation. The society that these children are constructing for themselves is the society that will become American society within the next two decades. The tragedy of Tiananmen Square represents a crushing blow to the aspirations of a generation of Chinese youth; the tragedies of development within specific environments in the United States will have profound consequences in the failure of our present society to be reproduced.

Is there a pattern that is discernible in the fabric that I have woven of the various strands of this commentary? No doubt there are loose ends and even holes. It seems essential that we achieve an understanding of development that overcomes the false dichotomies between the individual and society, between mind and society, between mind and environment, between cognition and environment, between "inside" and "outside," between "internal" and "external." This will occur not by assuming that each of these constructs enjoys an independent existence and then worrying about how they might interact. Rather, the various constructs must be understood as deriving their existence from the fact of their interpenetration. Given this standpoint, our responsibility as individuals for the defense of social environments against the loss of affordances — psychologically salient aspects — and for the reproduction of society as it will be constructed within the minds of the next generation becomes clear. The McCarthy era, Tiananmen Square, and the neglect of specific environments for development of the next generation are all of the same cloth.

REFERENCES

Chapman, M. (1986). The structure of exchange: Piaget's sociological theory. *Human Development, 29,* 181–194.

Furth, H. G. (1990). The "radical imaginary" underlying social institutions: Its developmental base. *Human Development, 33,* 202–213.

Gibson, J. J. (1979). *The ecological approach to visual perception.* Boston: Houghton-Mifflin.

Habermas, J. (1984). *The theory of communicative action.* Boston: Beacon Press.

Harre, R. (1984). *Personal being.* Cambridge, MA: Harvard University Press.

Kotlowitz, A. (1987, Oct. 27). Urban trauma: Day-to-day violence takes a terrible toll on inner-city youth; witness to endless brutality, Lafayette Walton, 12, has many emotional wounds; a comparison with Vietnam. *The Wall Street Journal,* pp. A1, A26.

McAllister, B. (1990, Feb. 12-18). The plight of young Black men in America. *The Washington Post National Weekly Edition,* pp. 6–7.

McCarthy, T. (1978). *The critical theory of Jurgen Habermas.* Cambridge: The MIT Press.

Meacham, J. A. (1984a). The individual as consumer and producer of historical change. In K. A. McCluskey & H. W. Reese (Eds.), *Life-span developmental psychology: Historical and generational effects* (pp. 47–72). New York: Academic Press.

Meacham, J. A. (1984b). The social basis of intentional action. *Human Development, 27,* 119–124.

Meacham, J. A. (1989). Discovering the social-cultural context of research: Listening to and learning from research participants. In D. A. Kramer & M. Bopp (Eds.), *Transformation in clinical and developmental psychology* (pp. 136–153). New York: Springer-Verlag.

Meacham, J. A. (1991). The importance of interpersonal relations for formal operational development. In J. D. Sinnott & J. C. Cavanaugh (Eds.), *Bridging paradigms: Positive development in adulthood and aging* (pp. 99–112). New York: Praeger.

Meacham, J. A., & Emont, N. C. (1989). The interpersonal basis of everyday problem-solving.

In J. D. Sinnott (Ed.), *Problem-solving: Theory and application* (pp. 7–23). New York: Praeger.

Piaget, J. (1971). *Biology and knowledge* (B. Walsh, Trans.). Chicago: University of Chicago Press.

Reed, E. S. (1988a). *James J. Gibson and the psychology of perception.* New Haven: Yale University Press.

Reed, E. S. (1988b). The affordances of the animate environment: Social science from the ecological point of view. In T. Ingold (Ed.), *What is an animal?* (pp. 110–126). London: Unwin Hyman.

Report raises alarm on children in poverty. (1990, April 5). *The Buffalo News,* p. A-5.

Vygotsky, L. S. (1978). *Mind in society.* Cambridge, MA: Harvard University Press.

Wall, W. L. (1985, Nov. 7). Growing up afraid: Farm crisis is taking subtle toll on children in distressed families; insecurity and tension affect personalities and grades; some become runaways; hauling the pet hogs away. *The Wall Street Journal,* pp. A1, A22.

11 Rumble or Revolution: A Commentary

William Kessen
Yale University

I begin with two stories; they can stand, like altar candles, to represent and to light my task. The first is about my son John whom we found, in his third year, walking up and down the living room saying over and over "I just can't stand it, I just can't stand it." Then he stopped, paused in his speech, and said "I wonder what 'I just can't stand it' means."

The second story comes from Francis Galton's (1853) description of his explorations into southwest Africa—he was the first European to make the trek. He came upon a tribal group in the interior that puzzled and aroused his scientific ardor—the Hottentots, in fact. He was especially interested in the pendulous buttocks of the women that were a major marker of beauty in the group; as a physical anthropologist (again, the first), he had to make the requisite measurements but, as an English gentleman, he saw no way to wind his tape measure around a sterling example of Hottentot beauty. After worrying about the problem for a while, he hit on a solution. From a discrete distance he observed a woman—Mrs. Petrus, by name—standing for a time in the sun. Galton set up his sextant, made the necessary angular measurements and, when he had paced off the distance between himself and Mrs. Petrus somewhat later, he solved the problem by triangulation. I return to both my stories.

STATEMENT

The chapters gathered in this volume have been a celebration of heroes—Piaget, Vygotsky, and Gibson—and they have been thoughtful exciting attempts not only to praise the heroes but to honor their wisdom and their impending victory. And Philadelphia[1] is an apt place for the articulation of a Developmental Declaration of Independence. I can cast Thomas Jefferson and John Adams and Roger Sherman (I have some difficulty with Benjamin Franklin, the prototypical yuppy of American life) but the joyful invention is to pick our George III. The obvious candidate is poor scapegoated B. F. Skinner, the corporate victim, but perhaps a better candidate is Réné Descartes, who surely has misled more people than anyone since Plato. But no, I think that the enemy—our George III—is the antique tradition of established science. This volume is, in fact, the setting for a Revolution and I want to collect my comments under three titles: (a) Crimes of the King; (b) What is left? With what timbers shall we build the New Republic? and (c) How is it that the enemy does not seem to care? Why are they not marching on Philadelphia?

CRIMES OF THE KING

There exist many tensions between the emerging intentions of developmental psychologists and the traditions of experimental science. There is neither room nor reason to examine the tensions closely here; what the next paragraphs will attempt is a calling off of *five* issues that have appeared, not always at the surface, in the preceding chapters. Of course, the resolution of some disagreements that I treat breezily will take years, if indeed they are susceptible to willful resolution.

The Persistence of Nature Versus Nurture.   The distinction has been around for millenia and was put in sharp focus by Galton, but it has some curious political implications that make it damnable. Nature-versus-nurture has had a long and ugly career as the carrier of racial prejudice. Again, let me tell a story. An American journalist, while interviewing Duvalier, the old dictator of Haiti, asked, "What proportion of Haitians are White?" Duvalier's immediate answer was "Oh, about 96 or 97 percent." Believing that he had misheard, the reporter repeated his question and, on receiving the same answer, asked for an explanation. Duvalier's answer poses our charge, "How do you determine who is Black in the United States?"

But the political utility of the nature–nurture contrast goes beyond skin color; the simplest skeptical statement of the case is: Nature has been used,

---

[1]The chapters printed in this volume were first presented at the meetings of the Jean Piaget Society in Philadelphia, Pennsylvania. The conceit that runs through my chapter is built on that coincidence.

almost without exception, as a weapon to *diminish the importance* of groups derogated by the culture—Blacks, Irish, Jews, women, gays, the handicapped, among them.

Not surprisingly, there are intricacies in the crime that make it difficult for the prosecutor to frame the charge. There are critical intellectual issues that can be cast in terms of ancestral influence on human beings; contemporary biology sings with the discoveries of genetics but, when the discussion leaves the laboratory for the street (or even for the textbook in psychology), it seems that some unfavored group of people will be put down.

Of course, the chief objection to the nature–nurture contrast is intellectual; it divides what cannot be divided and it contrasts what cannot be contrasted. Our conversations about children would improve mightily if the pair went away; one of the collective great strengths of the papers you have read here is the demonstration that the worthy and intriguing problems of the developmental psychologist can be framed without the encumbrance of the mean-spirited distinction.

The Universal Character of Knowledge.   The rage for uniformity of law and the universality of science has oscillated, too, over the last 500 years but, at the peak of modern scientific confidence, universality became one of the *defining characters* of human knowledge. Again, the skeptic can jibe merrily—if it is not true everywhere, it is not true. Yet, the true believer's terror of variety apparently shuts out the bewildering (and wonderful) texture and sheer puzzlement of the world. Sad to say, the lust for universality will not go away, so let us try a lesser test of the artificiality that the crime permits. Imagine an organization of the scientific community where several (say, national) divisions were established and where communication among them was eliminated. After 50 years or so, we would possess many different sociologies and different political sciences and different psychologies and, yes, different physicses, as well. Let us leave aside the question of what methods would be used to deal with the variation in solutions; the point would be clearly made that there is nothing inevitable in the growth of knowledge.[2]

There is another form of universalism that has plagued psychology in particular; the search for *cause.* One of the best defenses of the experiment as a part of method is that it is the only certain way to detect a "true" cause as against a casual or correlational connection. Psychologists have grumbled occasionally about the high cost of such surety but attacks on the

---

[2]Incidentally, it is one of the functions of cults (psychoanalysis, behaviorism, Department of Defense) to *encourage* the segregated development of answers to delicate questions.

fundamental epistemological status of cause have come from other sources over the last 20 years or so.[3] Suffice it to say, in our bound space, that the search for cause has not been a friend to developmental psychology.

Another far less important cost of universalism has been the psychologist's search for a permanent part of the person (and the earlier detected the better)—the *trait* or index or temperamental character which is held to define or to delimit a person. Until Neisser and Gould and Sternberg started their assorted critical examinations, the best example for us was the Intelligence Quotient, that ruby of person that lies in numerical guise behind our navels.[4] We may, in fact, be watching the slow demise of psychology's most celebrated and most heavily published-about creation. But, fear not; if IQ passes on, there will be attachment strength or shyness or cognitive flexibility to take its place.

One simplifying way of phrasing the crime is to speak of the desire for a *closed system*. There is not a new philosophical point here; the unavailability of closed systems, even in the tightest of sciences, has long been known. Rather, I call attention to the almost inevitable tendency of child watchers (and of intellectuals in general) to force their observations, first, into general principles and, then, into a system and, not infrequently, into a cult. It is almost inevitable, then, to leave the original observation untended and to defend the weak borders of the system. Alas!

Alas, too, that the commentator who sails too vigorously from Scylla spins into Charybdis. There are regularities in human behavior—universals, if you like—that keep us from falling in love with frogs and that make all languages intertranslatable (sort of!) and that keep our attention close to the task in hand. Yet, it is imperative that developmental psychology loosen its tie to the dream of the one best system, be it theoretical or methodological; in the finest and fullest of scholarly worlds, we will be no more than federated—never united.

Verbalism.   I gotta use words when I talk to you and language is the shared and essential province of poet and psychologist alike. Perhaps, however, it is worth attending to the fundamentally antiverbal (nonverbal, for a weaker assertion) moves of the chief shakers in psychology of our time—Freud and Piaget. Both of the great minds, in ways so different from one another that the heart of the commentator bounces in joy, saw as the

---

[3]The most sweeping (and the least carefully wrought) jeremiad against cause has been Michel Foucault's (1980). For a somewhat steadier, although hardly kind, analysis, see Feyerabend (1987).

[4]Once more, it is critical that the boundaries of my epistemological sourness be indicated. There is nothing *wrong* of itself with the notion of IQ; the reason for regret is the elevation of the number to the best single measure of humanity—the measure, astonishingly, by which we choose our physicians, our lawyers, and our senators.

basic target of his critique the *derivative, falsifying,* or *irrelevant* character of language. Skinner moved the problem of language out of the center in a radically different way; he trivialized language by making it a behavioral *phenomenon.* Only Vygotsky has made speech into an essential part of developing cognition.

Perhaps it was the pleasure of having language back in psychology as a proper object of study after its long reductionist exile that led us to forget the messages of several of our masters, but a developmental psychology that was overly behavioristic in 1955 has become overly verbal in 1990.

I seize on the commentator's right to gloss entangled and tesselated issues in order to remind you that the problem of verbalism is two problems — what we study and what we say about our study. It may be worth noting the *solidification of the word;* somehow, "attachment" or "intelligent" or "smile" or "eye position" have a specificity and a depth that were not present in most of our observations. Of course, the history of developmental psychology could be written as the story of our wrestle with the problem of moving from one domain to the other, from what we see to what we say; the down side of the story would be our collective inability to find fulfilling avenues.

The Ivory and the Abstract Tower.   Kings have had the charge often made against them that they occupy distant castles and talk only to other people in distant castles. As is seen in my summary comments, castle-talk is not all bad; how else could the society live and flourish?

But the fact of the matter in developmental psychology is that we have built our knowledge on the middle-class White American child who represents perhaps 1% of the world's population and probably not much more of the world's caretaking variety. It is the comic inversion of universalism: If it is true for us, it is true for everyone. Again, I beat an old drum, worn with pounding, but the tattoo has not much changed our procedures for finding out about the lives of children. The clinicians and the anthropologists (when they are not pressing for universal truths) show us the perplexities of our endeavor[5] but the boundaries of our working lives (how desperately we need a cartographer of that territory) forestall our *seeing* the perplexities and they make (to take only one example) our textbooks of developmental psychology *local* works.

Individuality.   The accretion of *individual* from adjective to noun to cultural principle over the century of psychology tells a mighty tale. It is not only that we act as though we believed that the history and experience of a

---

[5]A demonstration of the limits of our intellectual compass is contained in Lidz and Lidz (1989). They reported Herdt's observations on initiation practices in Papua New Guinea.

person is contained within the bordering skin (we all "know" the truth and discard such silliness) but, more, we seem to believe that we can discover what is there by an intense and scientific look at the singular person. Our obsession with studies of the infant child since Baldwin has many sources but, almost certainly, one of them is the conviction that, in the infant, we can approach the unsullied *individual*.[6]

But the news is good. Although the machinery of politics uses the metaphysics of individual responsibility to avoid recognizing the scandal of a society where one fifth of us are enslaved by poverty and injustice,[7] developmental psychologists move haltingly (because we do not possess a canonical method) toward the study of groups and of families.[8]

One last comment on individuality, a theme that could make either a psychological or an epistemological or a political or a historical treatise. The psychology would ask about the loneliness of the individual, the epistemology would open with a blast about academic arrogance, the politics would examine the streets of Bedford-Stuyvesant and Watts, and the history has already written its first chapters. The concentration of the technical student of children on the lives of particular persons measures important changes in Western culture over the past 200 years. As we slept fewer and fewer people to a room (even fewer and fewer people to a bed), the conceptual unit of psychology for the academicians (who had more rooms as well as a yen for pure science) could only be the individual (see Flandrin, 1979). In fact, Piaget and Gibson are as individualistic as my first-grade teacher, Miss Jencks.

It is not too much to say that Cartesian language, Cartesian psychology, and individualism are the dominant themes of American developmental study. With the 20th-century loss of clear transcendental commitment — for contemporary American scholars, there is no God, no devil, no fate, no destiny, no chance, no accident, no demons, and no tree nymphs — the belief in the epistemological purity of the individual is trying to fill the gap.

---

[6]Ben S. Bradley (1991), in his article "Infancy as Paradise," in *Human Development*, dissected the current professional attitude toward infants with a revealing scalpel.

[7]In 1859, C. L. Brace (1894), the executive director of New York's Childrens Aid Society, wrote "Each poor, deserted, unfortunate little creature in the streets is an *individual*, like no other being whom God has created; and this grand fact of his individuality must be considered in any methods of reform for his vices, or of education for his faculties."

Brace's intention was to remove each child from the mass of the "criminal" or the "immigrant" or the "lost" into which the nineteenth century (and we) cast outsiders. His was, in part, an ethical and religious statement, not an assertion about the sources of human variation.

[8]I leave it for a future commentator to amuse an audience with stories of the late 20th-century psychologist's renewed interest in the family just as the traditional family became an anachronism.

To move that belief aside, American society would have to be transformed.[9]

Let me turn for a moment from the aside that is my commentary to a smaller aside. Why do we have an emphasis on context, on specific environments *now?* There are probably several reasons, interconnected in curious ways. First, there are few living giants in developmental psychology. Piaget and Vygotsky and Gibson are memorial, not present, and that permits our open critique (by the way, there are few living giants in psychology at large). Second, and very important, the classical vision of social science is under keen scrutiny — by Foucault, by Gergen, by Feyerabend, by Rorty (with memories of our certain ancestor, John Dewey), most tellingly by Geertz — and we share some of their doubts.[10] Third, technological change bites at our heels — facsimile and computer chips, microwave and disposable diapers (which, by themselves, have changed the timing and psychological intensity of toilet training in the United States and added significantly to our problems of environmental pollution). And, at last, a factor we cannot yet fully assess are the recent changes in the status of women; the changes hold the germ of a Revolution that can reorganize all our lives and all parts of our lives. The Developmental Revolution lies in the shadow of that greater transformation.

I will hurry by these beguiling teasers to go to my second lemma. What's left? After we have convicted the King, what shall we build with? I confess that I feared for a moment that the only remaining sturdy planks in the wreck were statistics and the academician's lecture, but perhaps the tale can be happier than that.

WHAT IS LEFT?

The widespread reassessment of Piaget as developmental theorist, the attacks on narrow experimentalism, and the elevation of context that the present book captures — all represent a shaking of the foundations that have underlaid developmental psychology for decades. My guess is that the reconstruction will go on for several more years. In the past, such periods of doubt have ended either with the appearance of a fine radical mind (Piaget, in particular, gathered up many loose lines to engender a different American psychology) or with the appearance of a new method (the IQ test

---

[9]Our new here-focused attention to Vygotsky gives promise of wrenching us apart from the clutch of radical individuality. We shall see.

[10]In addition to the texts already cited, the case for revision has been made in: Foucault (1970); Gergen (1982); Feyerabend (1975); Rorty (1979); Geertz (1973), among many others; and, Dewey (1938).

and the Skinner box are examples). In the absence of either a new person or a new procedure, we will shuffle along with partial and conflicting visions, each of us attempting to pull some revealing truth from our unrevealing children.

The Study of Everyday Behavior.   Each new building block contains risk and perhaps none so much as the shift from the classical experiment to the observational study of everyday behavior. But we can be bolstered by the example of the four developmental giants and we can be guided by the success of our first attempts.[11]

The frightening prospect is chaos, a sort of psychological *Lord of the Rings.* But the risk is slight; consider, if you will, the hard database of Piaget's and Freud's and Vygotsky's observations. The only one of today's heroes who is an accepted experimental psychologist is Gibson and his use of his data was imaginative and against the grain. My emphasis, by the way, on the procedures for studying everyday behavior is no accident; just as we have learned that "language" can be studied in the laboratory, I am certain that we will discover the simplifying possibilities of studying skiing and grocery shopping and teaching in the comfort of the laboratory.[12] In fact, of course, we have.

But the intellectual reason for the study of everyday behavior is sweet in its simplicity: Everyday behavior is what we want to know about. Somehow, in the forest (garden? jungle?) of choices—Barker or Hull, Neisser or Anderson, Cole or Siegler—we lost sight of the core goal, the *understanding of what children do.* The present volume is testimony that we are back on track and that the long search for a theory of the environment will not emerge in full scholastic garb but will be constructed, one pant at a time, in the serious and careful study of children *where they are.*

The Contextual Emphasis.   The uniting joy of the chapters gathered here is their concern with context. Developmental study can break the bonds of universalism by the work that has been put on exemplary display here. Of course, contextualism is not without its risks as well; the concentration of 5,000 researchers, each on his or her own personal context, would make a joke of developmental study. The sharing of observations, the reach for connecting procedures, the chilling recognition that we all share a fairly coherent notion of reality, the acceptance of everlasting

---

[11]The lead of Neisser has been mirrored in developmental study by Rogoff and Lave (1984).

[12]With every assertion, I seem to require a retracting amendment. Of course, the laboratory experiment is a splendid human invention and one cannot understand many psychological questions without its use; nonetheless, the experiment can claim no *general* loyalty by people in 1990 who want to understand children.

ambiguity, all will modulate the dangers of personal science. Again, the peculiar role of conventions and seminars is to guard against the wildly exotic.[13]

Empiricism and the Language of the Academy. My screed about the crimes of traditional academic psychology should not paint over the procedural achievements of our discipline. The heart principle of developmental study lies in our conviction that we can find out some sort of answer to the questions we pose. We have seen in the foregoing chapters that we may have to twist our first graduate course in research method into somewhat unusual shapes but, *always,* the novelties are in the service of discovery.

We have another helper. Despite the attempts by several of the contributors to provide us with a special language for our work, we still speak an odd form of English. No one has written a grammar book for the psychological language (terrifying prospect, in a way[14]) but students of children possess a tongue that is rather fluent and that is widely shared.[15] If we are aware of the barbs and traps in what we can so easily say, the common language can keep us together and keep us working in translatable domains.

The Use of Narrative. A form for the expression of knowledge which we have usually seen only at the margins of the field (in the work of Barker, 1951, or of Coles, 1967), is *the interesting story.* Piaget gave us delightful narrative accounts of his children's behavior but shuffles them into a stuffy interpretative deck. Sometimes in book reviews or in summary articles, the developmentalist will escape the strictures of proper scientific discourse, but rarely.

Again, Clifford Geertz (appallingly for some of his colleagues) has shown that he can describe and interpret an observation with the color of the short story and still communicate effectively with most professional anthropologists. The use of narrative by students of children is an inviting opportunity to catch some of the complexity that eludes us (or that we want to avoid) without selling out to the Great Beast Slop. I recommend that we have the nerve to try it.

---

[13]Once more, beware. Perhaps the *only* characteristic that our heroes shared was their wild exoticism; but there is plenty of room for attendant lords.

[14]Mandler and I tried more than 30 years ago (Mandler & Kessen, 1959), in a burst of youthful confidence, to write a language for our field. The book is more a measure of the arrogance of that time than of Mandler's and my competence; it would be a very different book if we wrote it now.

[15]At the 10th meeting of the International Society for the Study of Behavioral Development, held recently in Finland and attended by developmentalists from numerous countries, there was little terminological or nomenclatural debate. Either we have a common language or we are kidding ourselves mercilessly.

Inner Certainty. Over the years, I have spent some effort arguing against the role of the developmental psychologist as *expert* in our culture but I stand in a minority. For most of us, our knowledge of children not only gives us the right, it gives us a positive obligation, to inform the world of policy about the right way to go. My guess is that the scholar as reformer, in a tradition older than our discipline, will continue to be a sustaining part of developmental study.

The reforming zeal of the children's scholar is tied closely to another root principle of American life, the unshakable belief in inevitable progress. Little as our times have helped to convince us of the validity of the belief, the conviction lives on, supported by our optimism and supporting it. It may be that the hopeful optimism of the American developmentalist is, right or wrong, one of the ties that binds us.

CONCLUSION: WHERE IS THE ENEMY?

There is enough good timber to build the New Developmentalism and this volume demonstrates that there is talent enough among the carpenters. But I have left unanswered my third question: Why are the enemy not marching on Philadelphia against us? The answer is tangled. For one thing, parts of the campaign have already been won; we even hear that we are in a post-Piagetian world. Second, conventional academic psychology is flush with achievement and with confidence; we have no march on Philadelphia because the redcoats are happily bound in another direction. Third, and it is good news, we do not have a grand edifice, either of work or of community. It may be in the nature of the reformulations discussed here that we *cannot* build grand social structures. Rather, our need is for the coming together of scholars, in meetings and in books, to tell stories about our children, to explore a prodigiously wide range of ideas, and to talk together cheerfully.

My opening stories carry my message. The world of developmental study will be as ambiguous for us as language was for my son John but, somehow, we, like Francis Galton, will solve our problems of knowing. Can we expect to do more? There is both promise and pause in James Mark Baldwin's aphorism (it too may be a cultural truth) —

The self insists — the world resists.

REFERENCES

Barker, R. G. (1951). *One boy's day: A specimen record of behavior.* New York: Harper.
Brace, E. (Ed.). (1894). *The life of Charles Loring Brace.* New York: Scribner.
Bradley, B. (1991). Infancy in paradise. *Human Development, 34,* 35–54.

Coles, R. (1967). *Children of crisis: A study of crisis and fear.* Boston: Atlantic Brown.

Dewey, J. (1938). *Logic: The theory of inquiry.* New York: Holt.

Feyerabend, P. (1987). *Farewell to reason.* London: Verso.

Feyerabend, P. K. (1975). *Against method.* London: New Left Press.

Flandrin, J.-L. (1979). *Families in former times: Kinship, household, and sexuality* (R. Southern, Trans.). Cambridge: Cambridge University Press.

Foucault, M. (1970). *The order of things.* London: Tavistock.

Foucault, M. (1980). *Power/knowledge: Selected interviews and other writings, 1972–1977* (C. Gordon, Ed.). New York: Pantheon.

Galton, F. (1853). *The narrative of an explorer in tropical South Africa.* London: Murray.

Geertz, C. (1973). *The interpretation of cultures.* New York: Basic Books.

Gergen, K. J. (1982). *Toward transformation in social knowledge.* New York: Springer.

Lidz, T., & Lidz, R. (1989). *Oedipus in the stone age.* Madison, CT: International Universities Press.

Mandler, G., & Kessen, W. (1959). *The language of psychology.* New York: Wiley.

Rogoff, B., & Lave, J. (Eds.). (1984). *Everyday cognition: Its development in social context.* Cambridge, MA: Harvard University Press.

Rorty, R. (1979). *Philosophy and the mirror of nature.* Princeton, NJ: Princeton University Press.

Author Index

Page numbers in *italics* denote complete bibliographic information

A

Alessandri, S., 86, *91*
Allport, G. W., 11, *40*
American Cartographic Association, 168
Anderson, J., 48, *73*
Acredolo, L., 51, *73*
Aries, P., 54, *73*
Arns, F. J., 184, *207*

B

Bachevalier, J., 113, *116*
Backhurst, D., 126, *150*
Baker, J., 133, *152*
Baker, J. G., 38, *41*
Baker-Sennett, J., 142, *150*
Bakhtin, M. M., 140, *150*
Bandura, A., 185, 187, *205*
Barker, R. G., 277, *278*
Barnard, K. E., 14, *41*
Bartlett, F. W., 47, *73*
Basalla, G., 55, *73*
Baumrind, D., 32, *40*, 212, *223*
Bearison, D. J., 130, *150*
Beckwith, L., 12, *40, 41, 42*
Bee, H. L., 14, *41*
Beilin, H., 94, *114*, 173, *180*, 227, *250*
Bem, D. J., 12, *41*
Bentley, A. F., 123, *150*

Berger, P. L., 139, *150*
Bidell, T. R., 94, 99, 104, *114*
Black, A. E., 32, *40*
Block, J., 12, 13, *41, 42*
Block, J. H., 12, 13, *41, 42*
Bloom, B., 231, 238, 240, *250*
Bovet, M., 123, *150*
Brace, E., 274, *278*
Bradley, B., 274, *278*
Bransford, J., 46, *75*
Brody, G. H., 222, *224*
Bronfenbrenner, U., 4, 7, 9, 10, 14, 16, 18, 20, 31, 33, 36, 38, *41, 95, 114,* 183, *205,* 225, *250*
Broughton, J. M., 94, *114*
Brown, A. L., 183, *205*
Brown, B. B., 21, *43*
Brown, J. S., 183, *205*
Brown, R., 59, *73*
Brun, J., 141, *151*
Bruner, J. S., 96, 104, *114,* 133, *150,* 193, 207, 225, 227, 232, 243, *250*
Bullock, D., 93, 97, 108, 111, 112, *114, 115*
Buss, D. M., 12, *41*

C

Carello, C., 123, *151*
Carnochan, 98, *115*

Subject Index